HUNTING GHISLAINE

HUNTING GHISLAINE

John Sweeney

HODDER & STOUGHTON

First published in Great Britain in 2022 by Hodder & Stoughton
An Hachette UK company

1

Copyright © John Sweeney 2022

A CIP catalogue record for this title is available from the British Library

Hardback ISBN 9781529375879
Trade Paperback ISBN 9781529375886
eBook ISBN 9781529375909

Typeset in Legacy Serif by Hewer Text UK Ltd, Edinburgh
Printed and bound in Great Britain by Clays Ltd, Elcograf S.p.A.

Hodder & Stoughton policy is to use papers that are natural, renewable
and recyclable products and made from wood grown in sustainable
forests. The logging and manufacturing processes are expected to
conform to the environmental regulations of the country of origin.

Hodder & Stoughton Ltd
Carmelite House
50 Victoria Embankment
London EC4Y 0DZ

www.hodder.co.uk

'The truth is, Epstein does know a lot about a lot of things. Just a few moments in his company and you know this to be true . . . And Ghislaine? Full disclosure: I like her. Most people in New York do. It's almost impossible not to. She is always the most interesting, the most vivacious, the most unusual person in any room.'

Vicky Ward, 2011

'I've got to get the nubiles.'

Ghislaine Maxwell, allegedly, according to Maria Farmer when a receptionist for Jeffrey Epstein in 1996.

'The girls. They are nothing! They are trash!'

Ghislaine Maxwell, allegedly, to Christina Oxenberg.

Contents

A word on pronunciation

Ghislaine Maxwell is hard to pin down, starting with the mystery of how to pronounce her tricky-to-get-right first name. When I began work on our podcast, 'Hunting Ghislaine', I could find no recordings of her or her family saying it. On her arrest on 2 July 2020 the FBI's Assistant Director in New York, Bill Sweeney – no relation – went with a hard G, calling her 'G-Len'. Ghislaine was born in France to a French mother. **G** has two pronunciations in French, soft in front of **E**, **I**, or **Y** or hard in front of **A**, **O**, **U** or a consonant. The **H** in Ghislaine is, I thought, silent, so when doing my podcast, I betted on how French grammar suggests her mother pronounced it, with the soft **G**, as in 'Zh-len'. My logic was that the FBI may know a thing or two but they're not her mum. But three months after the podcast was finished, in March 2021, Ghislaine's older brother Ian Maxwell went on BBC Radio Four's Today programme and pronounced it 'G-Len'. I bet wrong.

Proper names that end in 'stein' in Britain are generally said as 'stine', following received German and European pronunciation. But Jeffrey Epstein was a New Yorker where the 'stein' ending is pronounced 'steen'.

Robert Maxwell was known on Fleet Street by a lot of names, some of them unprintable, but most often 'Cap'n Bob' or Bob. I've called him Maxwell throughout and his youngest daughter Ghislaine, and having made that decision, it made sense to call the victims in the story by their first names too.

Introduction

The film flickers into life, a grainy black-and-white video from 1966. What you see is a Christmas scene like something from the Frank Capra movie *It's A Wonderful Life* or a fairy tale. A little girl, five years old, is standing at the very top of a stepladder, stretching as far as she can to tie a star onto an enormous Christmas tree standing in the great hall of a mansion. She turns at the top of the ladder and faces her father, who is back to camera. He's a giant of a man, lean, brilliantine-haired. He opens his arms and she jumps and he catches her and kisses her. Then there's a close-up, her face animated, her coal-black eyes a-glitter.[1]

The little girl in the film is Ghislaine, the father Robert Maxwell. She first caught the public eye on 5 November 1991 when she was chosen by the family to give the first expression of grief for Robert Maxwell, who fell off the back of the yacht he named after her. Standing on the *Lady Ghislaine*, a wretched Ghislaine read out her statement in a broken voice: 'I also want to take this opportunity to thank all the many hundreds of people who have sent messages of support to us at this very, very sad time.' World leaders vied to mark the passing of the great man. Mrs Thatcher, out of power, mourned his 'God-given talents', then Prime Minister John Major commended 'an extraordinary life, lived to the full', Mikhail Gorbachev was 'deeply grieved', President George H. W. Bush hailed Maxwell's 'unwavering fight against bigotry and oppression'.

We can set the pieties aside. Ghislaine's older brother, Ian Maxwell, tells the story of one Christmas morning when the family descended to the Christmas tree to find ripped up wrapping paper everywhere and all their presents opened. Ian explained: 'to understand my father you must realise he never had any presents to unwrap as a child.'[2]

The fancy palace Ghislaine was brought up in was a rickety sham, its master a monster, cruel, mad, as mad as a box of frogs. With her beloved father dead, Ghislaine flew to New York to woo Jeffrey Epstein. She lost everything when the first monster in her life died. Then she got everything back: private jets, swish parties, powerful friends.

All she had to do was feed the second monster with fresh children.

Ghislaine's supporters can plead that Epstein's victims must have known or should have known what they were getting into, that many came back again and again, that no one died on Epstein's massage tables. They can make the argument that what is happening to Ghislaine is a kind of witch-hunt, that society's anger and the media's obsession with her story is out of kilter with what actually happened. This is the essence of a series of interviews before her trial given by Ian Maxwell. He is, by most accounts, a decent man, defending his sister, who finds herself in the twenty-first-century equivalent of a dungeon: 'She is in effective isolation in a cell that measures 6 foot by 9 foot and which includes a concrete bed and a toilet. There is no natural light.'

Ian, speaking before the trial, believes his sister is no monster: 'The Ghislaine that we know has been buried in this caricature, this monstrous creature that has been invented as an abuser and a pimp.'[3]

The counter-argument is best put by one of the victims of both Jeffrey Epstein and Ghislaine Maxwell, Sarah Ransome, in her book, *Silenced No More*: 'Pardon me, brother Ian, but you have no bloody idea.'[4] The child sexual abuse was not the figment of a witch-hunt but all too real, and it is fair for the media to reflect this. The public's horror lies in the industrial scale of Epstein's perversion: that so many girls, hand-picked to be more child than woman, lost their innocence.

Ghislaine Maxwell has always denied knowledge of Epstein's paedophilia, both its nature and vast extent. But the scale of the operation to serve Epstein was like running a factory. Getting on top of the logistics must have been a nightmare and given that Ghislaine was in command of running Epstein's life and four homes, his mansion in Manhattan, his home in Palm Beach, his ranch in New Mexico and his private island, Little St Jeffs in the US Virgin Islands, that does not look good. In Epstein's house in Palm Beach, fresh children were processed like battery chickens all the live long day. The phone logs show Ghislaine at that house while under-age girls serviced Epstein. The flight logs of Epstein's Boeing, nicknamed 'The Lolita Express', show that Ghislaine shared journeys with very young women. If so, did Epstein's voracious sexual appetite for under-age girls never strike Ghislaine? His one-time lover, the one who had commissioned a comedy roast about schoolgirl crushes for Epstein? Not once? That seems hard – no, close to impossible – to believe.

The writer Christina Oxenberg, in her book *Trash*, alleges that in 1997 Ghislaine asked her to ghost her autobiography; a no-no. While stringing Ghislaine along, Christina says that Ghislaine started talking about how Epstein needed three orgasms a day, and that she had to drive around trailer parks in Florida, looking for girls. Christina, appalled, asked for an explanation, at which, she alleges, Ghislaine replied angrily, slicing the air with her hands: 'The girls. They are nothing! They are trash!'

Does Ghislaine rue the day she met Epstein? Ian Maxwell again: 'I know she wishes that she had never met him. He has ruined her life.'[5]

This book sets out the evidence that her life was ruined long before she met Jeffrey Epstein. She is in jail, her good name dross, her future haunted by horrors from her past, from 1980s Oxford to 1990s New York, Florida and the Caribbean. Had Ghislaine Maxwell not got entangled with Epstein, she would never have merited a book.[6] But she has become a mirror, broken, cloudy, shards lying on the ground, capturing the ugly truth about half-forgotten worlds of rotten beauty.

The life of Ghislaine Maxwell, then, is a dark fairy tale for the twenty-first century, told the wrong way round with the princess starting out in a palace and ending up in a dungeon. In traditional formula fairy tales – the one set out in Netflix's *Filthy Rich*, for example – there is only one monster. In this book, the twist is that there is definitely more than one.

chapter one

Daddy's Girl

When Betty Maxwell was heavily pregnant with Baby Ghislaine, the couple's oldest child, Michael, fifteen years old, funny, full of life, a natural leader but sensitive too, saw how exhausted she was. As Betty's husband Robert was away, Michael stepped in: 'Mummy, don't bother to cook lunch, leave the tribe to me, I'll take them all to Headington for fish and chips; they'll love that and you can have a rest.' The couple had had eight children deliberately to recreate Maxwell's family murdered in the Holocaust. But their sixth, Karine, had died from leukaemia at the age of three. The tragedy destroyed the harmony of four girls and four boys. 'So when my parents had another little girl it was really magic, it allowed the four boys and four girls to be recreated,' Ian Maxwell says.[1]

The ninth was born on Christmas Day, 1961, in a French maternity clinic run by Betty's sister near Paris and named Ghislaine Noelle Marion. Two days after Baby Ghislaine's arrival, Michael wrote a beautiful and loving letter to his mother. 'Mummy, this is the first time I really thought and worried about what was happening and I was terribly relieved when I heard that everything was all right.'[2] The next day Michael went to a dance in nearby Thame, enjoyed himself and was being driven home to Headington Hill Hall in Oxford by the family chauffeur Sam Swadling when the Rover ploughed into the back of a broken-down onion lorry with no lights on the Bicester Road.[3] The chauffeur survived; Michael was left brain-dead.

Betty, in her grimly fascinating memoir *A Mind Of My Own*, wrote how grief for her first-born son consumed her: 'there is no possible consolation for the loss of a child . . . I cried so much then that I have seemed to have exhausted the source of tears within me and have not been really able to cry since.'[4] Robert Maxwell was, Betty recalled, 'shaken to the very core of his being'. To Betty and the rest of the world, Maxwell kept his true feelings to himself, but a family chauffeur, Brian Moss, has since explained that, late at night, Robert would ask him to drive to the hospital where Maxwell would talk to his son in the vain hope that he would emerge from his vegetative state. Maxwell would even get the chauffeur to engage with the lifeless boy because he used to drive him to school: 'So I would try to talk to him,' Moss said, 'but there was never any response.'[5] When Maxwell went to court, suing the company that employed Swadling, he broke down in the witness box, sobbing over the loss of his son. Judge Edmund Davies told Maxwell, 'it is impossible for you not to be tortured'[6] as the boy was 'existing rather than living'.[7] The family was awarded £15,900 in damages. Later, the family set up the Michael Maxwell Memorial Fund for Brain Research.[8] He never recovered from his injuries and died seven years after the crash in 1968.

Michael's younger brother and sisters were scarred by the tragedy. Philip, the second son, never properly recovered from the death of his older brother. In later life, he rebelled against his father but didn't prosper greatly, repairing cell phones in a shop at Brent Cross; working at Curry's, a white goods store, in Staple's Corner, a not very fashionable part of North London; and being a maths tutor for the children of immigrant mini-cab drivers from Pakistan and Kurdistan. Perhaps not prospering greatly is Philip's point.

A girlfriend of the twins, Isabel and Christine, ten years old at the time, recalled the gloom that cloaked the house after Michael's accident.[9] Ian, six years old at the time, spent hours drawing blood-spattered figures in cars and ambulances, Betty wrote. The tragedy so overwhelmed Betty that Ghislaine, who should have been the centre of her mother's attention, was overlooked. She became anorexic. When she was just three years old she said: 'Mummy, I exist.' From then on, Betty continued, she was so fussed over she became spoiled.

True, Ghislaine was born with a silver soup spoon in her mouth, her father extraordinarily rich, his publishing company worth £3 million in 1963, around £50 million in today's money, her mother good and good-looking, the family home a fifty-three-room mansion where Oscar Wilde had once danced at an all-night summer ball dressed as Prince Rupert of the Rhine. But it's also true that from three days old Ghislaine lived under the shadow of a much-loved older brother made lifeless in the grimmest possible way, and that shadow itself was thrown into a deeper gloom by the fact that the boy in the coma was named Michael after his grandfather Mehel, murdered by the Nazis along with most of the family and much of Europe's Jewish population a decade and a half before. Ghislaine Maxwell has been accused of doing some terrible things, but before we approach judgement on that, it is fair and proper to say that she had a cruel start to her gilded life. And not just the start.

To understand Ghislaine Maxwell, you have to take proper account of the two greatest influences on her life: father Robert and mother Betty. They were both extraordinary people, he a monster, she a kind of saint, but far too often Betty's essential goodness yielded to Maxwell's narcissism, deepening her own agony and that of all their children, Ghislaine, perhaps, most of all.

I call Robert Maxwell a monster because I met him. Back in the mid-1980s I was working on a piece about Fleet Street's royal ratpack hounding Princess Diana, some time before her death, for *Time Out* magazine. I turned up at London's most famous children's hospital, Great Ormond Street, knowing that Diana was expected. But standing on the steps to greet her was Robert Maxwell, then the self-publicising owner of the *Daily Mirror*. He was a great fat bear of a man, twenty-two stone, more, in a brilliant powder-blue suit, white shirt and red tie, his hair dyed creosote black. Just like the hideously creepy Nazi spy General Vagas in Eric Ambler's

1938 thriller, *Cause for Alarm*, Maxwell wore make-up – certainly powder on his face and I suspect rouge on his cheeks. His hair oil gave off a sheen that glistened in the camera flashes. Diana arrived in a Jaguar, the door opened by a detective. She looked down the barrels of her eyes at us, the hacks, and was immediately and stunningly the most beautiful thing in sight. Then the ogre Robert Maxwell pounced on her, his chops slavering, his face beaming that he had the beautiful princess in his paws. His joy was both unconfined and calculated, weighted. There's a moment in Fred Zinnemann's film *A Man for All Seasons* when Robert Shaw, playing Henry VIII, leaps from the royal barge into the Thames' mud and his stockings are made filthy by the slime. He turns and stares back at his courtiers, daring them to snigger at their lord and master. Everyone freezes. Then the king starts to roar with laughter and all his half-men jump into the mud and roar with laughter too. Maxwell's sense of humour was just like that of Henry VIII. He was a narcissist, the man who must be the bride at every wedding, the corpse at every funeral. I can remember thinking when I first clapped eyes on him: 'this man's a monster'. You could see through him immediately, that he was fake, not to be trusted, and from then on I observed the British Establishment's stately gavotte with this beast, endlessly fascinated, endlessly appalled.

Pretty much everyone who came across Maxwell thought him a monster too. Most held the tongue until they were released from the bonds of fear thanks to him falling off – or jumping from – his own poop-deck. Pandora Maxwell, the former wife of Kevin, stands tall in English folklore for one of the funniest TV soundbites of all time when, nine months after Robert Maxwell's death, she found some people from the lower orders knocking on her door at a very early hour. In front of massed TV cameras and Fleet Street's finest, she barked out in her crystal-cut posh accent: 'Piss off, we don't get up for an hour. I'll call the police', only to be told: 'Madame, we are the police.' They had come to arrest her husband over, at the time, the single biggest fraud in British criminal history but Kevin and brother Ian were both found not guilty. The Maxwells are survivors. Pandora reportedly called her father-in-law 'that fat fraudster' and bemoaned his cruel hand forever on Kevin's shoulder: 'He always expected Kevin to put him before me and the children. He was endlessly demanding. No matter what we had organised with the children, RM' – Robert Maxwell – 'would snap his fingers, and Kevin would drop everything.'[10]

'He was a monster. And a crook' – that was the verdict of former Tory MP and novelty knitwear guru Gyles Brandreth, who wrote in his diary, *Breaking The Code* on 6 November 1991, the day after Maxwell was fished out of the sea: 'I know: I sat in reception at Maxwell House for hours on end, saying, "I'm not leaving without a cheque in my hand," and meaning it – and getting it – after months and months and months of waiting.' Brandreth recorded that Tory grandee and convicted criminal Jeffrey Archer had 'witnessed Captain Bob put his bear-like arm around the Queen and keep it there. Not even Her Majesty was able to freeze him off. Well, he had chutzpah. And for the children it is a tragedy.'[11]

Mike Molloy was the *Daily Mirror*'s editor in 1984 when Maxwell gobbled up – sorry, acquired – the paper. In his Fleet Street memoir, *The Happy Hack*, he noted: 'the strangely orange colour of his complexion, his ink-black hair and enormous eyebrows gave him the look of a music hall comedian; but his smile was like that of Richard III'.

Roy Greenslade was the last but one editor of the *Mirror* on Maxwell's watch. In *Maxwell's Fall*, he wrote that Maxwell 'was arguably the greatest confidence trickster the world has ever known . . . What makes him so fascinating is that everyone knew he was a dodgy character. You did not have to work next to him to know that he was up to something: he was so transparently a man with a lot to hide.'[12] Greenslade went on, that Maxwell liked to play Uriah Heep, claiming 'I am only here to be of service.' The editor reflected: 'the cruelty, the rudeness, the aggression, the rapaciousness saddened him . . . It was a lie, and it was his truth.'[13]

Richard Stott, who was in the chair at the *Daily Mirror* at the time of his master's death, wrote in his biography, *Dogs and Lampposts*, that Maxwell: 'was, in every meaning of the word, a monster, untameable, dangerous, unpredictable, with power over all he surveyed, and he revelled in it.' Stott continued: 'The first thing you noticed about Robert Maxwell was the smell. It came from his hair, not the jet-black dye but the bay rum he used to oil it. Then there was the sheer size of him – enormous body, of course, but a huge head too, with small, even teeth. Small, almost dainty feet and green-brown eyes, fierce and primeval.'[14]

Perhaps the most compromised – although the competition is stiff – of Robert Maxwell's biographers was the late Nicholas Davies, a *Daily Mirror* reporter and not to be confused with the *Guardian* journalist Nick Davies, author of *Flat Earth News*. Davies was the foreign editor of the *Daily Mirror* at the end of Maxwell's reign. Infamously, when he was accused of being in cahoots and in business with an American arms dealer based in Ohio, Davies claimed that he had never, ever been to Ohio. Then a photo turned up on the *Sun*'s front page of Davies with the arms dealer from Ohio in Ohio. Davies bested Maxwell for the love of a woman a third of Maxwell's age. His nickname among other reporters was 'Sneaky'. I knew him a little from the time in the 1980s and 1990s when I worked as a war reporter for the *Observer*. He had a habit of cupping his hand over his mouth, leaning into you and oozing secret confidences, very much like Private Walker, the spiv in *Dad's Army*. But just like the spiv, Davies oozed charm and had stuff – stories – to sell.

Davies on Maxwell can be very funny: 'His vanity knew no bounds. The only time I ever saw Maxwell panic, and it was always for the same reason, was when he realised he was heading out without his powder puff.'[15]

Davies tells the story, not long before Maxwell's mystery death, of Ghislaine wrestling with her father to make her new sinecure inside the family empire work. Maxwell had created a corporate gifts company and appointed her managing director. Davies recalls that Ghislaine was going to New York and was thinking of dropping in on Donald Trump to sell him her corporate gifts. She asked Maxwell if he would phone Trump, as they were friends, to get her an appointment. Maxwell, said Davies, exploded: 'Have you got your bum in your head? Why the fuck would Donald Trump want to waste his time seeing you with your crappy gifts when he has a multimillion-dollar business to run?' Ghislaine, said Davies, couldn't win.[16]

The killer witness against Robert Maxwell is his own widow. Betty Maxwell writes in a preface to her book that Maxwell was just a man, not the monster invented by the press. She then spends much of the rest of the book setting out in grim detail how he tortured her and the children and how he held near absolute power over them. Flying around the world, meeting world leaders, Maxwell soared like an eagle over the ordinary constraints of family life, she wrote, and that was a powerful drug for someone already hooked on megalomania.[18]

Ghislaine's flights on the Lolita Express, hobnobbing with two US presidents, Bill Gates, Prince Andrew and all, and her habit of appearing superior to ordinary folk, echo her father's flaws so faithfully that one begins to worry about the idea of free will.

Befittingly for such an ogre from a dark fairy story, he was born in Transylvania, then Czechoslovakia, a child of a dirt-poor Orthodox Jewish family. Maxwell set out a version of his life story in an edition of *Desert Island Discs* in the summer of 1987. After the first track, from Mozart's Symphony no. 40, Maxwell recalls his childhood: 'I came from a very poor family indeed. My father was an unemployed farm labourer. We didn't have enough to eat. I've only had three years' primary education.' Parkinson asks what effect that had on him and Maxwell replies: 'All I remember is being hungry most of the time. It has had no effect on me in any way.'

That was not true. He gorged on food his whole life, while his youngest daughter starved herself. Problems with food stalk father and daughter.

Eleanor Berry is a former mental patient who once, attended by her own Harley Street psychiatrist, tried to beat up the editor of *Private Eye* Ian Hislop. The editor's offence had been to run an *Eye* cover showing Maxwell's funeral in Israel with the headline: 'A Nation Mourns' and speech bubbles from various rabbis at the grave saying: 'Here lies Bob Maxwell' and 'He lied everywhere else.'[19] Eleanor Berry stormed past the receptionist, marched into Hislop's office and gave him a smack. She is the daughter of Lord Hartwell, the former owner of the *Daily Telegraph*. When she was twenty, she suffered a mental breakdown and ended up in hospital. She was infatuated with Robert Maxwell and wrote three privately published books about him, the most recent being *My Unique Relationship with Robert Maxwell: The Truth at Last*. It is a very strange book, finely written in parts but not a little odd.

Eleanor Berry describes how Maxwell, who 'looked like a beautiful big black bear', rescued her from her 'mental hospital', as she calls it, just as the electrodes were in place on her head and the current was going to be switched on to start a course of electric shock treatment.

'"Turn that fucking machine off!" shouted Bob . . . If I had had so much as one more treatment, I would have become a vegetable. Effectively, Bob saved my life.'[20]

Eleanor Berry became a guest at Headington Hill Hall and lived there for a year, according to her account, when Ghislaine was nine years old. Eleanor was in an extraordinary position to describe life under Maxwell from the perspective of being an insider but tied neither by family bonds nor by employee's anxieties. Once, she saw a padlock on the larder door and asked Betty how come. Betty, according to Eleanor, replied: 'We have to lock it to keep Bob out, whenever we put him on a diet. Otherwise he breaks in and eats everything there is. He broke in, only the other day, I'm sorry to say.'

Eleanor writes: 'I listened, fascinated. Betty continued: "He ate a pound of cheese, a jar of peanut butter, two jars of caviar, a loaf of bread and a chicken in one go."'[21]

Maxwell told Nick Davies: 'All I can ever remember about my childhood is the awful feeling of hunger in my stomach, going to sleep hungry, waking up in the night hungry, and scavenging for bread in the mornings, looking for anything to eat.'[22]

Davies describes Maxwell scoffing beluga caviar at the Paris Ritz in the spring of 1989.[23] Another time, he watched his boss stuff five or six small sandwiches into his mouth so that he could hardly chew the food: 'It was like watching a starving man, driven mad by hunger, unable to control himself as he forced handfuls of food into his mouth. He must have sensed me there, because he turned and saw me standing in the doorway. For a split second he was like a cornered animal, as though I had caught him thieving.'[24]

Davies noted how though he doted on Ghislaine, Maxwell once ordered the locks of the kitchen to be changed just to stop her helping herself to a tiny amount of the vast hoards of food that were kept there.[25]

At the time of his death, he was monstrously obese, over 22 stone (300 pounds or 140 kilograms). Virtually everyone who met Maxwell has a story of him gorging himself on food.

Gyles Brandreth, who was at Oxford with Anne Maxwell, Robert's oldest daughter, recalled seeing Maxwell in the late 1960s, 'going down the table eating everything with his hands, piling it into his mouth. I'd never seen anything like it before. It was as if he was hungry for life, as if he couldn't get enough of it.'[26]

There is a telling scene in *The Master*, the film about a fiction-alised version of Scientology's founder, L. Ron Hubbard, in which the son of the fake messiah figure warns a disciple: 'You do realise he's making it up as he goes along, don't you?' Run-of-the-mill confidence tricksters tell lies they know to be untrue to get them past the next hurdle in life, but the really brilliant ones, like L. Ron Hubbard, Robert Maxwell and Donald Trump breathe their lies. (Trump was rude about me when I asked him why did he buy the concrete for Trump Tower from Anthony "Fat Tony" Salerno, boss of the Genovese crime family, so I can be rude about him[27].) Narcissists live inside their own fiction. The grinding poverty that the young Robert Maxwell endured seems to have cut off his emotional or psychological development. He grew up to be an enormous toddler, self-obsessed, solipsistic, the complete narcissist. Such men can, for a time, be extraordinarily successful in life, in terms of material success, in getting their own way, but narcissists make bad fathers. Their children grow up learning that what is real and what is fake is contingent on Daddy's mood and that can change in a flash. It becomes impossible to develop a proper sense of self, to learn to know what is right and what is wrong.

Her father's narcissism is the first act, if you like, of Ghislaine Maxwell's tragedy. She suffered from living at the whim of an all-dominating alpha male who didn't know his own mind, was never happy at rest in his own skin and who never had a proper sense of self. Molloy recalls: 'It took only a short while to realise that Maxwell lived in a parallel universe where his own opinions rode roughshod over the logic of the real world.'[28]

Ghislaine's mother, Betty, née Meynard, was as kind as her father was cruel, good as he was monstrous, noble as he was mean-minded. Her people were 'old money', her father's great-great-grandmother, Manon de Nérac, having smuggled herself into the Bastille to steal the revolutionary order calling for her lover's execution, so saving him from the guillotine. Betty's family were Protestant but well integrated into the grain of French high society, her father a rich cavalry officer, who became a gold prospector, then a silk manufacturer, before being ruined by the 1929 crash. Betty was sent to a convent in Acocks Green, Birmingham, aged nine, to learn English with her sister. In 1944, when she met Maxwell, she was beautiful, fun and clever. She swooned on second sight. Betty describes in her book how she caught sight of a wild-looking British sergeant, tall, sunburnt, in knee-length boots, pistol in a holster at his thigh, infantry black beret angled on his dark brown hair. She fainted.[29] Food was scarce in newly liberated France and Betty was constantly hungry. Her Sir Galahad watched her, amused, as she fed ravenously on beans on toast and sausages. He had food and money and had been fighting the Nazis. Game over. From the very start, Betty saw two opposing sides of him, writing that his lips sometimes suggested luxurious fresh fruit, sometimes thin lines of blood, telling of death and carnage.[30]

After that first meeting in the autumn of 1944, Maxwell went back to the war. In January 1945 he stormed a Nazi machinegun post and his raw courage was recognised. He was decorated by General Bernard Montgomery with the Military Cross.[31] In March 1945 he learnt that most of his family had been murdered in the Holocaust.[32] He told *Desert Island Discs*: 'The sorrow of those losses are ever before me ... I don't hate as I did during the war, but I cannot forget or forgive.'[33]

With the war almost over, he took the surrender of the mayor of a German town. But when a German tank opened fire, he, according to a letter to Betty, took revenge: 'Luckily he missed, so I shot the mayor.'[34]

I've seen enough of the chaos of battle to make a judgement. To me, to shoot an unarmed civilian because of the unrelated action by a third party is a war crime.

After the war was over, Maxwell, fluent in half a dozen languages, got a job with the British military occupation in Berlin, then bought a German scientific publishing company, seeing the opportunity of selling its back catalogue to American and British readers. He made a killing.

The official line that Maxwell was a wonderful family man can be found in *Maxwell* by Joe Haines, the great man's approved biography: 'The greatest wealth Maxwell possesses is the love his family show for him.'[35] It's a fairy tale and not a happy one.

After Maxwell died, Betty found the courage to set out the truth. Her book *A Mind of My Own* describes what should have been a glorious summer holiday in 1966. The family often hired a luxury yacht and sailed through the Mediterranean, visiting Elba, Corsica, Sardinia, Naples. On this cruise they were exploring the Greek islands. The row was over food. Betty writes that Maxwell forced Kevin, then seven years old, to eat French beans. Kevin refused for two days, then in floods of tears, sobbing, surrendered, telling his father that he was giving in but only because he was bigger and stronger, and for no other reason. Betty recalls that her own heart was torn to shreds.[36]

Ghislaine was five years old at the time.

Maxwell was horrible to all his children. The late Bridget Rowe was appointed editor of the *Sunday Mirror* in 1991, a Fleet Street bruiser as insensitive as they come. Her office walls boasted a photo of Pamela Anderson's cleavage opposite a shot of John Wayne Bobbitt's chopped-up penis, never published on grounds of taste. Rowe recalled Maxwell swearing at Kevin, then explaining to her: '"The trouble with him is that he never ate his beans as a child . . . Go away, go away and eat some beans!" Still without saying a word, Kevin walked out of the room and shut the door behind him.'[37]

Maxwell was a sadist who loved sadism as spectacle. Stephen Clackson, managing editor at Maxwell's *London Daily News* in 1986, recalls him humiliating a new executive: 'This letter you have sent out, this is shit, cunt. My old grandmother, who could never speak a word of English, brought up in the mountains of Carpathia, could write better English than this.' The hapless executive was ordered out of the meeting to write a memo explaining his purpose in the company. 'The poor bastard left the room, nearly in tears. It was torture and the torture was very public.'[38]

Like all bullies, Maxwell went to great lengths to shut critics up. Reporters who tried to investigate were threatened with libel writs and some were sued, so much of Fleet Street and the broadcasting media kept well away from what was really going on inside Maxwell's houses. When a tiny minority of journalists fought back, Maxwell played dirty.

In the dismal story of Robert Maxwell's hold over the *Daily Mirror* and a big chunk of the British Establishment from banking to publishing to politics, there are a tiny handful of heroes who stood up to him, come what may. The longest-lived of these is Richard Ingrams, the second editor of *Private Eye* throughout the 1960s and '70s up to 1986. The *Eye* was sued so often by Maxwell that he can't remember quite how many times. Such resistance to Maxwell's menace was vanishingly rare. Ingrams reflected on his old enemy's contempt for ordinary people: 'There was a famous example when he had this helicopter pad on the top of his Mirror building and it was known that he actually peed off the edge of the roof onto the poor, innocent people passing down below in the street.'[39]

Ingrams continued: 'Maxwell also had the habit common to megalomaniacs of going to the loo and leaving the door open so that people waiting to see him would have to listen to the sound of him evacuating or whatever you care to call it.'

I first met Richard Ingrams when I went to my first *Private Eye* lunch in 1984 and I have never known him tell a story without there being something to it, what they call at the magazine 'the *Private Eye* ring of truth'. In what has been perhaps my most peculiar inquiry in investigative journalism, I went hunting for people who might corroborate Richard's extraordinary allegation. The first is Patrick Forbes, who was a director on Thames TV's weekly television financial show, *The City Programme*, when he and his team interviewed Maxwell sometime in the late 1980s. He recalls: 'we were setting up the camera, waiting for him to turn up. And suddenly there was this enormous eruption from the room next door. What the hell was that? And then we slowly began to realise that we were right next door to a lavatory and somebody had just done the largest and most audible shit in their life. Just think of a large amount of marble dropping onto a lot of plate glass, volcanic rumbling, a succession of fast toilet flushes. Shortly afterwards, Maxwell turned up to do the interview without saying a thing. He did this a couple of times before interviews. He was just saying: "Fuck you."'[40]

Jenni Frazer spent months getting an interview with Maxwell, finally succeeding in 1986: 'we could hear but not see him because there was a bathroom off the office area. The doors were open and he was quite evidently using the lavatory very, very noisily. Splashing noises. It was all done for our benefit so it was a power play. I am in no doubt that he knew we were there, and that he put on this display deliberately. And the photographer and I were looking at each other like, what the hell's going on? But, you know, what could you say?'[41]

And the publication Jenni worked for? *The Jewish Chronicle*. Robert Maxwell was, then, a monster at both ends.

Jenni Frazer had been trying to find out why Maxwell had previously denied the fact he was born a Jew, with little success. David Kessler, former chairman of *The Jewish Chronicle*, explained to Sam Jaffa that the *Jewish Year Book* was updating its list of Jewish MPs shortly after Maxwell had been elected to parliament in 1964. They sent Maxwell a form but instead he called Kessler: 'You know I'm not Jewish.' Kessler had the impression that Maxwell, like many central European Jews, denied his religion so that he could get on in the world. 'I reminded him that this was England and that here people preferred others to be honest about their origins, however humble they might be.'[42]

For most of his life Maxwell claimed he wasn't Jewish, perhaps fitting in with, or not opposing, the anti-Semitism he grew up with. But during the mid-1980s he would switch to being Jewish some of the time and from the late 1980s he became an ardent supporter of Israel. Some of this peculiar behaviour may, perhaps, have been driven by survivor guilt. He lived but nearly all his family were killed. Betty records how he once told his his oldest surviving son, Philip, that nothing he had achieved in life would ever match his greatest regret, not being able to rescue his family. Maxwell added that he kept the door to his haunted inner chamber locked.[43]

Noreen Taylor, then a star feature writer on the *Mirror*, recalls the time in 1984 when, after Maxwell had bought the paper, she first met him. There had been rumours that she was on the point of quitting and Maxwell called her up to his office. There was only one problem: she had been out with two colleagues. 'We were all pissed. The three of us, suffering from the effects of a liquid lunch.' This being proper Fleet Street, back in the day, the feature writers had been on the drink for five hours. Maxwell had heard rumours that Noreen was leaving the *Mirror*. When she pledged to stay, Maxwell replied: 'You're not leaving me, I'm so glad; that makes me so happy. It was the worst news I heard since my grandparents were murdered in Auschwitz.'[44]

That's a crass thing to say but Maxwell was a crass man.

A bully at work and a bully at home. Sunday lunch at Headington Hill Hall was a torture. He would have lunch with the whole family, but, most often, he would bring along an eminent guest: a chemist being published by his scientific publishing company, Pergamon; a politician from the time between 1964 and 1970 when he was a Labour MP for Buckingham; or someone from the world of banking and business. Maxwell would rant and rave at the children, making Sunday lunch a torture, reducing them to tears, Betty recalls in her memoir. As the seventies drew on, things got worse so the whole family would dread what Betty calls the Maxwellian drama.[45]

Maxwell's children reacted to their father's monstrous behaviour by sticking together, to try and look after each other as, individually, they suffered the lash of their father's tongue. Many commentators noted how well Ghislaine's sisters and brothers supported her at the trial in Manhattan. Of course they did; that's what they had always done. One should note, however, that Ghislaine has six brothers and sisters. The two oldest, Philip and Anne, did not turn up in New York. Their age suggests the obvious reason for that but they are also the two who clashed most bitterly with their father when he was alive; who, perhaps, had little sympathy for Ghislaine's adoration of Robert Maxwell.

Betty deplored his cruelty but did not do anything effective to stop it. In December 1965, when Ghislaine was approaching her fourth birthday, Betty wrote to Maxwell, calling him nagging, bad-tempered, despotic, saying she would give up everything but not her love for him.[46]

There was something self-destructive in Betty's passion for Maxwell. In one letter she wrote to him: 'I want to drown my soul in your desires . . . You will only need to say what you want and it will be done, or to express a desire and I will satisfy it. Perhaps you will discover that the half-flayed creature you have stripped naked still deserves to be loved.'[47]

Maxwell picked on Betty, and then on each child in turn. Philip, the oldest surviving boy, never properly recovered from the trauma following the death of his older brother Michael. He was a brilliant mathematician, winning a scholarship to Oxford when he was sixteen, before fleeing to Argentina where he met and married a woman whom Maxwell did not approve of and disappearing from his father's view. Anne, the oldest daughter, aspired to be an actress but Maxwell was contemptuous of her ambition. She was, Betty wrote, very often on the receiving end of his temper. Anne's acting career was by not a disaster. She had been in a movie with Sean Connery,[48] but Maxwell was openly contemptuous, demanding why she was not doing as well as Glenda Jackson or Judi Dench.

Ian Maxwell was promoted by his father at Pergamon Press, the engine room of the Maxwell publishing empire, but was sacked when he failed to meet him at Charles De Gaulle Airport in Paris. Ian recalled Maxwell's rage to Rosie Kinchen of *The Sunday Times* in 2018: 'He said, "You're fired. You're fired as of this minute. I can't trust you with a burnt box of matches."'[49] Maxwell held a board meeting in the middle of the night to promulgate the sacking. Ian was, Betty recalls, humiliated when Maxwell used to gloat about sacking his son in public.[50]

The torture of Sunday lunch continued even though the children were adults. The children hated being humiliated but he would accuse them of selfishness and lack of loyalty.[51] Betty, torn between her hopeless love for Maxwell and her maternal instincts, froze, paralysed when he demanded answers from her. She realised that he had no emotional maturity, that he was more child than man.[52]

Ghislaine was his favourite child but even she did not avoid his wrath. Betty writes of an utterly miserable Christmas Day, 1981, spent at a fancy hotel in San Francisco in the penthouse suite overlooking the Golden Gate Bridge. This time Ghislaine, normally his favourite child, was the prime scapegoat.[53]

From the start of the 1980s Betty and Maxwell started living separate lives. At the end of her tether, Betty wrote him a savage letter, bemoaning that he boasted of deals costing millions of pounds while blasting her for spending money on doing up Ghislaine's room. Betty called him 'harsh, cruel, uncompromising, dictatorial'. She accused him of taking a sadistic pleasure in crushing and humiliating everyone who loved him the most.[54]

The same dismal pattern repeated itself, time and again. Betty was driven to set out her misery on paper. Maxwell would make some amends and then abuse her or the children again and the cycle continued. His cruelty to Betty became a commonplace in his circle. Estranged from Betty, he found comfort elsewhere. One of his long-time lovers was the late Wendy Leigh, a feisty and much-loved hack. When she requested an interview with Maxwell for a book about sex, power and money, lunch at the Savoy Grill followed, which she described as 'an audition for the role of mistress'.[55]

Wendy Leigh wrote a thinly disguised novel about the affair called *Unravelled*, with Robert Maxwell re-baptised as 'Sir Robert Hartwell'. The hero's favourite food? 'The waiter . . . hands Robert Harwell a large tin of beluga, plus a crystal spoon, with which he proceeds to demolish the entire contents of the tin.' There is a novel inside her novel that the narrator reads out to Sir Robert and it just so happens to be sado-masochistic: 'I pick up the crimson velvet blindfold from next to the rug and put it over my eyes . . . my legs spread, bottom in the air.' In the novel proper, there's more of the same: 'For what seems forever, he spanks and spanks, then spanks more.'[56]

You get the drift.

Towards the end of his life Maxwell developed a passion for one of his secretaries, Andrea Martin, who was a third of his age. She was blonde, cool and, for a time, thought she could handle his eccentricities. But eventually, as we will see, he tried to force himself on her, and she fled.

There was one final mistress, a forty-seven-year-old Russian journalist, Kira Vladina, who he first met in November 1990. Kira was interviewed by Tom Bower in his second book on Robert, *Maxwell: The Final Verdict*. He comes across in her account as a manic depressive on steroids: 'I'm so lonely. The people around me only want my money, even my children and especially my wife.' There's no serious evidence that Betty was ever greedy. He told his Russian mistress, according to Bower, that gold was not his thing: 'I wouldn't mind if I lost all my money. I'd be just as happy and I'd start again. In any case, my family won't inherit anything.' That, at least, turned out to be true. 'The only ones who deserve anything are my youngest, Ghislaine and Kevin. I adore both of them. Kevin is so much like me and Ghislaine is a friend.'

Maxwell continued: 'Ever since childhood I've been traumatised by love. I was crazy about my mother. I loved her to utter distraction and I wanted the same from my wife and family. But I didn't get it.'[57] The spectre of this loveless, desperate, depressed man makes you feel sorry for him until yet another witness pops up to remind you that he was routinely horrible to everyone around him.

Davies recalled visiting Paris in the 1980s when he accompanied Maxwell and Betty as they returned to their tiny flat in the City of Light, one which he had kept for forty years. It was chilly and Maxwell, who had had one lung removed after a cancer operation years before, was poorly. Betty tried to help him on with his coat. Davies recalls: 'Maxwell exploded. "I have told you to fuck off, now fuck off," and he grabbed the coat and stormed out of the flat. I looked at the floor in embarrassment and Mrs Maxwell, to her credit, barely reacted, just pulling a face, shrugging her shoulders and then following him.'[58]

In February 1981 Betty wrote Maxwell a fireball of a letter, condemning his dependence on 'Maxwellian drama', an absurd vortex of 'exorcism, yelling, threats, tears, gnashing of teeth, repentance and contrition.' She concluded: 'When I think that I wanted to recreate your murdered family, you make me regret it now that I see each one in turn become the object of your fury.'[59]

But, hopelessly, she concludes the letter with the phrase: 'I will not stop loving you.'

Of all of his children, one stood out as having managed to develop a coping mechanism to deal with her father: Ghislaine. All the witnesses agree that Ghislaine could charm her father to forget his anger and get him to do what she wanted. Davies writes in *The Unknown Maxwell*: 'Undoubtedly she was spoilt as a child and she was always the apple of her father's eye . . . Maxwell, always the sexist, was proud that she was a good-looking woman too. Ghislaine's photograph was the only one he kept on his desk.'[60]

Peter Thompson and Anthony Delano, two former *Mirror* journalists in their twice-sued book *Maxwell: A Portrait of Power*, tell the story of the great man's sixty-second birthday party. Maxwell announces his family one by one: 'when he came to the last name Maxwell's voice softened noticeably . . . the raven-haired, lovely – and undoubtedly his best beloved – Ghislaine . . . Whatever his mood, she was always welcome, to hug him, to slide behind his desk, slip into his lap and cajole for favours: a trip to St Moritz, a new BMW, a new business.'[61]

Eleanor Berry writes that when Ghislaine was an adult, 'Bob kept taking Ghislaine on his knee, cuddling her and smothering her with kisses.'[62]

Roy Greenslade told me: 'I remember I was alone with Maxwell when the door opened and she came in.' One of the quirks of Maxwell's office was, just like the Sublime Port under Abdul the Damned, supplicants for preferment would wait for hours, sometimes a whole day, before they would be allowed into the presence. Editors like Greenslade could jump the queue; family, especially Ghislaine, did not register the concept of a queue at all. Greenslade recalls her coming into the office and Maxwell, playing the loving grump, worried about some adventure in Italy when she had fallen off a yacht. It runs in the family. Greenslade described how father and daughter interacted: 'She giggled and didn't take him too seriously. She laughed a lot and went over, gave him big kisses. And it was obvious that he doted on her and that he didn't treat her in the same rude way as he did Ian and Kevin. She was daddy's girl.'[63]

But at what terrible cost did Ghislaine's power over her monstrous father come?

Ghislaine loved her father and her father loved her so much that he named his yacht the *Lady Ghislaine* after her rather than, say, the *Lady Elisabeth* after his wife, the mother of his nine children. Ian Maxwell recalls the 'big mystery' of the naming ceremony, how the family was woken up at the crack of dawn and flown to a boatyard in the Netherlands. 'Ghislaine was given this bottle, she crashed it against the side, the wrap fell off and there it was: the *Lady Ghislaine*. She was stunned. We all were stunned.'[64] The superyacht became Robert Maxwell's favourite toy, but it's important to note that he bought it second-hand from arms dealer Emad Khashoggi. Various branches of the Saudi family will pop up through this saga.

Towards the end of his life, Ghislaine became Maxwell's escort too, the woman he would bring along to parties and events instead of his wife. But long before that there is a witness to the closeness of the relationship between father and daughter. This being Maxwelliana, the source is the former psychiatric patient, Eleanor Berry. In her third book on the subject, *My Unique Relationship with Robert Maxwell: The Truth at Last*, she writes about an incident when Eleanor is staying at Headington Hill Hall after her successful escape from electro-convulsive therapy. Ghislaine, then nine years old, who has been away staying with friends, returns. Eleanor writes: 'Ghislaine was wearing blue jeans, tennis shoes and a white T-shirt. She clambered onto her father's knee and put her arms around his neck. She had large brown eyes and brown hair, taken back into a ponytail. She was very pretty. While she was on her father's knee, I became agonizingly jealous of her.'[65]

Later, Eleanor and Ghislaine are on their own when the little girl tricks the twenty-something-year-old. Eleanor explains that Ghislaine talked about her father giving her a hiding and then showing a row of things in an empty room: 'Daddy always allows me to choose what I prefer to be beaten with.' Eleanor, who has something close to a photographic memory, noted the following punitive instruments arranged in a row on a table: 'a riding crop, a ruler, a stick, a cane, which made a swishing noise on being brought down through the air'.[66]

Eleanor Berry sets out a second story in her book, of Betty lending her a satin-bound copy of the Marquis de Sade.[67] A spokeswoman for Eleanor Berry said that she could not respond to my questions for this book because of ill-health.

Francis Wheen, the deputy editor of *Private Eye*, recalled the time she came to the *Eye*'s office after Maxwell's death in 1991 and roughed up Ian Hislop: 'What makes me think that she's not a complete fantasist is that her description of the *Private Eye* office is spot on. The front office, she writes about this threadbare sofa with springs sticking out, she's appalled by the clutter and the general mess. And I'm afraid she's exactly right.' Wheen noted that when Betty Maxwell's memoir came out years later, recording Maxwell's cruelty to her and the children, it tallied with Eleanor's picture.[68]

Ghislaine's older brother Ian Maxwell said in 2021 that Eleanor Berry's story was 'utterly implausible. We were all physically punished, girls and boys; the girls were smacked and the boys belted, mostly for poor grades, laziness and lack of application at school.'[69]

For the Hunting Ghislaine podcast, I asked a number of questions of the Maxwell's family public relations man, Brian Basham. After he heard the episode reporting Eleanor Berry's claims that Maxwell used to beat Ghislaine when she was nine years old, he opened fire: 'Dear John, I guess you must have been desperate for some cash when you got bumped out of the BBC but this is no way to rebuild your reputation. It's a lazy clippings job that reads as though you put it together in your dressing gown with a bottle in your hand.'

For the record I did not, at the time, own a dressing gown. Basham continued: 'Your attempt to criminalise Ghislaine by implying that she abused others because she was abused herself is a disgusting canard. Desperate for employment or not, you should be ashamed of yourself. Regards, Brian Basham.'[70]

Eleanor Berry added one more detail in her book, that years after the death of Robert Maxwell, Eleanor was visiting Betty at her flat in London. Eleanor over-indulged on the G&Ts and Betty let her snooze on her sofa. Eleanor writes that she woke up when the phone rang and feigned sleep. She recalls hearing Betty comforting Ghislaine who was in New York. Although only getting Betty's side of the conversation, Eleanor deduced that Ghislaine was clearly upset. Betty said: 'Are you seeing a psychiatrist about Daddy's canings when you were little?' Then Betty realised that Eleanor was listening in: 'Ghislaine! I'm afraid we can't continue this conversation. Eleanor's here! She was asleep. Now she's woken up. She's heard everything.'

Richard Ingrams described Eleanor Berry as a very eccentric woman, but went on to say: 'I believe it, but I also believe that Ghislaine's behaviour is partly due to the fact that she had this very peculiar upbringing with this monster as her father. People need to connect the Ghislaine story with this nasty man who is her father.'[71]

Eleanor Berry could well be a complete fantasist but, aside from her account, the evidence that Robert Maxwell was a monster to all his children, Ghislaine too, is overwhelming. And from one of her father's greatest enemies in life, Richard Ingrams, there is, for the monster's daughter, for daddy's girl, a measure of pity.

chapter two

Making Diana Cry

When Ghislaine Maxwell was growing up in Headington Hill Hall, she was surrounded by a wall of money. Robert Maxwell was rich, very. There were helicopters and limousines and a private yacht named after her and newspaper journalists who wrote down her father's truths or woe betide them. Did Ghislaine ever get a sense of the alternative narrative: that far from being colossally rich, she might, in fact, be living inside a massive confidence trick? That her father was a crook? That, if you dared to press against the marble it would wobble because it was really plywood scenery? That she might be locked inside an English country house version of *The Truman Show*?

There were some clues that all was not well inside the fabulous land of Maxwelliana. Take the family mansion, Headington Hill Hall. Built for the brewing family, the Morrells, it hosted a grand ball in the back half of the nineteenth century for, among others, Oscar Wilde, who was later jailed for, effectively, being homosexual. Come the Second World War, Headington Hill Hall was requisitioned for War Office use and ended up as a rehabilitation hospital for gravely wounded soldiers. It was sold by the Morrells in 1953 to Oxford City Council but continued to be used for looking after the critically injured until 1958 when it was closed down. For two years it was left to rack and ruin, then, spotting a deal, Maxwell swooped, paying Oxford a pitifully small rent for what he liked to boast was the 'best council house in the country'. He even commissioned a stained-glass window depicting 'Samson at the Gates of Gaza' for his home, the word being that the model of

Samson was Maxwell. However, the downside of living in a council house is that there's little point in doing it up because you don't own it. The result was that, grand-sounding as it might seem, it was a bit of a dump.

'It was awful and I wouldn't have lived there if you paid me.'[1] So says Gerald Ronson, one of the very, very few people who have admitted to liking Maxwell after his death. This being Maxwelliana, Ronson is a controversial businessman who befriended Maxwell, advised him to buy the *Lady Ghislaine*, and took Maxwell and Betty on their first trip to Israel. Ronson got involved in an infamous share-dealing scandal in the City, was convicted, went to prison, appealed to the European Court of Human Rights, which ruled that his conviction had been unfair, re-appealed through the British courts but didn't win the final match. You win some, you lose some. Ronson had a soft spot for Maxwell: 'He was quite a character and, personally, I liked him.'[2] But that fondness did not prevent critical judgement of the man on a number of points, including his mansion.

Nicholas Coleridge – Eton, Trinity College, Cambridge, and, naturally, an ancestor of the poet who wrote the rhyme about the ancient mariner killing the big bird – has known Ghislaine Maxwell for more than forty years since she was a student at Balliol College, Oxford. Coleridge found Headington Hill Hall 'peculiar . . . like an enormous municipal town hall'.[3]

Mirror editor Mike Molloy – a working-class lad from the wrong side of the tracks in West London was similarly dismissive of Headington Hill Hall: 'Like every building I'd seen that Bob had taken over, it was decorated and finished with an eye to economy. The fabric of the building was grand, but the reproduction furniture looked as if it had been bought at the closing-down sale of a failed country hotel. There were also some of the worst paintings I've ever seen on anybody's walls.'

Nothing was quite right at Headington Hill Hall. Everyone lived inside the madness of Robert Maxwell, three-year-old Ghislaine too. Her anorexia frightened Betty but eventually a solution was found, courtesy of one of the great scientists who dined at the hall. Daniel Bovet, an Italian Nobel Prize winner, suggested: ' "You must treat her just like I treat my rats." ' Betty tells the story that his rats, given a week's food supply in one go, gorged on it to begin with but then worked out that steady eating was the better way. And so Betty took Ghislaine's place from the table and let her eat whatever and whenever she wanted. Betty remembers Ghislaine gorging herself on chocolate and peaches, fearing that she would get diarrhoea. But after a week or so Ghislaine pleaded to be allowed to eat normally with the other children. Betty noted how, in later years, Ghislaine loved to tell the story of how this brilliant professor had cured her of her eating disorder because she was treated like his laboratory rats.[4]

Given this story of little Ghislaine's recovery from anorexia when she was three years old, it is striking to read reports of her losing 15 pounds while in prison waiting for her trial.[5] Her older brother Ian suggested that this was because of the wretched quality of the food provided by the remand prison she has been kept in, the Metropolitan Detention Center, Brooklyn, and there is overmuch evidence corroborating his complaints about the food there, and a lot besides. Stepping back and looking at Ghislaine's life, pre-prison, it's true to say that her disturbed attitude towards food is an echo. On this, like so many other things, she is her father's daughter.

Families develop their own way of dealing with trouble. Life at Headington Hill Hall for the Maxwell children could be fun, too. Betty tells the story of how she would ask the children to help entertain the guests and, in return, she would help out with their French homework or other bits and bobs. Betty recalls entertaining two eminent German astrophysicists, Professor Foch and Dr Penish. The children 'would go out of their way to say, "Have some more nuts, Professor Fuck", or "Another drink, Dr Penis?" '[6]

Maxwell's roller-coaster career hit three troughs in quick succession. The first was Rupert Murdoch snatching the *News of the World* from his grasp in 1968. The sitting editor wrote a leader rejecting Maxwell's advances, 'it would not be a good thing for Mr

Maxwell, formerly Jan Ludwig Hoch, to gain control of this news-paper ... which I know is as British as roast beef and Yorkshire pudding'.[7] The anti-Semitism was not heavily disguised. The second trough was when he lost his Labour seat at Buckingham in the 1970 general election. He had talked too much, too often in the Commons, earning himself the nickname 'gasbag', so it wasn't much of a political career to lose. But the third trough was bad – very. It happened in July 1971 when Department of Trade inspect-ors concluded their report on a financial scandal that centred on his Pergamon Press. The inspectors wrote what should have been Maxwell's business obituary: 'Notwithstanding Mr Maxwell's acknowledged abilities and energy, he is not in our opinion a person who can be relied on to exercise proper stewardship of a publicly quoted company.'[8]

Maxwell never surrendered. One banker, Nat Rothschild, said: 'I have shot Mr Maxwell through the forehead seventeen times. But he kept on coming.'[9] He won a new nickname, the Bouncing Czech. The human cost of this very public disgrace took a terrible inner toll on Maxwell and his family. The worlds of business, high society, politics, entertainment shunned the whole family. Used to lots of money and high society, the family was suddenly on its uppers. Betty recalled that the family had been treated like kings. Now they were shunned, abandoned by friends and facing finan-cial ruin.[10]

Pergamon was based in the outbuildings of Headington Hill Hall, so to prevent Robert Maxwell interfering the new management erected a mini-version of the Berlin Wall. One morning Betty woke up to see workmen hammering in fence posts then lining them with coils of barbed wire.[11] The younger children had to cope with the fact that their very famous father was now attracting all the wrong kind of headlines. Kevin, then aged eleven, had to face down callous and anti-Semitic remarks from fellow schoolboys.

Ghislaine had started at Oxford High School for Girls in North Oxford, a very posh crammer for the super-bright daughters of Oxford dons. Ghislaine was too young to understand exactly what had happened, but Betty reports that she started misbehaving at school.[12]

Fellow pupils included Cressida Dick, former Commissioner of the Metropolitan Police in London, and the sister of Ben Macintyre, the acclaimed writer on spies and columnist for *The Times*. Macintyre recalls that Ghislaine was 'a bird of paradise in a successful academic battery farm ... envied, admired, teased for her money, and mocked for her slow reading. But she was more than capable of bullying, perhaps inspired by her father.'[13]

Ghislaine was yanked out of Oxford High because she was disruptive and, as Betty reported the headmistress's view, 'not very bright'.[14] She spent the next four years at Edgarley Hall boarding school in Somerset. Four years later she was back in Oxford, this time at Headington Girls School where, according to the *Oxford Times*, she was 'very sporty at tennis, hockey and athletics'.[15] For her sixth form, Ghislaine went to Marlborough, where one younger boy recalled: 'She was very much one of the in-crowd, fashionable, beautiful. I had a bit of a crush on her.'[16] She played football in midfield for the girls' team, The Grannies. Her A levels did not go as well as hoped and she struggled to get into Oxford. Hey presto, Maxwell funded a bursary at Balliol and she went up to the family college in 1981 – but the ease with which she did so provoked gossip that her father's gold had eased her passage. Ben Macintyre commented in *The Times* in 2020: 'When she went on to Balliol some sniggered that it was only because her father had endowed the college with the Maxwell Fellowship; they still do.'[17] The current Maxwell Fellow at Balliol is Dr Daniel Butt, whose speciality is 'Theories of distributive and rectificatory justice, with particular reference to historical injustice'.

No irony at Balliol, then.

Ghislaine studied modern languages, French and Spanish, and scraped a third, suggesting that the headmistress at Oxford High who thought her a bit thick was on the money. But no one ever bothers about what kind of degree you get. It was going to Oxford that mattered and making the right kind of connections and by that yardstick Ghislaine got a starred first. Her father demanded success and that became her goal too. She once wrote an unpublished piece about the importance to her of winning things: 'I could hang in the loo. I "qualified" as a magician's assistant and pool lifeguard. I learned to bake cupcakes, crochet and speak new languages . . . I have to learn something new every year.'[18]

Nothing, there, about the life of the mind, of loving books for the worlds they help you explore, of using your intellect to help others.

On Ghislaine at Oxford, one strange omission, a peculiar absence of evidence, is that the student journalists do not seem to have written a word about Ghislaine. Researcher Daisy Bata went to the Bodleian Library to scour through back copies of the *Cherwell* and *Isis* and found nothing at all about Robert Maxwell's youngest daughter. Ghislaine was bright-eyed, rich, threw wild parties at the family home and had an infamous old man who lived in Oxford, but none of the student journalists thought any of that would make a story. One wonders whether Daddy's money or his fancy lawyers had helped her news value vanish. Perhaps Ghislaine's antagonistic attitude to scrutiny started long before her father died.

A good number of people from Oxford days point to what they saw as Ghislaine's essential likeability – most often anonymously. One such source, a girlfriend of Ghislaine, told Mark Edmonds of *The Tatler*: 'Nice girl, and her father was a complete c**t. We'd go to Headington Hill Hall and have lunch; there'd be two Filipinos behind his chair, piling up the food for him.'[19]

Another close friend of Ghislaine's told *The Sunday Times*: 'All her energy went into impressing her father, but she never quite managed it. I went to her parents' house once and I was shocked by how hard she tried to get him to love her, notice her, to recognise her by giving her a serious job, like her brothers. But all she got, along with all she materially desired, was charity projects, social stuff.'[20]

Ghislaine made good friends in her Oxford years but often with people who had no connection with the academic world, such as

Prince Andrew, the Duke of York and Susannah Constantine, who, although the daughter of an Old Etonian landowner, worked at Harrods for a bit before going on to become 50 per cent of the Trinny and Susannah fashion combo. Constantine has since said: 'I knew Ghislaine well, before I married in the nineties, but have hardly seen her since then. She was a sweet, kind, loyal friend back then.'[21]

Other pals she made at the university include Ariadne Calvo-Platero, Tania Rotherwick – who went on to found the Wilderness Festival in Oxfordshire, otherwise known as 'Poshstock' – and Nicholas Coleridge, who described the naffness of Headington Hill Hall so nicely. He was moved to defend his old friend in an email to me, written before the trial: 'I always liked her, and I'm sure still do. It wouldn't have occurred to anyone that friendly, smiling, warm Ghislaine would find herself in a cell like now. She never struck me as remotely depraved.' However, Coleridge noted the number and severity of the charges: 'The whole episode has elements of Greek tragedy about it. Don't be too hard on Ghislaine, she had mitigating characteristics and she was a generous, including sort of person. Ghislaine had a large circle of British friends, and I doubt anyone would have had the slightest conception of how her life might become, after her father died. It is impossible to correlate the Ghislaine we all knew in the early eighties with the heinous crimes of which she stands accused.'[22]

Coleridge is exceptional in that he is ready to admit to his old friendship and defend the woman he knew all those years ago, albeit in a qualified way. The norm among Ghislaine's friends at her four schools and Oxford is silence. Francis Wheen, the deputy editor of *Private Eye*, reflected on the sealed lips of the English upper class when I asked him why so many people have closed ranks and don't want to go on the record. Wheen said: 'I'm not sure it's entirely loyalty that is keeping her friends or acquaintances quiet. An awful lot of people knew her socially. I think it's also fear of embarrassment.'

Another friend or rather acquaintance who is willing to go on the record about knowing Ghislaine is Nicky Haslam, the English interior designer and socialite. 'I vaguely remember her being around London, always quite chic if a trifle "ostentatiously" dressed, and bright, with a desire to please mixed with a certain standoffishness, and sort of conspiratorial. I went once to that house in Oxfordshire and recall an on-tenterhooks, explosive atmosphere though Robert Maxwell wasn't there or didn't appear.' Haslam noted that the furnishings were banal but Betty was sweet.[23]

There are a tiny number of people who knew Ghislaine but didn't like what they saw and are willing to talk or write about her on the record. One such is the writer, Anna Pasternak – yes, of course her great uncle Boris wrote *Dr Zhivago*. Ghislaine Maxwell was a slightly older contemporary from Oxford days. 'I vividly remember that she was the kind of person who would say "hello" to you while looking over your shoulder for somebody more interesting, more influential, more powerful. She came across as quite brittle.'

Is she surprised where Ghislaine is now? Anna told me: 'I'm not surprised. It has a lot to do with her relationship with her father. She was the ultimate daddy's girl who had to please daddy at all costs. She seems to be the only member of the family who could sort of wind daddy around her little finger, but that would have come at a cost.'

The journalist Anne McElvoy recalls a Ghislaine who was very much part of the public school set at Oxford, 'striking, with a great mane of glossy dark hair and a fondness for showing off her lithe figure in bright clothes, adorned with proper jewellery, as the rest of us were scouring second-hand shops.' One morning she bumped into Ghislaine who confided that she was going straight from an all-night party to the library. McElvoy wrote that a mutual friend told her that Robert Maxwell was making her love life nigh on impossible. She was encouraged to have a fancy social life, one that would reflect well on him, but Maxwell was squeamish about the idea of her having boyfriends. He 'wanted his daughter to be the ultimate prize and marry accordingly.' McElvoy thought Ghislaine a bit of a bully. She was 'armed with a self-confidence so bullet-proof that she could joke about "making Diana cry" in a world where "teasing" about everything from the wrong boyfriend to the wrong designer could come uncomfortably close to bullying'.[24]

How did Ghislaine Maxwell end up 'making Diana cry'? Charlie Spencer, Viscount Althorp, nowadays titled the ninth Earl Spencer, got into Magdalen College, Oxford, when Ghislaine was in her last year at Balliol, so it's very likely she met his sister, Diana, through him. Ghislaine refers to 'Charlie Althorp' in her black book of contacts.

There is one more hostile witness to the brittle glitter of Ghislaine's Oxford years: George Monbiot, the environmental guru. I met him at a literary festival and found him to be sweet and likeable, with a deft and funny way of self-deprecation. Anyone who has been declared *persona non grata* in seven countries and sentenced *in absentia* to life imprisonment in Indonesia gets my vote. The day after Ghislaine was arrested by the FBI in July 2020, he wrote a Twitter thread:

> For a few months at university, I was in the same social circle as Ghislaine Maxwell. I knew her fairly well. At first, it was fun. Then, almost overnight, I saw it for what it was: a networking nightmare of bright laughter and false friendship, with a howling void beneath. No one gave a damn about anyone else. It was all about climbing the social ladder. I felt I had seen an X-ray of power and wealth in this country: the grinning skull and empty sockets beneath the peachy skin. It was terrifying. It set me on the path I've been on ever since. I spiralled into a pretty dark place after that. I withdrew completely, and started the process of working out what a good life looked like, and how it could be lived. The experience inoculated me against ever again wanting to live the high life, or rub shoulders with that crowd.[25]

Boris Johnson went up to Balliol in 1984 when Ghislaine was in her final year. Another student was Boris's friend Darius Guppy, a dodgy socialite. The two pals were once recorded discussing the possibility of murdering an irritating journalist. One pal ended up going to prison for insurance fraud; the other became prime minister.

Boris Johnson's sister, Rachel, wrote in November 2021, shortly before the trial: 'As a fresher, I wandered into Balliol JCR one day in search of its subsidised breakfast granola-and-Nescafé offering and found a shiny glamazon with naughty eyes holding court astride a table, a high-heeled boot resting on my brother Boris's thigh.' Rachel went on that Ghislaine: 'gave me a pitying glance but I did manage to snag an invite to her party' held at Robert Maxwell's mansion in Oxford, Headington Hill Hall. 'I have a memory of her father, Bob, coming out in a towelling robe and telling us all to go home.'[26]

What is weird is the timing of this piece, a few days before Ghislaine was tried for being a paedophile's apprentice. Why on earth would the sister of the former prime minister – they are believed to be on good terms – want to further tar Boris Johnson's reputation by volunteering that Boris and Ghislaine were, to put it mildly, friendly back in their Oxford days? One possible scenario is that Rachel has deliberately outed the friendship because her big bro suspected it would appear somewhere else. Dot, dot, dot . . .

Shortly after the last episode of the Hunting Ghislaine podcast was broadcast at Christmas 2020, I was contacted by someone who had been at Oxford at the same time as Ghislaine. She had stayed in touch with friends from that time and picked up a peculiar piece of gossip from one of her gang – someone in the City, a high court judge – that kind of tier. My contact's source had said that what was odd about Ghislaine was that when she was up at Oxford she would frequently disappear and return with beautiful posh but dim slightly younger girls and take them to Headington Hill Hall to meet her father. That was considered a bit weird by people who knew her. It was only when the allegations emerged that she had been Epstein's pimp, finding very young women for him, that the penny kind of dropped. What if Ghislaine had become an enabler not first for Jeffrey Epstein, but for her father, long before? I wrote to Ghislaine Maxwell's PR, Brian Basham, and put this story to him and he replied: 'I don't believe it.'

The Ghislaine described by the men and the Ghislaine described by the women seem to be two quite different people locked in the same chassis. The attractive and generous woman to the men was a brittle 'mwah-mwah' princess to Pasternak, forever craning her neck for someone more interesting to talk to and, where Ghislaine found weak or not-well-connected women, she could be, says McElvoy, as cruel and bullying as her father.

That, certainly, is the opinion of Anna Pasternak: 'It's my view that she grew up in a form of an abusive family environment; that, yes, there was a lot of money; that, yes, these children were encouraged to have their places at Oxford, to mix within a certain set. But actually, there was a lot of fear; Robert Maxwell and his moods generated an awful lot of fear.'[27]

Before leaving Oxford, Ghislaine started working part time for the family business. In 1984, Robert Maxwell got himself a fabulous new train set, the Mirror Group. David Seymour worked for Joe Haines as the deputy leader writer of the *Mirror* and, at Maxwell's command, he had to show the leader column to the boss every time he wrote it. Seymour would knock off the draft leader – Mrs Thatcher was bad, President Reagan worse, the royal family in a pickle over Diana, blah blah blah – and then wait for the boss's sign off. And wait. And wait. Seymour spent long hours in the ante-room to Maxwell's cavernous office, peopled by his personal assistant, Jean Baddeley, the assistant-assistant, as it were, Andrea Martin, and Peter Jay who, according to Seymour, had no desk but had to stand in a corner. Jay had once been the British ambassador to the US but was now down on his luck. Maxwell humiliated him but Jay, to be fair, had a liking for the old monster. Supplicants for Maxwell's ear were stacked up like jets coming into Gatwick. And, coming and going with rights of privileged access were the children who were working closely with

Maxwell. Ian was helping out with the *Mirror*; Kevin was running the publishing business, the Maxwell Communications Corporation; and Ghislaine was flitting about. Seymour said: 'I don't want to sound sexist about it but she was extremely attractive, clearly highly intelligent. And, I suppose most of all, she was humble with it. She didn't do "I'm the boss's daughter." I think she was just one of those people who were always friendly.'

Seymour was a relatively important figure in Maxwell's new train set, and a man, so Pasternak's observation would not have applied to him. That autumn Maxwell threw the traditional *Daily Mirror* party at the Labour Party Conference, which was being held in Blackpool. At the end of the party Ghislaine and her brother Ian were both, Seymour recalls, standing around, 'looking a bit spare', so he invited them to join the rest of the *Mirror*'s political team for dinner out on the town. Dinner over, the group returned to the hotel for late night drinks. Seymour recalls that Ghislaine was paralysed with fear about missing a meeting at eight o'clock in the morning the next day. He suggested that she get an alarm call from the hotel. She was still worried, so he gave her his own alarm clock and promised to call her at seven thirty, so she had three separate alarms. 'She looked amazing, I have to say, for somebody who had just woken up and she said, "Thank you so much. I can't be late. I'm having breakfast with my father." And that was a real shock that somebody should be so terrified of being a little bit late, particularly a daughter. She was terrified of him.'

She also loved him, of that there is no doubt. The journalist Tim Willis profiled her for *Tatler* in 2019. He told the story of a male friend of her brothers who took her out for a disastrous date when she was at Oxford. To avoid fuss, he took her out to a restaurant in the countryside, away from prying eyes. He need not have bothered: 'All she talked about was her father: how great he was, how great it was to be his daughter; how she loved reading about him every day in the papers. And all in a very loud voice. By the end of dinner, the whole place was silent. All the diners – and the staff – were listening in.'[28]

Throughout her teens, when she turned twenty-one and even later, Maxwell was protective of Ghislaine to the point of being proprietorial – and beyond. Ian Maxwell talks about an incident when he was at Oxford University and Ghislaine, then aged fifteen, maybe a year older, met some of his fellow student friends. There's a suggestion that one clicked with his younger sister. 'One of them called for Ghislaine at Headington and my father picked up the phone. Ghislaine heard the conversation and it went like this, "Who is this? How old are you? Twenty-one? You are far too old for my daughter." Then he hung up.'[29]

Maxwell policed his children's choice of partners and did so unpleasantly. Greenslade told *Vanity Fair* how after Philip suffered a nervous breakdown in the late 1970s, he went to Argentina and fell in love with Nilda, and had a child with her and married her: 'Maxwell was incredibly enraged, and a massive argument began. I saw Philip once in Maxwell's office, and he had tears in his eyes, and his face was pressed into his father's arms. I said, "Philip, you're not looking too well," but he wouldn't enter into any discussion.'[30]

Maxwell, more child than man, used to show his disfavour to people he didn't approve of by getting their names deliberately wrong. He used to call Nilda, 'Dildo', for example, and Pandora, Kevin's ballsy squeeze, 'Pandura'.[31] He wanted Kevin, Pandora said, to marry into a publishing dynasty or to marry a girl with a title: 'An irony, really, given how badly the Establishment treated him.'

She recalls that the atmosphere at Headington Hill Hall was rather like a demented version of *Downton Abbey*, everyone nervous, taking their positions, before RM (her term for Robert Maxwell) arrived. When Kevin introduced her, she said of Maxwell, 'He always talked at you, not to you.'

Pandora was appalled by how much he had bullied his children: 'He used to beat Kevin with a shoe or a belt whenever he had a bad school report or even one implying that he could have tried harder. Kevin was terrified of him.'[32]

After Maxwell's death, his former mistress Wendy Leigh

interviewed Pandora. She explained that Maxwell had done his best to end the relationship by sending Kevin to America on business. 'He always rang at any time of day or night, irrespective if we were awake or not, and when I answered at 3 a.m., he knew I was there with Kevin.' Maxwell threatened to sack his son unless he gave her up. In what Pandora today terms 'Kevin's finest hour', Kevin stood his ground and Maxwell fired him on the spot. For Kevin it was a brave decision.[33]

Pandora has space in her heart to recall, too, moments when living inside Maxwelliana could be fun: 'We did used to have happy times at Headington when we'd all pile on to his vast bed and on his gigantic screen watch James Bond or Charlie Chaplin films with him. He adored Chaplin.'[34] The irony here is that Maxwell was not like the little tramp but the fat baddie, played by the British actor Eric Campbell, whose signature trick was bending a lamppost.

The hard fact was that if you were Maxwell's child, you did what you were told. And of all the children, Ghislaine had the biggest problem in finding a suitable boyfriend because no man ever seemed good enough for her father. Nick Davies recalls: 'He was always choosy over her boyfriends and would tell her so, often saying that she should "forget" whoever her current beau was and find someone more suitable.'[35]

Ghislaine's twenty-first birthday party should have been a joyous occasion. It was anything but. One young woman – let's call her Katy – who had just left Oxford, was going out with a young academic at the university. Katy got in touch after listening to the Hunting Ghislaine podcast, explaining that she was dating 'a rather beautiful young man' who had been invited to Ghislaine's twenty-first birthday party. Katy had not been invited but went along with him, partly out of fascination. 'The moment Ghislaine saw me, her hackles rose. She was like a cat arching her back, in pre-hiss mode. We ran away but I will never forget her animosity towards me. The thing is, she was very pretty and the family had all this money, but she didn't have a bloke and she wanted mine and she treated me as if I didn't count.'[36]

One schoolfriend of Ghislaine explained that the party started to get a bit out of hand; there was, perhaps, a little too much drinking, cocaine: 'And Robert Maxwell simply closed it down. He'd had enough. Ghislaine was incredibly upset, as you can imagine. But she was in awe of her father and just had to accept it,' – just as she had to accept her father never letting her bring boyfriends home.[37]

Perhaps there was a reason for this, and a creepy one at that.

There are multiple witnesses who echo David Seymour's observation that Ghislaine was in the mid-1980s a very attractive woman, and a sub-set of them say she was fully aware of the power of her sexual attraction. Mark Edmonds in *Tatler* interviewed one anonymous young man of 1980s London: 'She was a bit naughty. Mischievous and a bit spoilt. I remember her coming up to my flat in her tennis gear – that was sexy.'[38]

Puritanism sickens the soul and I am no Puritan. But the evidence is clear that Ghislaine's sexuality was charged, unusually so. One friend said: 'Ghislaine ran with a fast crowd. She was more like a man than a woman, and that's why men liked her.'[39]

A student at Oxford Poly who worked in The Emperor's, a wine bar on Broad Street, got in touch with me after the Hunting Ghislaine podcast was first aired. He has a specific memory of Ghislaine's crowd: 'she used to hang around with these outrageous toffs, people like Gottfried von Bismarck and Olivia Channon.' They would hire the top room at The Emperor's. Once, when the Poly student came in, laden with drinks, he heard Ghislaine boast: '"I give the best blow-jobs in Oxford."'[40]

'She was one of the boys,' one of Ghislaine's American friends told *The Sunday Times*, 'she spoke the language of men.' A New Yorker, at Oxford with Ghislaine, said: 'At university whenever we went on a boys' night out, she would be the only girl with us. Guys always loved hanging out with her. She was naughty, funny and very worldly. She was as comfortable at Buckingham Palace as she was at a hip-hop convention – a chameleon who fitted in everywhere.'[41]

Someone else who knew her later on in life said that Ghislaine was obsessed by sex. 'Bumping into her maybe a decade ago, she was selling "stainless-steel mini dumb-bells that you put up your fanny". She was giving seminars in LA, teaching women how to exercise their vaginal muscles, power up their pelvic floor, learn the Singapore Grip. "They all turn up and I tell them, this is how you keep your man." '[42]

The schoolfriend who had gone to her twenty-first birthday party said that she was 'a great laugh at that age – one of my friends had a fairly serious relationship with her and she was very flirtatious and sexy. She was definitely up for it.'[43] That last phrase pushes me to take stock. Who wasn't definitely up for it when they were twenty-one? It's even said that people older than that age have sex too. Collating this evidence, checking it out and thinking about it, the counter-danger strikes me that there could be something of *Malleus Maleficarum* – the Hammer of the Witches – about some of the comments on Ghislaine's lusty nature. *Malleus Maleficarum* was the work of a sex-obsessed fifteenth-century German Catholic cleric Heinrich Kramer. His book set out the ideological case for burning witches. It's probably the most powerful misogynist text of the Middle Ages. That part of Ghislaine's defence case is that she has been the victim of misogyny does not necessarily make it untrue.

Ghislaine's most striking university friend was Count Gottfried Alexander Leopold von Bismarck-Schönhausen, an extraordinary figure in 1980s Oxford, in any time. The great-great-grandson of Prince Otto, Germany's Iron Chancellor and architect of the modern German state, he was a brilliant student but a broken human being. He was named Gottfried after a great uncle who had taken part in the July 1944 plot to assassinate Hitler, and had been sent to a concentration camp but survived because of the spell cast by the family name. Ghislaine's Gottfried, known as 'Max', was said to have found his ancestry a burden. He was clever, funny, and could be kind, outrageous, often wasted by too much alcohol or heroin, militantly self-destructive. His obituary in the *Daily Telegraph* sets out some of the issues that troubled him and some that troubled the newspaper: an 'extravagant host of homosexual orgies . . . [he] hosted a dinner at which the severed heads of two pigs were placed at either end of the table. When not clad in the lederhosen of his homeland, he cultivated an air of sophisticated complexity by appearing in women's clothes, set off by lipstick and fishnet stockings.'

The obit concludes: 'He never married'[44] – the *Daily Telegraph*'s not-very-hard-to-decrypt code for he was gay, exotically so for that time.

Von Bismarck was a pillar of the Piers Gaveston Society, set up to honour the courtier and probable bedfellow of Edward II – 'a worthless king' according to the only history book worth reading from cover to cover, *1066 and All That*.[45] Medieval chroniclers suggested Gaveston had a homosexual relationship with the king. To be fair, Gaveston mocked his fellow nobles, calling the Earl of Lancaster 'The Fiddler', the Earl of Lincoln 'Burst-belly', the Earl of Pembroke 'Joseph the Jew', and the Earl of Warwick 'The Black Dog of Arden'. Gaveston was captured by nobles jealous of his influence and killed in 1312; Edward II later came to an untimely end, the said medieval chroniclers implying that he had been murdered by the insertion of a red-hot poker up his bottom, a death so hideous that it inspired Christopher Marlowe's grisly tragedy, *Edward II*, first performed in 1592, and the punk-rock band Eddie and the Hot Rods from Canvey Island in 1975. The Piers Gaveston Society was set up at Oxford University in 1977 and attracted rich and/or very posh sexual exhibitionists, often gay or bisexual, some of who were also heavily into hard drugs. One former head of the society, Nick Richardson, described in the *London Review of Books* how the club worked in his day. The society appealed to those who 'only went to Oxford to feel as if they were in a pornified Evelyn Waugh novel.' Members chose their own names, Richardson recalling a Fellatrix, an Irrumator, a Raging Horn and a Mr Whippy. The head of the Piers Gaveston Society is known as the Lord High Spanker – 'Spanks' to his mates. Richardson recalled one party in the countryside near Oxford. The drug dealer came in a white cowboy outfit and had a large suitcase full of powders and pills.

People had sex and drugs and rock'n'roll. 'No one, as far as I know, fucked a pig's head.'[46]

This last point refers to an initiation rite at another Piers Gaveston party, in which prime-minister-to-be David Cameron, then of Brasenose, Oxford, allegedly inserted his penis into a pig's head. Mr Cameron has pooh-poohed the story; the pig denied any wrongdoing.

To celebrate the end of their finals in June 1986, von Bismarck and Olivia Channon, the twenty-two-year-old daughter of Paul Channon, one of Margaret Thatcher's cabinet ministers, went on a massive bender involving huge amounts of champagne, Black Velvet and sherry. Then Olivia overdosed on heroin. Her corpse was found amid a sea of broken bottles and party wreckage in von Bismarck's rooms at Christ Church college, Oxford, the following morning. He was not there. Von Bismarck was charged with possessing amphetamine sulphate and cocaine and was later treated at a £770-a-week rehab clinic in Surrey. At Olivia Channon's funeral he was said to have 'wept like a child'. In disgrace, von Bismarck vowed: 'My days of living it up are all over.' That turned out to be a lie. He left Oxford so quickly that he did not have time to settle his bills. His father, Prince Ferdinand von Bismarck, sent a manservant, who went round his son's favoured watering-holes, restaurants and his tailor with a fat chequebook.

Von Bismarck was often described as having perfect manners, but carried on living on the edge. He set up in London and threw extraordinary all-night parties at his £5 million flat at Draycott Place, Chelsea, not far from Sloane Square. In 2006 one of his male guests, Anthony Casey, fell sixty feet to his death, triggering rumours that von Bismarck might be the victim of a family curse. Scotland Yard's Detective Inspector Mike Christensen investigated. He told the coroner that police officers had discovered 'buckets of sex toys', vodka, butane lighter fuel and 'a substantial number of syringes' in the living room of Count von Bismarck's apartment. A large rubber tarpaulin covered the floor, and there were mirrors propped up against three of the walls. A television and video player had been set up to show 'scenes of a pornographic nature', said the copper. Paul Knapman, the coroner, said: 'In common parlance, in the early hours of the morning there was a gay orgy going on.' He told the court that most if not all of the men present had been wearing jockstraps and boots.[47] Von Bismarck told the inquest that he had not seen any homosexual activity taking place.

One year later, in 2007, von Bismarck was selling his flat but wasn't answering calls. His father asked the estate agent to check up on him. He was found lying on a mattress with his arm exposed and blackened. He had injected himself with cocaine every hour for a period of nearly twenty-four hours before his death. The pathologist, Professor Sebastian Lucas, said the amount of cocaine in the count's body was the highest he had seen in his career. He found traces of morphine in the body too which most likely came from heroin. His liver was frazzled from alcohol and drug abuse and he had HIV and hepatitis B and C. The coroner, Paul Knapman – who had presided over Casey's inquest one year before – recorded death from a heart attack caused by drug dependency and overdose. Knapman said: 'I think this is a very regrettable story. The reckless behaviour with cocaine has caused his death.'[48]

Ghislaine Maxwell never featured in the press reports at the time of Olivia Channon's death and the gorgeous, sick depravity of von Bismarck's circle at Oxford. That is odd because von Bismarck and Ghislaine were close. Both the barman at The Emperor's wine bar and Anne McElvoy said so. McElvoy concluded her article: 'I met her once again a few years ago. We talked about the Balliol years and how much we missed our old friend von Bismarck, who died of a drug overdose . . . "We had a great time," she said ruefully. "It's tragic how things turn out." '[49] That phrase could headline Ghislaine's own obituary.

There is one more piece of evidence that Ghislaine kept up her contact with von Bismarck after his first disgrace in 1986. In 1996 Kevin Maxwell and his brother Ian were tried for the then biggest fraud trial in British criminal history, accused of helping their father steal £400 million-plus from the Maxwell pensions funds. After walking free from court, Kevin Maxwell set up Telemonde, a telecoms firm based in the United States. Who better to be Telemonde's company secretary than heroin-injecting, coke-addled, amphetamine-guzzling Gottfried von Bismarck, the man at whose parties over the years not one but two people died? Perhaps surprisingly, perhaps not, the company boasting both the Maxwell and von Bismarck brand names collapsed in 2002 with debts of £105 million.[50]

Did Gottfried von Bismarck, Oxford's professor of debauchery, teach his friend Ghislaine a few party tricks when, back in the day, they were having such a great time? Members of the Piers Gaveston Society were divided into two categories: 'Masters' and 'Minions'. Years later, one of the victims of Jeffrey Epstein told *Vanity Fair* that Ghislaine Maxwell 'would call people her minion . . . So you felt like you were nothing.'[51] The worry is that she took a joke for posh twits in the Piers Gaveston Society and lived its sick, elitist gospel to the letter.

Ghislaine is a fabulously elusive character. But also, perhaps, there was another factor at work here. There are no stories about Ghislaine in the Oxford student papers and nothing remotely critical in the newspaper archives while her father remained alive. As the daughter of a press baron, *un capo dei capi*, she enjoyed a mafia-style protection from scrutiny by the red tops. Rupert Murdoch's *Sun* didn't dig into the private life of Robert Maxwell or his children; Robert Maxwell likewise; ditto, Lord Rothermere who owned the *Daily Mail* group.

Back in the late 1980s Kelvin MacKenzie, former editor of Rupert Murdoch's the *Sun*, was door-stepped by *Tatler*. The editor phoned up the *Sun*'s news desk and complained that some 'fat cunt' was shouting through his letterbox.

I was that fat cunt.

For this book I tracked down my old enemy. MacKenzie explained to me that the newspaper owners back in the day had an NPP, a 'Non-Pissing Pact. If you own a newspaper you have immense power to piss all over people, but you can get your own leg wet into the bargain. So Rupert Murdoch, Robert Maxwell and Harmsworth at the *Mail* had an agreement, nothing signed, nothing said; that they wouldn't turn over each other and the kids were covered too.' MacKenzie's view that is that despite the informal NPP, had Maxwell been around today he would not have been able to protect her from the Epstein blowback. 'The story's too big.'[52]

Roy Greenslade agrees with his old sparring partner:

> I don't think there was a formal deal of any kind, probably more of an unwritten, unacknowledged acceptance by all concerned not to invade each other's privacy. And it wasn't just about 'the kids' but about each other. I was witness to the *Daily Mail* editor, David English, commiserating with Murdoch about his estrangement from Anna, but the *Mail* didn't carry the story. As for Ghislaine, she was such a minor figure at the time – youngest daughter, not outwardly involved in the business, not known as a wild child – that there was no reason to write about her.[53]

Ghislaine at Oxford exhibited the following character traits: first, she could be extraordinarily sensitive to another's wishes, especially if they were male; second, she could be coldly dismissive of people who did not merit her attention and – to weak and vulnerable people such as the late Princess Diana – outrightly cruel, especially if they were female; third, she was sexed up, big-time; fourth, she was afraid of her father, morbidly so; fifth, she loved him or was so in thrall to him she would obey him, come what may.

In the back half of the 1980s, Maxwell, along with buying the *Mirror*, started throwing his money at English football, specifically the local team, Oxford United. It worked for a time and, under Maxwell's ownership, in 1986 the Yellows won the Milk Cup. Maxwell and Ghislaine were photographed celebrating their victory. The camera catches her hugging him in a way that looks more than a little bit creepy.

While making the Hunting Ghislaine podcast, I was put in touch with a psychotherapist in the United States, Wendy Behary, the author of *Disarming the Narcissist*. The book describes a syndrome where the daughters of narcissistic men become in some measure their partner. Two photographs help to illustrate the syndrome. One is of Donald Trump, long before he is president, in a white suit looking like Don Johnson in *Miami Vice*, and he's got a girl leaning against him. She's wearing a short denim skirt and a skimpy top, and it's his daughter, Ivanka, who looks to be around twelve or thirteen years old. In the background are palm trees and two cement parrots shagging; on grounds of aesthetic taste alone, then, it was almost certainly taken at Trump's Mar-a-Lago estate on Palm Beach. And the second photo is of Ghislaine and Robert Maxwell hugging each other when Oxford United won the Milk Cup.

Such women can be defined as 'the hostage princess in the palace', said Wendy Behary. She explained that for women like Ghislaine Maxwell or Ivanka Trump the attachment with daddy warps how they see the world: 'you're going to take it, accept it as a child because it's a survival mechanism and you get a lot of goodies that come with that . . . But you're vying for the power and the privilege that comes with staying closely attached and so you will commit yourself to the daddy figure. And you get kind of addicted to having all the privileges that come along with that.' In other words, they become addicted to daddy or a daddy figure. The approval from daddy gives a sense of worth, of value, and that, Wendy said, provides some meaning in the world. She went on to discuss what happens when daddy dies. 'It can happen in some cases where the child of a man like this may gravitate towards a polar opposite type of partner, but in so many cases, people are a creature of habit. It's the familiarity. It feels like, smells like, sounds like, looks like . . . And it's a mirror. Daddy dies. I've lost my mirror. I've lost my capacity to see my reflection of who I am and how I matter and what my position is. And so I seek that same or similar position of power.'[54]

Nicholas Coleridge, I believe, is exactly right in that Ghislaine's story has the feel of a Greek tragedy to it and that sense was enhanced when I read a Twitter post by James Marriot of *The Times* quoting from *The Art of Psychotherapy* by the late English psychiatrist, Anthony Storr, on the character flaws of someone with a depressive personality. Storr noted 'the absence of an inner sense of worth . . . being so dependent on the good opinion of others and so vulnerable to criticism often has the consequence that the depressive is less than normally assertive with other people, and over-anxious to please them'. Storr theorised that some depressives, so anxious to avoid blame and obtain approval, become hyper-sensitive to the needs and wishes of others: 'This kind of sensitivity is not unlike that demanded of their secretaries of over-burdened executives, who expect that they shall know, without being told, exactly in what mood the boss may be, and treat him accordingly.'[55]

Storr seems to sum up Ghislaine's hopelessly servile, horribly abusive relationship with her monster of her father in a nutshell.

At this point in the tragedy of Ghislaine Maxwell, her father is still very much alive. But something happens that throws her volatile, potentially self-destructive mix of character traits – servile to men, cruel to women, highly sexed, fear and love for Robert Maxwell – into spasm. While Daddy goes further round the bend, Ghislaine falls in love.

chapter three

The Currency of Sex

Count Gianfranco Cicogna Mozzoni, nicknamed the 'Turbo Count', was handsome, charming, Italian, old money. Variously described as 'Italy's Rockefeller' and 'an old-fashioned smoocher', he was, by all accounts, deeply loved by Ghislaine. The Mozzonis date their family tree back to the eleventh century, but they hit the big time in 1476 when one of the gang, Agostino Mozzoni, obliged Duke Galeazzo Maria Sforza by killing a ferocious bear, although he got wounded in the process. The duke granted him and his descendants tax exemption *ad infinitum*. The Cicognas go further back to Tacitus and boast former Doges of Venice in the family tree.[1] The family was rich but Gianfranco's father, film producer Bino Cicogna, facing financial troubles, gassed himself in Rio in 1971, another reminder that gilded cages can be grim. A brother, a war photographer, was killed in Afghanistan. Gianfranco, who was one year older than Ghislaine, went to the University of Buckingham, then worked in finance. In 1992 the *Mail on Sunday* described Ghislaine's affair with the Turbo Count: 'A dashing, charming member of the [now defunct] Ciga hotels clan, Cicogna was the man who moulded the Ghislaine we now see. He told her where to get her hair cut, and what to wear.'[2]

The Turbo Count was an adrenalin junkie, racing cars and motorbikes, loving speed, flying, danger. 'Gianfranco was a thoroughly nice bloke,' Simon Mann, the Old Etonian mercenary jailed in Zimbabwe and Equatorial Guinea in 2014 for his role in the failed 'Wonga' coup told me. 'I had a drink with him the day before I left South Africa to do the coup.' The attempt to depose the leader of Equatorial Guinea, President Teodoro Obiang, failed spectacularly when Mann and his mercenary crew were arrested in Zimbabwe. It was not an ignoble failure, Obiang being one of Africa's nastiest tyrants. Allegedly, he once ate the testicles of someone who had displeased him. While in prison in Zimbabwe, Mann reportedly wrote an unsigned letter by hand setting out who had funded the coup: 'Scratcher' – his nickname for Mark Thatcher – and 'Cicogma', a misspelling of Ghislaine's ex. Mark Thatcher has always denied that he knew he was funding a merce-nary-led coup or anything like it. [3]

Mann told me that the letter was a red herring, that the count had been approached but said no. Mann described him as very good-looking, tall, six foot something, dark hair, lean, athletic, a polo player, a charming Italian aristocrat. 'I remember that last drink I had with him, I was nervous, he knew where I was going, and he very graciously said, "You're going through the mill now but it will be fine once you get stuck in." He was spot on. Lovely chap.'[4]

Ghislaine's love affair with the count ended in 1990. In 2012, Cicogna was doing aero-acrobatics at an air show in South Africa when his plane crashed, killing him instantly in front of his wife and two small children. In his obituary, the Italian newspaper, *Il Fatto Quotidiano*, noted his charitable work in Africa and at Lourdes and went on to write: 'He loved the high life and its excesses. Gianfranco Cicogna Mozzoni was reckless but he had such a big heart . . . He cultivated the myth of the superman and always had his foot down on the accelerator pedal of life. As a top gun, he did everything for the thrill of speed. Until his last fatal flight.'[5]

It's hard to know why the love affair ended. Suffice to say that the Turbo Count, from the sound of him, had the grace, the social capital and the raw courage to take on Ghislaine's father. Simon Mann said: 'I do feel that Ghislaine would have been much better off with Gianfranco than the man she ended up with.'

In the summer of 1990, the writer and devoted party-goer Vassi Chamberlain bumped into Ghislaine at a restaurant in Soho, London. Ghislaine was, Vassi recalled, 'loud and great fun; dressed in black shorts, sheer tights and a top hat, with a touch of gold, possibly a scarf. She looked naughty and sexy, but tomboyish too, markedly at odds with the Dianaesque taffeta femininity around us. She was intriguing, an anomaly. After that I became a keen Ghislaine-spotter.'[6]

She could be extraordinarily manipulative. Vassi Chamberlain tells the story of a younger woman that summer of 1990 arranging with Ghislaine to go to a party. Ghislaine insisted the younger woman drive her car even though she hadn't passed her driving test and didn't have a licence. The younger woman said that Ghislaine, to help her new friend, put her hand on top of hers but it stayed there the entire journey. The experience could have been erotic, the friend recalled: 'It was so weird. Coerced is too strong a word. She was more a bulldozer. If she could get someone like me to do something like that, which was illegal, with that natural skill set, she was capable of anything.'[7]

Apart, that is, from standing up to her father. Nick Davies recalls that when in a very bad mood Maxwell could be horrible to Ghislaine, the apple of the monster's eye: 'She'd go in, give him a big kiss, say "Hello, Dad", and Maxwell as often as not would say "Bloody stupid woman – fuck off." And she'd go off in tears.'[8]

You can make the argument that Robert Maxwell was mad his whole adult life. His *modus operandi* of suing critics for libel made sure that people held their tongues. But not all. In his elegantly written memoir of Fleet Street, *The Happy Hack*, Mike Molloy describes a lunch he had at Langan's with a friend, psychiatrist Tom Pitt-Atkins, who firmly declared that Maxwell was not eccentric but mad.

'I've got people inside who are less crazy than him.' The psychiatrist asked the editor whether Maxwell had a group of people who fulfil the following functions: someone who was the repository of all his secrets; a person he only uses for sexual gratification; a group of executives who are bitter rivals and only answer to him directly; a devoted dogsbody he treats like shit. Molloy answered yes to every question. The shrink asked how Maxwell treated his family and Molloy answered, 'like slaves', adding that he wanted to leave a great heritage for his children. Pitt-Atkins replied: 'He'll leave nothing to them, just ashes. He'll probably die unexpectedly, perhaps in some kind of explosion.'[9]

Tom Pitt-Atkins wasn't just a psychiatrist but also a bit of a Mystic Meg. As the 1980s wound on, Robert Maxwell became madder and madder until his failure to grip reality destroyed his fortune and ended up killing him. For a time, his insanity was masked by the fact that he had become a national joke. He abused the readers of the *Daily Mirror* by forever popping up in its pages, trying the patience of everyone who came into contact with him, and routinely sued or threatened to sue anyone who dared question his word. Or his sanity.

Everyone had to bend the knee before Robert Maxwell's bullying ways. If you didn't, you were dead to him. When Roy Greenslade was running the *Mirror*, his rival Kelvin MacKenzie was editing the *Sun*. Greenslade recalled Maxwell demanding a temporary secretary to call MacKenzie so that the three men could talk. There was a long silence and nothing happened. Maxwell demanded that the temporary secretary, who was obviously very young and inexperienced, come into his office, Greenslade recalling he was physically intimidating and she was scared. Maxwell wanted to know why she had failed to get hold of MacKenzie and she stammered that he did not want to talk to him. Maxwell growled: 'What did he say *exactly*?' She said: 'I can't use those words.' '*Tell me what he said.*' 'He said: "I don't want to talk to that fat Czech cunt."' The next day she'd gone.

Maxwell reminded Roy Greenslade of another figure from our time: 'Trump and Maxwell, two peas in a pod: the narcissism, the changes of mind, the throwing aside of all responsibility for any of their actions despite the consequences. The maverick, mercurial behaviour. All of it is just exactly the same.'[10]

Having a dad who was being constantly lampooned in the pages of *Private Eye* as a crook and a monster must have been mortifying. But standing up to Robert Maxwell was not cost-free. *Private Eye* issued some fifty apologies to Maxwell over the years. Perhaps the most insane piece of mockery was for the *Eye* to feature Maxwell in their joke lookalike competition. The letters page would regularly run letters from readers with funny names whom one suspected were made up, suggesting that two famous people were in some way related. In February 1983 one Ena T. Courtauld wrote: 'Sir, Have any of your readers noticed the remarkable likeness between Robert Maxwell, chairman of BPCC, and Ronnie Kray, the famous East End gangster? I wonder if they have anything else in common?'[11] The letter was headlined 'Kray Twins' and under a black-and-white photo of Maxwell was the caption 'Kray' while under a photo of Ronnie Kray was the caption 'Maxwell'. Ronnie Kray was a psychotic gangland boss who ruled over London's East End in the 1960s. Rivals were killed; witnesses intimidated; juries nobbled; bent coppers paid off. Infamously, after rival villain George Cornell reportedly called Ronnie 'a fat poof', Ronnie tracked him down to the Blind Beggar pub in Whitechapel and shot Cornell dead in front of all the drinkers. Witnesses in the pub refused to testify to the police because they were so scared. Eventually the Krays were jailed for murder and while in prison Ronnie was diagnosed a paranoid schizophrenic. In 1979 he was sent to Broadmoor, Britain's oldest high-security prison for psychiatric patients.

For *Private Eye* to compare Robert Maxwell to Ronnie Kray was, to put it mildly, sticking their heads into the lion's gob. No one before had threatened to sue on a lookalike – what the *Eye* saw as a funny joke safely inside the historic British tradition of teasing the rich and the powerful. Maxwell fired up his libel lawyers and the *Eye* grovelled, telling its readers that it entirely acknowledged that no such likeness between Ronnie Kray and Robert Maxwell existed. The *Eye* added that the line suggesting that Maxwell and Kray might have other things in common was also deliberately offensive and a wholly fictitious insinuation.[12]

Maxwell accepted the apology for the Kray lookalike gag but a while later the *Eye* returned to the fray, suggesting that Maxwell had been funding foreign trips for the Leader of the Opposition, Labour's leader Neil Kinnock, in return for influence – perhaps a peerage – an accusation that was stoutly denied by Kinnock's office. Maxwell sued and when he was giving evidence in court brought up the Ronnie Kray lookalike story. Maxwell, the *Eye* reported in its court coverage, was asked if he found anything funny in this lookalike. He replied: 'Not only was I not amused, but, far worse, Mrs Maxwell and all of our children were utterly shocked to have me, their father, compared to a major gangster.'

Richard Hartley QC, for Maxwell, noted that after the apology the *Eye* had taken to signing lookalike letters 'Ena B. Maxwell' of Headington Hill Hall. Hartley then showed Maxwell a lookalike of the late Duke of Edinburgh and Adolf Eichmann, the Nazi war criminal, as an example of a letter signed in this way. The *Eye* reported: 'Maxwell suddenly burst into tears, producing a handkerchief from his pocket, while explaining that his "family was destroyed by Eichmann".'[13]

What had happened is that two unrelated *Private Eye* jokes – one mocking the late Duke of Edinburgh for his right-wing views and the other mocking Maxwell for his dislike of the Kray lookalike – had come together in what seemed an ugly manner and Maxwell had played a blinder. Any British jury when confronted with the grief of a Holocaust survivor would give that person the benefit of the doubt. It was also true that throughout his career, especially in the City of London, Maxwell had faced anti-Semitic prejudice. But *Private Eye* had Jewish contributors and regularly attacked far-right anti-Jewish groups like the National Front. However, the damage had been done. Tom Bower, like Ingrams another heroic journalist who stood up to Maxwell under heavy fire, wrote in his definitive book *Maxwell the Outsider*: 'Maxwell performed a remarkable somersault. Maxwell the ogre and bully became Maxwell the underdog . . . Maxwell was winning sympathy as the victim of gross insensitivity.'[14]

Ingrams had run the libels but then had stepped down, making way for the new editor of the *Eye*, Ian Hislop, who told me: 'I'd like to say a personal thank you to Richard Ingrams for leaving me when I became editor with so many writs from Maxwell. Richard said, "Sorry, it's a bit of a ticking bomb."'

The *Eye* lost £55,000 in damages and had to pay £250,000 in costs. Maxwell ordered a team at the *Mirror* to cook up a spoof copy of the *Eye* called *Not Private Eye*. It was pretty crude stuff, showing on the front cover Ingrams' head stuck onto the torso of a Nazi general chatting to Hitler with a speech bubble reading: 'And if anyone objects, we say we were only doing it for a laugh.'[15]

Peter Cook sensed that the *Mirror* team working on the spoof might only be obeying orders. So, in a stroke of genius, he sent a case of whisky to them and they duly started drinking it. Cook then sought and got an invitation to join in the fun. A team from the *Eye* got in a taxi and hurried around to the Mirror building, including Ian Hislop, the new editor of the *Eye*. While the *Mirror* crew fell asleep, paralytic on the *Eye*'s whisky, Cook stole into Maxwell's office, scribbled 'Maxwell is a wanker' on the office walls, opened Maxwell's fridge, drank his booze and then called Maxwell, who was in New York, on his own office telephone to tell him exactly what he was doing, how indeed, he was bemoaning the *Eye*'s defeat by drinking Maxwell's own champagne. Maxwell, in a fury, called security. The gang from the *Eye*, Cook too, vanished, Stott hid the drunken *Mirror* culprits from the search teams and Maxwell's trans-oceanic rage was unconfined.

Robert Maxwell's staff at the *Mirror* found working for him by turns maddening, surreal and unbearable. Noreen Taylor, the feature writer on the *Daily Mirror*, once found herself in the same Manhattan hotel as Maxwell and his entourage. She was feeling under the weather after an exhausting set of interviews and only wanted a good night's sleep before flying back to London, but Maxwell had other ideas. He got his butler to wake her up, dictated some article to her, decided to leave for London, changed his mind. 'He spent nights like this, in constant flux, dragging people into this nightmarish maze and making demands and then cancelling the demand, then making fresh demands. But not because he could get joy out of it. He was lost in his own swirling nightmare.'[16]

For all Maxwell's madness, Noreen bravely admits to liking him because he wasn't an accountant and was genuinely interested in what his reporters were up to. He was, she says, fascinated by storytellers. But she did not like his daughter. Noreen moved from the *Mirror* to Maxwell's new toy, *The European,* in 1990 and bumped into Ghislaine as she was leaving Maxwell's office. Ghislaine asked Noreen where she was going – Hungary – and Ghislaine said: ' "Well, do your best. The paper deserves it." It was a headmistressy thing to say, or the sort of thing a netball captain might say. Idiot. She hadn't done a day's work in her life.'[17]

Noreen is one of the great feature writers of our time. She's interviewed Nelson Mandela, Donald Trump, Paul McCartney, Mick Jagger, Muhammad Ali and Jackie Kennedy. For Ghislaine to treat her like a shopping assistant at Boots tells you far more about Ghislaine than Noreen: that she can't read the room; that a haughty manner is her default position when dealing with other women who she might find threatening; that like her old friend Count Gottfried and her pals in the Piers Gaveston Society, other people outside her set were not masters but minions.

The forces – real and imaginary – raging against Robert Maxwell were closing in, and as they were doing so the pressure on him was taking its toll. Maxwell started making mistakes: small ones, gigantic ones. In 1988 Maxwell, to show he was top dog over Rupert Murdoch, bet the farm on going big in the United States. The deal to buy Macmillan, an American publishing firm, for $2.6 billion, was mad. The price he paid was probably a billion dollars over the going rate and as the world entered recession interest rates hit 15 per cent. His whole empire was going bust and he started robbing Peter to pay Paul and then robbing his own pensioners when Peter had no money left. And still he couldn't pay the banks the interest he owed them – never mind the capital. Soon the banks started asking for their money back and there was no way out.

At the same time, the world he'd known since 1945 was breaking up. In his pomp, Maxwell had been a noisy player on the international stage, publishing a series of ghastly vanity books, *Leaders of the World*, his craven interviews with mostly Eastern European strongmen. The worst one was called *Nicolae Ceaușescu: Builder of Modern Romania and International Statesman*. It ends with an interview between the two great men of ditch-water-quality dullness. Maxwell

concludes: 'Mr President, I feel dutybound to express my deep gratitude for the time you have given to answering my questions, for this
interesting, frank and comprehensive talk. I wish you good health
and power to continue your constant, tireless activity for the good of
your country, for the success of peace and détente worldwide, for
understanding and collaboration among nations.'[18]

As it happened, I spent the Christmas of 1989 with the
Ceaușescus, kind of. Reporting for my old paper, the *Observer*, I
crossed the country on Christmas Eve while the regime of Nicolae
Ceaușescu was overthrown. On Christmas Day, Romania's revolu-
tionaries shot him and his wife.

Maxwell's most perceptive interviewee in the *Leaders of the World*
series was the Polish dictator General Wojciech Jaruzelski, he of
the opaque spectacles, worn after he suffered sun-blindness under
Soviet captivity in Siberia. Jaruzelski told Russell Davies in his
book, *Foreign Body*, that Maxwell had two or even four souls: poor
Jewish boy; multi-millionaire who had climbed Mount Olympus;
leftist who would address one as 'Comrade'; and arch-capitalist
who had made 35 per cent of his workforce redundant.[19]

Back in the day Maxwell had been able to trade on his contacts
with the old monsters of eastern Europe. Now they were being
carted off to the museums of statues or getting machine-gunned.
Noreen Taylor has a vignette of Maxwell's slow demise as his grip
on his old levers of power starts to weaken. It was winter at the fag-
end of the Soviet Union – 1989, 1990, she wasn't quite sure – and
Maxwell announced that they were off to Moscow on his private jet,
he to interview Mikhail Gorbachev, Noreen to interview his wife,
Raisa. Noreen was feeling poorly, her voice afflicted with laryngitis,
perhaps her own anxiety about the trip worsening her condition.

'Halfway through the flight,' Noreen told me, 'Maxwell came
down and sat next to me and said, "What do you know about
Gorbachev?" I replied so weakly he couldn't hear me and he
shouted at Joe Haines, his writing factotum, "She's no fucking
use" and stormed off.'

Noreen Taylor liked Maxwell for his swashbuckling style but
was fully aware of how he could turn nasty on a sixpence.

Gorbachev, his back against the wall, could not find time in his diary to see Maxwell, so the team returned with their tails between their legs.[20] The failure of Gorbachev to make time to meet Maxwell was a sign that the old man's powers were waning. Andy McSmith was a *Daily Mirror* political reporter who, to his intense misery, was ordered to act as Maxwell's personal PR man in the summer of July 1990. McSmith realised that Maxwell was falling apart mentally. One day, at the start of McSmith's brief tenure, he and Robert Maxwell were in a lift when Maxwell introduced him to one of his sons. 'Maxwell said: "This is Ian Maxwell." Without thinking, McSmith burst out, "No it's not, it's Kevin." Kevin looked furious that an employee had to point out to his own father that he'd got the wrong son.'[21]

'Suddenly,' observed McSmith, 'I realised I was talking to a tired old man who didn't know what was going on.'[22]

And all the time Maxwell's two-billion-dollar bet on Macmillan Publishing in the States was killing him. What no one on the *Mirror* or in the family knew was that, by the start of the 1990s, Maxwell's business empire was in terminal trouble, but his favourite child was on hand to help. On 5 November 1990 – a year before Robert Maxwell went overboard to the day – Ghislaine flew by Concorde from London on a mission for her dad. In New York she picked up paper, ten million shares of the Berlitz language school company worth $200 million, owned by the Maxwell Communications Company, a publicly quoted company. Tom Bower, in his book *Maxwell: The Final Verdict*, writes that Ghislaine spent the night partying in New York, flew back the next day and handed the shares over to her father, who put them in his safe and from there into one of his private companies. Ghislaine didn't know it but she had just helped her father steal $200 million.[23] He would blow that money on secretly buying the shares of the Maxwell Communications Company to bolster their value, to no avail because the price kept on going down.

In Tom Bower's BBC documentary, *Maxwell: The Downfall*, there is a clip of Robert Maxwell telling his workers their pensions are safe. 'As chairman of the Maxwell group of companies' pension funds, I'm addressing you today for the purpose of persuading you that it is in your and your families' best interests to remain a member of whichever pension scheme you are a member of in our group.'

That was bollocks. Behind the scenes, Maxwell was robbing some £400 million from his staff pension funds and robbing more from the banks, perhaps two billion pounds in all. To keep himself ahead of the pack, he started a surveillance operation against the very people he was stealing from. Roy Greenslade, his last but one editor, was one of the people whose private phone calls were snooped on by Maxwell's security goons: 'Like all mega-lomaniacs, but particularly like somebody who is a conman, he was paranoid, fearing that he might be found out, so he wanted as much information as he could get on everyone around him.'

Roy Greenslade often called his rival at the *Sun*, Kelvin MacKenzie, for a gossip: two newspaper editors chatting over the Fleet Street garden fence. But was someone else listening in too? Greenslade told me: 'I remember saying one time, "Oh, that's the helicopter landing above. I'd be really pleased if it fell out of the sky one day." And Kelvin said, "Careful." And suddenly I thought that Kelvin may be right, maybe Maxwell could have been listening in. And he was doing exactly that.'[24]

In 1991 Maxwell had one last throw of the dice. As his debts piled up, he went on a final spending splurge, buying the ailing *New York Daily News* from its owners, who were getting frustrated with the corrupt practices of the printing and distribution unions. Maxwell didn't know who, exactly, he was dealing with. He had sent Ian Watson, editorial director of *The European*, to discuss the nitty-gritty for the job cuts necessary to make the New York tabloid a going concern. Nick Davies recalled how one union official asked Watson, who was Scottish, in a broad Brooklyn accent if he was a New Yorker. Watson said no he wasn't and asked what was the point of the question. The union boss replied: 'If you think you can push us into an agreement, you'll end up in the East River with your throats slit. All of you.'

Maxwell gave New York's underworld an easy ride. His play

with the *New York Daily News* was all about keeping up appearances, not turning the paper into a money-maker.

By late 1991, Kevin and Ian Maxwell were doing their best to keep the plates spinning in the air, but the rest of the family, Ghislaine too, found Maxwell impossible to deal with. Physically, the old monster was in a bad way. 'He couldn't breathe,' said his chauffeur John Featley. 'He couldn't talk properly. He had a sore throat. If he'd been a horse, you would have put him down.'[25] The banks were snapping. They wanted their money back. At the very head of that queue was the Swiss Bank Corporation – SBC – which had lent Maxwell £60 million to buy a company, expecting him, as per contract, to hand over some collateral holdings as security. The bad news was that the holdings intended for SBC had already been sold.[26] The Swiss were threatening to call in the Fraud Squad. Maxwell's grip on reality was disintegrating. His memory – for people, for numbers – was failing him. His old party boss chums? Jaruzelski disgraced, Erich Honecker on trial, Gorbachev out of power, Ceaușescu shot.

Betty and Maxwell at the end were living apart, his children, Ghislaine included, finding it extraordinarily difficult to have any half-pleasant interaction with him. In May 1991, Ghislaine flew with Maxwell by Concorde to New York. They were in the Big Apple to attend a gala evening honouring the Nazi hunter Simon Wiesenthal. But Maxwell changed his plans at the last minute – a constant nightmare for his children – and flew to Moscow for business talks. Ghislaine called her father, telling her how the evening had gone. She wasn't sufficiently effusive and he bawled her out. Tom Bower got hold of her written apology where she abased herself: 'I am very sorry that my description of the dinner was inadequate and made you angry. I should have expressed that I was merely presenting you with a preliminary report and that a full written report was to follow . . . Please forgive me.'[27] She then gave gushing descriptions of guests at the do fawning over Maxwell. Such was the power of his despotism over her.

Keen to get out of her father's orbit, in 1990 Ghislaine started to spend more and more time in New York. It was there, at the wedding between Andrew Cuomo and Kerry Kennedy, that she bumped into

Christina Oxenberg, the daughter of Princess Elizabeth of Yugoslavia. Christina is a gifted writer, funny, bitchy, a little mad and an ocean-going snob. She suspects that she may have been the lovechild of JFK. She tells the story of her first meeting with Ghislaine in *Trash: Encounters with Ghislaine Maxwell*. Ghislaine called Christina 'Ox' and Christina called Ghislaine 'Max', all very jolly hockey sticks. But *Trash* suggests that Christina disliked Ghislaine from the get-go. Ghislaine first met Christina at the wedding party in the company of Christina's then husband, the English painter Damian Elwes. Damian and Ghislaine were friends from Oxford days. After Ghislaine and Damian had mwah-mwahed, Ghislaine turned towards Christina and said to Damian, 'What is this?'

Christina said nothing, Ghislaine laughed and walked off with Damian. The slight, writes Christina, meant little because Christina was set on divorcing Damian but you get an inkling of how Ghislaine could behave with the male partners of women she didn't rate. Christina writes: 'I did not like Ghislaine from that first encounter. Specifically, what I did not like about her was the absurd display of overconfidence combined with a total lack of self-awareness.'[28]

By autumn 1991 Ghislaine was twenty-nine years old, with her days of licensed wickedness at Oxford University retreating in the rear-view mirror. This makes the evidence of one more witness to Ghislaine's strange hyper-sexuality before her father's death all the more striking. Nicola Glucksmann, then a TV producer, was invited to Headington Hill Hall in September 1991 for a stay-over dinner party. She knew who Ghislaine was but did not know her personally when she was invited as a plus-one by a mutual female friend who was visiting Britain. Nicola was struck by the drab, utilitarian outbuildings of Robert Maxwell's Pergamon Press squatting in the grounds of Headington Hill Hall in a kind of mini-industrial estate:

> entirely unsuited if the effect you are seeking is grand country house. The house itself was odd, unloved, municipal, not shabby chic but shabby, dark, a lot of very dark wood, a bit run-down. I have an image of a

blue-patterned carpet on the staircase up to the bedrooms, a bit like a pub carpet, and a full suit of armour on the half-landing like a prop from a film. It didn't feel like a house that had any real history. It felt more like the abandoned set of a *Carry On* movie.[29]

Neither Maxwell nor Betty were present at the house that weekend. There were around twenty or so other guests for the dinner party, all of them upper class, wealthy. Nicola doesn't remember much about the other people. Susannah Constantine and Steve Wyatt were the only two she could place. 'Susannah was delightful. Steve Wyatt – the heir to a Texas shopping fortune and former lover of Sarah Ferguson, Duchess of York – was straight from central casting, an eligible bachelor with a handsome face, an easy manner and a body the triangular shape of a comic book superhero.'

Nicola's recollection was first aired when she took part in an online *Tortoise* 'think-in'.

Ghislaine, who she had never met before, made a real impression:

> charming, elegant, beautiful. Her mind was obviously very very quick but I remember being aware that she didn't seem to focus long on anyone, there was a sense of hyper-alertness, something a bit on edge. She was constantly assessing the room, as if anxious about missing something in another corner and, although she was very quick to laugh, any real conversation wasn't welcomed – at least not with me.

After a perfectly nice meal, Ghislaine announced that she was in charge of games. She came out of the next room, where she'd disappeared briefly, with blindfolds for the men, explaining that the women were to take off their tops and their bras and present themselves to the men, who were to identify the women from the size and feel of their breasts.

Nicola and her friend made their excuses and left so she doesn't know how the game played out or even if it happened at all. She was shocked and embarrassed, discomforted by the peer pressure, the public element, to be either bullied into it or shamed for being a killjoy: 'but there was no joy in that game. If this betrayed how Ghislaine viewed her own body, and what she felt she had to do with it to entertain men, then it's haunting. She was a beautiful and intelligent woman but where was her sense of her own worth?'

Nicola reflected on Ghislaine's stark disassociation between sexuality and intimacy, treating nakedness as only a game: 'If she wasn't worthy of a healthy equal relationship with a man, but instead was only there to service their needs, then perhaps she might simply expect other women to do what she herself had always done. It's no excuse but it might go some way to explain it.'

Nicola remains unsettled by the evening at Headington Hill Hall because of the shadows cast by the tragedy of the charges against Ghislaine: 'There was something about her seeming to see sex as simply a currency that stayed with me. She had a kind of performative studied superficiality about her, very sassy and upbeat, but also something urgent and strangely anxious about her management of people.'

There is one more element to Ghislaine's tragedy that Nicola, who herself is Jewish, has thought hard about:

> Like her father, Ghislaine was an outsider trying to get in. The Americans find the closed ranks of the British class system particularly hard to understand – they see Ghislaine, not as the daughter of a Jew and a foreigner, but as upper class. But her hyper-vigilance and relent-less social networking were, I suspect, hard-wired and rooted in a fearful fantasy – shared by her father – that she could be rejected and abandoned at any moment. If she didn't constantly assert her value to the opportun-istic circle she courted, the door could close in her face. Just being Ghislaine was never enough and therein lies the tragedy. She was both terrified and ruthless. We are dealing with a very troubled human being.

That observation comes from someone who met Ghislaine once, in September 1991, while her father was still alive. Ghislaine was broken long before she moved to New York. Nicola believes that ghastly as her father was, the contrasting 'saintliness' of her mother, Betty, has been over-egged. 'What kind of mother are you if you don't stand up to a man who is so psychologically so abusive to your children?' asks Nicola. 'Betty Maxwell's devotion to Maxwell meant that in one major respect she failed all her children, Ghislaine most of all. Their protection took second place to her desire to appease Robert.'

Ghislaine's last time with her father was in his London office before he flew off to Gibraltar. 'He was looking for an apartment in New York — a sort of pied-à-terre, where he could talk and have meetings — and he wanted me to help him. He asked me to go see a particular apartment. He said, "If you like it, I'll make time to see it and come to New York." '30

By the autumn of 1991, her father was running out of road. For a time, he had pursued his secretary Andrea Martin until he learnt – most likely from having her phone bugged – that she was having an affair with the *Daily Mirror*'s foreign editor, Nick Davies. The reporter recorded one ghastly scene between the ageing Lothario and his extremely reluctant target. Davies recalled Andrea phoning him from the King David Hotel in Jerusalem, in tears, distraught, frightened: 'She told me that Maxwell had walked into her room that morning while she was only in her dressing-gown and had tried to force himself on her, trying to kiss her as he fought him off, shouting at him to stop, hitting out at him as she struggled to escape his bear-like arms.'31

Eventually she quit, but Davies said that Maxwell would phone up Andrea Martin most days, sometimes just chatting, sometimes begging, beseeching her to come back, to no avail.

Maxwell was no longer taking care of his personal hygiene. In his penthouse flat, he was using cloth towels to wipe his bottom, discarding them on the floor for his Filipino staff to clear up. He'd run out of love, pity and money, full stop.

Time, then, to go for a short cruise in the middle of the Atlantic on the *Lady Ghislaine*.

chapter four

Lost At Sea

On 5 November 1991 Kenny Lennox, the star photographer at the *Daily Mirror*, was preparing to go on a routine assignment. Kenny is Scottish, brave and a Fleet Street legend. One year previously he had captured the moment when Margaret Thatcher left Downing Street for the very last time as prime minister by car. Kenny managed to get a shot of her through the window of her limousine, sitting in the back, weeping her eyes out. It's a stunning image of how power, or the loss of it, can break the strongest of people.

Kenny recalls in his lovely Scottish burr: 'I was just about to leave the *Daily Mirror* to go on a job, and the editor's secretary said don't go anywhere, "Richard wants to see you."' Richard Stott was the editor of the *Daily Mirror* at the time. 'Close the door,' he said, 'Nothing I'm saying to you must get out of here. It will affect the future of the *Daily Mirror*. The old man [as Stott called Maxwell] has gone overboard from his yacht in the Canaries.'

Stott asked Kenny to accompany Betty Maxwell on the flight down to Tenerife.[1]

When Kenny Lennox arrived in the Canaries with Betty, he was taken aside to make the first identification of the body. He told me what Maxwell looked like when alive: 'Giant of a man, huge man. He must have weighed at that time in the region of 20 stone.' (Roughly equivalent to 280 lbs or 127 kilograms.) 'He was big, raven haired, jowly, protruding tummy, but very imposing. A big, big man, with a big, big personality.'

Betty recalls landing and being immediately confronted by a throng of press photographers and, to her horror, seeing a helicopter land nearby and a large stretcher with a white blanket being removed and taken into the base.[2]

Kenny was taken to the mess of the air-sea rescue people to identify Maxwell. They asked him if he had any identification marks and Kenny suggested a black mole behind his left ear. That confirmed it, the corpse was Maxwell: 'He only had one mark on his shoulder, one broad graze, not a narrow thing, tapering off, on his left shoulder. Otherwise – I know this sounds ridiculous – he looked great. He was lying there, his tummy had flattened out. And there were no distortions. He wasn't bleached. He wasn't in the water that long. I know this sounds ridiculous but he looked good.'

Betty locked up her grief and retained her composure the whole time. But Ghislaine, then aged twenty-nine, suffered the loss of her father hugely. Kenny Lennox recalled: 'she was decimated. She was weeping really hard about her daddy. She did everything with her daddy. I think he decided everything she did in her life. She went to football matches with him, she was dressed up as his escort some nights when he did stuff in the city. He decided everything about her life. She lived the life of an adult but Robert Maxwell treated her like his baby.'

The family decided that Ghislaine should meet the press and she rehearsed her speech, over and over again: 'every time she got to bits about her daddy, the poor thing just fell apart again. It was very moving to watch a young girl do all this.'[3]

Only one of Maxwell's seven surviving children believes he was murdered: Ghislaine. In 1997, *Hello!* magazine's cover story was its interview with Ghislaine in which she said there was no evidence of suicide or a heart attack. 'I think he was murdered. One thing I am sure about is that he did not commit suicide. That was just not consistent with his character.'[4]

Ian Maxwell disagrees with his youngest sister on this critical matter: 'Ghislaine is very clear that she believes that he was murdered. She is the only member of the family to my knowledge who holds that position and she has never demurred from it . . .

Because I disagree with her on that subject and because she is immovable, we have stopped discussing it.'[5]

Let's examine the theory that Robert Maxwell was murdered. There were two autopsies, one immediately after the body was found in the Canaries, and a second, more professional job, carried out in Israel shortly before his burial on the Mount of Olives by local pathologists and Britain's then leading forensic pathologist, Dr Iain West. Two months after his death, *Paris Match* reported that the Israeli autopsy found several bruises on Maxwell's face, shoulders, stomach and calves, pointing to him being beaten before he went over the side. *Paris Match* quoted Loïc Le Ribault, a French police forensic expert, who said that, 'according to the photos, it is highly probable that the victim was hit on the back of the head with a blunt instrument'.[6]

But remember Kenny Lennox saw only the graze on his shoulder – and that points to the 'bruises' or 'injuries' having been caused after death by the first, Spanish, post mortem. Kenny Lennox is a reliable witness.

Could Maxwell have been bumped off by Mossad? To rehearse Henry Kissinger's zinger, 'Just because I'm paranoid doesn't mean that there aren't people out to get me,' Maxwell had both paranoia and enemies in spades. Ari Ben-Menashe spent ten years working with Israeli military intelligence, Aman, from 1977 to 1987. Ben-Menashe claimed that Maxwell had been assassinated by Mossad for trying to blackmail it. He is quoted in a book, *Epstein: Dead Men Tell No Tales*, as saying that he ran Robert Maxwell as his agent and that Maxwell introduced Ghislaine and Epstein to Israeli intelligence, after which they engaged in a blackmail operation for Israel. '[Epstein] was taking photos of politicians f**king fourteen-year-old girls – if you want to get it straight. They [Epstein and Maxwell] would just blackmail people like that.'[7] Ben-Menashe claimed that Robert Maxwell had been assassinated after attempting to blackmail Mossad. 'He really lost his compass once he started playing these games with people.'[8]

There is no documentary evidence, no piece of paper, no photograph, no email chain, no other source backing up the claim that

Jeffrey Epstein and Robert Maxwell ever met. The critical question
is how reliable is the word of Ari Ben-Menashe? He did work for
Aman, true. This has been corroborated by his former boss,
Aman's deputy director, Moshe Hebroni: 'Ben-Menashe served
directly under me . . . He had access to very, very sensitive material.'[9] But Ben-Menashe also testified that he personally witnessed
George H. W. Bush meet members of the Iranian government in
Paris in October 1980, part of a secret Republican Party plot to
keep the fifty-two US hostages held in Iran for longer until
President Jimmy Carter would lose the 1980 presidential election
to Ronald Reagan. This was Ben-Menashe's so-called 'October
surprise'.

A committee of the US House of Congress investigated and
concluded: 'Ben-Menashe's testimony is impeached by documents and is riddled with inconsistencies and factual misstate-
ments which undermine his credibility. Based on the documentary evidence available, the Task Force has determined that
Ben-Menashe's account of the October meetings, like his other
October Surprise allegations, is a total fabrication.'[10] ABC News
said he failed a lie-detector test, big-time: on a scale of reliability
from zero to minus eight, he scored minus seven. The journalist
Craig Unger wrote of Ben-Menashe: 'Listen to him, trust him,
print his story verbatim — then sit round and watch your career
go up in flames.'[11]

That said, there is credible evidence pointing towards – but not
proving – Jeffrey Epstein running a blackmail operation against
powerful men and there is also credible evidence pointing towards
– but not proving – his links to United States intelligence agencies, most likely the Central Intelligence Agency, and that he may
have used those connections as leverage with law enforcement.
But the source is not Ari Ben-Menashe.

When the FBI raided Epstein's mansion in 2019, they found a
fake Austrian passport in Epstein's safe, with a photo of Epstein
but a false name. The home address given in the passport was in
Saudi Arabia. Business associates in the late 1980s said Epstein
was close to Adnan Khashoggi, the Saudi arms dealer uncle of

Jamal Khashoggi, the dissident who in 2018 got hacked to bits
with a bone saw by a group ultimately reporting to Saudi Crown
Prince Mohammed bin Salman, also known as MBS, also known
to the opposition in exile as Mr Bone Saw. The crown prince firmly
denies this charge. We shall turn to the evidence on whether
Epstein was working in some capacity for the CIA in greater depth
later.

On Robert Maxwell being murdered, there is no evidence on
means, none at all. And the evidence on motive is tin-hat stuff.
Robert Maxwell was a monster in the way that he dealt with his
family and staff, but there's no evidence that he crossed the Soviet,
Israeli and/or British intelligence services. The Soviets and the
Israelis had lots of far more important targets to worry about
than a crooked media mogul they quite liked. The idea that MI6
would knock off anyone like Robert Maxwell is silly. He probably
helped MI6 back in the day. Besides, the service is far more risk-
averse than painted by John le Carré; Ian Fleming was a fantasist.
The boring version, that Britain's spies spend their time sipping
mineral water in meeting rooms and are led by conformists and
milquetoasts, the kind of people who always thrive inside great
British institutions, is less exciting but more credible.

Roy Greenslade – no friend of the British state or its intelligence agencies – has studied the context. By late 1991 Maxwell's
finances were in dire trouble, the banks closing in. Goldman
Sachs, long-time buyers of Maxwell stock, were dumping their
shares. The Maxwell Communications Corporation was tanking
so badly it was about to crash out of the FTSE 100, which would
mean that the big institutions, the pension funds and the like,
would cash in their shares robotically. The Swiss Bank Corporation
had told Kevin Maxwell and he had told his father they would go
to the Fraud Squad unless £60 million capital was repaid in full
on 5 November, the day Robert Maxwell was lost at sea. Maxwell
was about to be revealed as broke – and worse. Greenslade noted
that, the day before, Maxwell had enjoyed watching his private jet
tip its wings as it flew past the *Lady Ghislaine*: a rather sombre fare-
well gesture for someone with his life ahead of him.

Murder or suicide? I asked Greenslade. 'I'm absolutely convinced that it was suicide. The overarching theme is that this was a man who could not face the ignominy of jail, of being found out as a liar and a fraudster.'

Greenslade listed three factors that point to suicide. First, his cabin, the state room, was locked from the inside by a man used to walking about naked on the boat. He took the trouble to get up, put a dressing gown on and lock his cabin door. That suggests to Greenslade intent, that he obviously wanted to conceal from the crew that he was going over. Second, the background of a man who is about to be found out. Third, his strange behaviour the previous day, watching his plane fly over, his generally good mood with the rest of the crew, which was unusual. 'All of this suggests that for me, this was a man who committed suicide when the balance of his mind was finally *undisturbed*. Reality suddenly kicked in. And for me the murder theory is a nonsense.'[12]

Nick Davies recalls, towards the end, how not just depressed and self-pitying Maxwell had become in conversation, but sometimes suicidal: 'Sometimes,' Maxwell said, 'I don't know why I go on. Everything I try, people turn against me . . . I've got no friends, no-one I can turn to . . . no-one to share my life with . . . sometimes I think I should just end it all, throw myself out of the window . . . I sometimes feel I can't go on.'[13] Davies believed Maxwell killed himself: 'He knew he was finished and he couldn't bear the ignominy of being torn to shreds by the wolves. That, and the one person he wanted' – Andrea Martin – 'he couldn't have.'[14]

There is a third possibility favoured by Richard Ingrams. Maxwell's old enemy never thought he was murdered. Ingrams believes there are good grounds for thinking it could be suicide, but prefers a different ending: 'one of the things we know about Maxwell in his later years was that he had a habit of peeing all over the place, wherever he was. So I think he started to pee into the sea off the back of his boat and because he was a bit drunk, he fell off and there was no way that he could have been rescued because no one was aware that he was there.'[15]

The night Maxwell's corpse was found in the Atlantic the *Mirror* team looking after Betty and Ghislaine slept on the *Lady Ghislaine*. With space tight, Kenny Lennox ended up sleeping on Robert Maxwell's bed. 'He would get up in the night to pee. And he didn't pee in the loo, he pulled the door open and stepped out onto the transom to pee off the back.' There was not a rail but three wires, Kenny explained. 'They would have come up to the top of my thighs' – Kenny is of average height, a lot shorter than Maxwell – 'so there's a lot of weight above the wires. He used to go around naked by the way. Now if that boat lurched at sea . . . I'm a dinghy sailor and my bum is always in the water. I know that in the flattest of seas, sometimes you can get up a bump coming from nowhere.'

Suicide or murder, I asked Kenny? 'Neither. Accident.' Kenny acknowledged that the pressures on Maxwell were immense but 'Robert Maxwell thought he was bullet-proof, that he could wriggle out of it eventually.'[16]

The summer after Maxwell went overboard Gyles Brandreth was aboard a pal's gin palace in the Mediterranean when they came across the yacht that had been called the *Lady Ghislaine*: 'In the harbour we passed Robert Maxwell's yacht; it is smaller than I imagined, but I don't think he could have toppled over the ship's rail by accident. Either he jumped or he was pushed.'[17]

Heading the list of people who are convinced that Maxwell killed himself is his ancient enemy, Rupert Murdoch: 'I remember I got a call one morning saying that he had disappeared off his boat. I said straight away, "Ah, he jumped." He knew the banks were closing in. I can't give any other explanation.'[18]

If he jumped, then how come the graze on the shoulder noted by Kenny Lennox? What could be the explanation for that?

Chester Stern in his book *Dr Iain West's Casebook* sets out some possible scenarios written in a report by West's wife, also a pathologist, Vesna Djurovic. She theorised that the shoulder muscles got torn because Maxwell's immense weight was born by one hand hanging on to the rail. The pathologist Dr West found no evidence for homicide, but it remains a possibility because he could not exclude it. He did not think Maxwell died of a heart attack: 'Without the background of a man who was in financial trouble, and who knew it, I would probably say accident. As it is, there are probably only a few percentage points between the two main options, but I favour suicide.'[19]

The insurance syndicate running Maxwell's life policy accepted his verdict. It just so happened this meant they believed they didn't have to cough up £20 million to the Maxwell family.

For what it's worth, my view is that I cannot rule out accident and it is possible that Maxwell fell to his death while pissing off the side of his yacht; like Richard Ingrams, I get the dark poetry of that particular ending. But suicide is much more common than people think it is, ten times more likely than murder. (There are roughly 10 suicides per 100,000 a year in the UK[20] and roughly 11 murders per 1,000,000 in England and Wales.[21]) Men kill themselves more often than women. Ex-soldiers kill themselves more often than civilians. Maxwell knew he faced not just disgrace but prison. People who intend to commit suicide often change their minds in mid-attempt, so it's entirely plausible that he did try to kill himself, climbed over the rail, stood unsteadily on the slippery bit of the hull beyond the rail-wires, had second thoughts, but then the yacht hit a bump and over the side he went. He clung on to the rail wire for as long as could hold out, then slipped into the sea, his screams for help drowned by the roar of the mighty ocean, the lights of the *Lady Ghislaine* slowly fading to black . . .

From this point onwards, Ghislaine sheers off from the rest of her family in believing that dark forces killed her father. There's no good evidence of that. She is detached from reality. There was something cultish about Robert Maxwell's hold over Betty and the whole family. Reflecting on a letter he wrote to her in 1945, Betty acknowledges that the whole family were somehow locked into his personality cult.[22]

So Ghislaine's own mother suggested that her daughter had been in a kind of cult, its kind-of-messiah her father. Robert Maxwell's was not a classic cult. He didn't have a horde of suckers on their knees in a kind of church handing over their money in return for fake enlightenment. He didn't need to. He was conning the banks and stealing from his workers' pensions. But the unconditional love he demanded, the fear he generated, the messiah-like intensity of everything he did, the constant humiliation of his underlings, his wife, his children, of all those close to him, the paranoia, the spying on people, the hyperbolic legal aggression, firing off writs here, there and everywhere: all of that is very cultish.

In 2007 I went toe-to-toe with the Church of Scientology, infamously losing my temper with Sea Org high priest Tommy Davis[23] – bear with me, there is a point to this diversion. It is fair to report that the Church of Scientology says that I am a liar, a bigot and psychotic. For my part, I believe Scientology to be a brainwashing space alien cult masquerading as a religion to avoid tax and scrutiny. Ranged against me at the time were a host of private eyes, lawyers and Scientology celebrities. Among them were the Church's former head of its Office of Special Affairs, Mike Rinder, and the Hollywood actor, Leah Rimini. Both Rinder and Remini have since left Scientology along with a host of others. What is striking about those leaving Scientology is that it takes them years before they fully leave, before their minds are clear of the brainwashing. Rinder, for example, was still honouring the wisdom of L. Ron Hubbard when I met him three years after he walked out on the Church. Now, he is far more critical. I described people who had just left as 'Outs' and people who had properly washed their brains – this takes time – as 'Out-Outs'.

Betty Maxwell in her memoir reflects the self-doubt and the agonising that afflicts so many ex-cult victims when she writes about 'Bob'. In her Introduction, he was 'not the degenerate monster the press has invented',[24] but once she starts setting out the facts he becomes 'messianic ... despotic ... sadistic ... monstrous'.[25] What is so troubling about Ghislaine is that there is no evidence that she ever left the cult of Robert Maxwell and some – her belief that he was murdered – that she is a still a believer.

Ian Maxwell recalled the moment he found out that his father was dead, having been lost at sea, to Rosie Kinchen of *The Sunday*

Times in 2018. Ian felt 'exhilarated to be free of this extraordinary alpha male presence in my life and at the same time incredibly scared as to what the future would look like without him.'[26]

Robert Maxwell's legacy has poisoned relations for the surviving children. Ian Maxwell tiptoed around this when he spoke to *The Sunday Times*. Anne and Philip Maxwell, the two oldest children, were said to have suffered horribly at his hands. Ian replied: 'I think it is fair to say that there are some within the house who are more critical and prepared to enunciate that criticism than others.' Where would he put Ghislaine? 'I'm nearer the positive than the negative end of that scale. I think she would be with me.'[27]

I suspect that the truth is it's worse than that, that Ghislaine still loves her father and has never come to terms with who the real man was, an abusive monster, a thing of evil. This is the second act, if you like, in her tragedy. She is charming, extraordinarily well connected, but suffers from a fundamental disordering of her grip on reality. Her father buried, she goes to Manhattan where she is about to step on the same rake twice.

chapter five

Manhattan

One month after the death of her father, disgrace boomeranged into Ghislaine Maxwell. The *Daily Mirror* discovered that Maxwell had been looting their pension fund to the tune of £400 million – more. The newspaper group that had mourned 'The Man Who Saved the *Mirror*' now discovered that he had been a monster all along. The *Daily Mirror* called her father 'rogue', 'crook', 'bully', 'thief', 'megalomaniac', 'gangster' – what is known in the Fleet Street milk bars as a reverse ferret, when you argue with a passionate ferocity against exactly what you had been saying the day before yesterday with the same passionate ferocity.

The shame broke her, for a time. A friend of Ghislaine was reported saying: 'Now she was the shattered child of a man described as a monster, his name forever equated to scandal. "She was catatonic," the friend said. "It hit her in a way that scared people."'[1]

Recovery, closure over his death, was all the harder because no one knew for certain how he had died. The conspiracy theories about his death spiralled out of control. *Vanity Fair* picked out five: one, that he committed suicide rather than face his financial crimes; two, he died aboard his yacht while engaged in sex with a mistress; three, he fell overboard during his regular post-midnight piss over the railings; four, he was murdered by British security agents panicked that he had taken possession of tapes that could incriminate the MI6 intelligence service in crime and espionage; five, he was injected with a poisonous syringe by frogmen sent by his Mossad spymasters to silence him from revealing their secret arms deals. I believe the first and think number three is possible.

The *Guardian* ran a nonsense story suggesting the corpse identified by Kenny Lennox and Betty Maxwell was a body double and that Maxwell had absconded to some far-flung destination. The nastier British tabloids told lurid tales of her father's sex orgies with midget Filipino hookers.[2]

It was a grim time for all the Maxwells. The year 1992, Betty writes in her memoir, was the worst in her life, describing the experience as like being raped in public.[3] Note that Betty does not regard the year in which her husband died as the worst year.

Down the track, the James Bond scriptwriting team started work on *Tomorrow Never Dies* in which the baddie, a megalomaniac British media baron, ends up 'falling from his yacht' in a punchline delivered by Judi Dench playing 'M' as hardcore as they come. A tribute, then, but not a good one. Ghislaine, who had been completely protected from negative newspaper coverage by the power of her father, by what Kelvin MacKenzie calls the 'Non-Pissing Pact', now got it with both barrels. When she was spotted flying back from London to New York via Concorde, a ludicrously expensive way of crossing the Atlantic, the *Mirror* pensioners howled with rage.

Peter, Lord Mandelson, the oleaginous consigliere of Tony Blair, was a very close friend of Ghislaine Maxwell: 'I think she had a very tough time when she arrived in New York. Someone told me she had nothing and literally had to remake herself from scratch.'[4]

Ghislaine was evicted from the Maxwell company flat in New York, telling a friend: 'They took everything – everything – even the cutlery.' The friend tells reporter Ed Klein from *Vanity Fair*: 'She was broke, the family was broke. This girl who was brought up in luxury, and – *bang* – everything was taken from her.' Klein visited her in her New York apartment shortly before Christmas, 1991. He described a picture of human misery, the floor strewn with newspaper clippings about her father, hundreds of letters of condolence on a desk, waiting for a reply. Klein had heard about a 'racy, glamorous social flibbertigibbet' squired by actor George Hamilton at the Derby, who skied with him at Aspen, who had attended the Kerry Kennedy–Andrew Cuomo wedding. The broken woman in front of him was not that person.

Ghislaine told Klein: 'He wasn't a crook. A thief to me is somebody who steals money. Do I think that my father did that? No.' She bemoaned her lot: I'm surviving — just. But I can't just die quietly in a corner. I have to believe that something good will come out of this mess.'[5]

She turned out to be wrong about that.

Vassi Chamberlain, who had first met Ghislaine in London in 1990, renewed the acquaintance in New York around this time. Back in London, Ghislaine had been the life and soul of fun. Not in New York. This time, talking to her was hard work: 'If a piece of the puzzle was missing when I first met her, it was firmly in place by the time we met again, in New York in 1992, at a party in a downtown loft, not long after her father's death . . . At this party Ghislaine looked unkempt, shell-shocked, vibrating with anger and bitterness.'[6]

Grief and anger yes, but at least some of Ghislaine's Cinderella act was a show. She enjoyed a trust fund established in Liechtenstein by her father, yielding an income of about £80,000 a year.[7] So, to put it mildly, she wasn't flat broke. And when she met Klein, the reporter from *Vanity Fair*, shortly before Christmas 1991, she didn't let on her big news. She did tell him that the Maxwell family would regroup and get back on track: 'It's sad for my mother. It's sad to have lost my dad. It's sad for my brothers. But I would say we'll be back. Watch this space.'[8]

What she didn't say was that the space had already been filled by one of the richest men in New York City. A photograph captures Ghislaine at an event honouring the memory of Robert Maxwell on 24 November 1991, just three weeks after his death, in the Trump Plaza hotel in Manhattan. Ghislaine is sitting at a table populated with champagne glasses. She's wearing a brilliant blue kaftan thingy over her top. To the right of the picture is *The Odd Couple* TV star Tony Randall looking like the most uncomfortable gooseberry on the whole planet. To the left, laughing at a joke, is Jeffrey Epstein. Ghislaine is staring at Epstein, fascinated by him. They look like lovers or people about to be lovers very soon. The photograph proves that Ghislaine Maxwell and Jeffrey Epstein knew each other in the same month that her father died.[9] But not how long the relationship had been going on.

Like Robert Maxwell, Jeffrey Epstein came from a poor Jewish family very much on the wrong side of the tracks, but made his own way in life. Like her father too, Epstein had cunning, drive, intelligence. Epstein was born in 1953 and grew up in Sea Gate, Coney Island, which is one of the furthest parts of Brooklyn from Manhattan and therefore one of the most working class and least fashionable. His dad was a gardener for the parks department, his mum a school assistant. He had one younger brother, Mark.

Epstein went to ordinary local schools, was strikingly good at maths and ended up at New York University, but dropped out in June 1974. He started the autumn term teaching at Dalton School on the Upper East Side of Manhattan, one of the poshest private schools in the United States. Former pupils include Tony Blinken, President Biden's current Secretary of State, Anderson Cooper, the CNN journalist, Claire Danes, the actor in *Homeland*, and Sean Lennon, son of John and Yoko. The headmaster who is believed to have appointed him was Donald Barr, the father of President Trump's Attorney General William Barr. Like everywhere else at the time that autumn of 1974, the school was going through what we now call 'culture wars'. Nixon had just resigned, conservative values were mocked. Barr was strict, keen on stopping marijuana use, beefing up the academic side of things.

There is a photograph of Epstein in front of a blackboard at Dalton, his incisors glinting in the light, his hair a dark shag, a wolf in wolf's clothing. Former students told the *New York Times* that he used to show up at parties where students were drinking. Epstein stood out for his attention to girls in hallways and class-rooms. 'I can remember thinking at the time, "This is wrong,"' said Scott Spizer, who graduated from Dalton in 1976. Fellow student Millicent Young remembered observing Epstein flirting with girls at the school: 'There was a real clarity of the inappropriateness of the behaviour – that this isn't how adult male teachers conduct themselves,' Ms Young said.[10]

What was really going on inside Epstein's mind when he was teaching at Dalton School came to light when Ghislaine Maxwell commissioned a comedy roast by entertainer Christopher Mason for Jeffrey Epstein's fortieth birthday in January 1993. Mason is now uneasy at the memory of the roast: 'She wanted me to mention that when Epstein was teaching at the Dalton School, he was the subject of many schoolgirl crushes.' At the time Mason thought it was 'kind of an odd thing to want in a song about a man who appears to be your boyfriend. But she clearly thought that that was something that was going to amuse him. Another odd thing that she wanted me to say was that he had 24-hour erections.' Mason went along with this stuff feeling it to be 'brash, possibly hyperbolic ... She had a mischievous wit.' When the night came, Mason was surprised that the party was tiny, only Epstein, Ghislaine and six or seven men, including Les Wexner, the billionaire boss of the Victoria's Secret chain.[11]

Here's the roast, so wittily delivered.

> *Poor Jeffrey Epstein is 40, oy vey!*
> *Life must be tough his hair is already so gray*
> *He sure looks older but it's clear from his smile*
> *The older he gets, the more juvenile*
> *Ghislaine is lavishing him with her affections*
> *She claims he has 24-hour erections*
> *Sounds like he's busy, now ain't that berserk*
> *How does he find the time to get off to work . . .*

Mason read out some of the roast for a video for the *Mail Online*. But the recitation stopped before the end of the poem. The *Daily Mail* printed the ending and it went like this:

He wakes when the cock crows while everyone slumbers
He rivals Einstein when crunching those numbers
He taught at Dalton: the naughty boy blushes
To think of schoolgirls and all of their crushes.[12]

On the evidence of the Chris Mason's roast alone, you would have thought Ghislaine might have picked up that Epstein had a thing about under-age girls and that thing was not good.

Epstein could not have got away with what he did for so long without two things: his money, tons of it, and Ghislaine Maxwell. New York investment banker Euan Rellie used to hang out with the couple back in the 1990s. The *New York Times* reported Rellie found Epstein elusive to the point of imperiousness, only appearing at dinner parties when all the guests had sat down. For Rellie, the attraction was Ghislaine, the 'charming, likable front person. A big part of the reason people talked to him was because of Ghislaine.'[13]

Let's look at how Epstein became a multi-millionaire. It's a mystery, made more puzzling by the gossip that Robert Maxwell's ill-gotten gains are lurking somewhere below the surface. In June 1976 Epstein was asked to leave Dalton School for 'poor performance' under something of a cloud: a characteristic of the young Epstein. But a second personality trait surfaced at the same time: his extraordinary ability to manipulate rich and powerful men, to bend them to his will. One of the parents at Dalton was Alan C. 'Ace' Greenberg, of Bear Stearns, the bank that later went bust in 2006 for borrowing too many billions against the junkiest of junk bonds. Back in the 1970s, Greenberg offered Epstein a job and the boy from the wrong side of the tracks was on the make. Smart, clever, Epstein was doing well when five years after joining the company he was asked to leave because of a violation of compliance rules – naughty but not, on the face of it, criminal.

Epstein set up his own company, Intercontinental Assets Group, the pitch being to help clients get back stolen money from bent brokers and lawyers. Epstein was, in effect, a high-end bounty hunter and he was good at picking up scalps. One grateful punter was the Spanish film star Ana Obregón, best known for her role as Bo Derek's pal in the 1984 movie *Bolero*. She hit the British tabloid headlines sometime later when rumours about an affair with then Real Madrid and England international football player David Beckham surfaced. Beckham's wife Victoria gloriously challenged her – 'Why would he be interested in an old lady like you? Leave my husband alone' – amid unflattering descriptions of the then fifty-year-old as a 'geriatric Barbie'.[14] Ana denied any impropriety. In the early 1980s her father had lost a ton of money invested in Drysdale Securities Corporation when it went bust. Epstein stepped in to help out in 1982 and got power of attorney – another trait emerging – from Ana over any monies he recovered, and her gratitude. Later, Ana said: 'I know he's had some problems. I don't want anything to do with that.'[15]

The reporter Edward Jay "EJ" Epstein – no relation – first met Jeffrey Epstein at a large Halloween party in Manhattan in 1987. The journalist found him bright and charming but not that well-off. He lived on the Upper East Side but in a one-bedroom apartment for free because there was a rent strike at the time. Very quickly, Jeffrey Epstein's cool veneer started to crack. He conned people into thinking that he lived in the penthouse by inviting guests up to the communal roof garden and getting a deli to deliver food. He told EJ that he was a financial bounty hunter but his talk of tracking down money for shady people in sunny places such as Andorra, Fiji, Gibraltar and the Cayman Islands made the reporter wonder that he might be hiding money in those places too.

Jeffrey Epstein was a business partner for a time with Steven Hoffenberg, who ran Towers International, a bailiff company with dreams of grandeur. EJ Epstein found Hoffenberg striking because he had a bodyguard who carried a gun.

Jeffrey Epstein was smart with the new tech, which was beginning to change everything in finance, in the world. But not that smart. To impress EJ, he gave him a programme that allowed the reporter to access his computer remotely via a telephone modem. That was very state-of-the-art but it provided a window into Jeffrey Epstein's business that was not good. EJ logged in to read letters from people demanding money. One New York financier wrote that a cheque from Jeffrey Epstein for $83,000 had bounced for a second time.

In early 1989, EJ Epstein fell out with Jeffrey Epstein because he didn't trust him. For example, once EJ was flying to Spain, cattle class. Jeffrey magically converted his ticket into a first-class one. The free upgrade didn't work because at the airport EJ was told his ticket was fake. What Jeffrey had done was get hold of a cache of first-class upgrade stickers and attach one to EJ's cheap ticket, hoping that the check-in staff wouldn't notice.

EJ wrote in the *Daily Mail* decades later: 'Everything about Epstein was a con. I never thought: "Here's an honest guy." '[16]

Around the end of the 1980s, Jeffrey Epstein split with Hoffenberg and created his own financial management vehicle, J. Epstein & Company, the spin being that he only looked after clients with $1 billion in assets or more. I put to Hoffenberg a rumour going round the houses that Robert Maxwell and Jeffrey Epstein had been in business together. Hoffenberg told me: 'Yes, they were friends. I was involved with, working with and being part of Jeffrey Epstein's world for nine years. Robert Maxwell was a very important social and business connexion of Epstein's.'

This raises the possibility that Epstein helped hide Robert Maxwell's dirty money away from the *Mirror* pensioners and that the true source of Epstein's wealth was Maxwell's dark gold rather than his debt-collecting malarkey. Is this story that Epstein may have ended up with pots of Robert Maxwell's crooked money – the Holy Grail of Maxwellology – true?

The *Daily Telegraph* filed the rumour, 'an apocryphal, but tantalising, story' that Ghislaine had searched her father's papers on the yacht the day after he died, and she found a reference to a New York financier who had helped Maxwell squirrel away 'misbegotten funds offshore'. His name was Jeffrey Epstein.[17]

Ghislaine's old friend from London, Vassi Chamberlain, was astonished to discover that the daughter of a disgraced crook was now living the life of Reilly in New York: 'I remember thinking, but with what money?' Chamberlain had a source, a New Yorker working on and around Wall Street, who told her 'my personal belief is that Epstein had been hiding money siphoned off by Robert Maxwell . . . I believe it was Jeffrey who laundered Maxwell's money.' The source set out their logic, that Epstein was never a money manager but someone who structured off funds, to hide or recover money. The source noted that the second Ghislaine landed in New York, she was all of a sudden 'very chummy with Jeffrey. Then he started spending on a different level, suddenly buying these extraordinary townhouses.'[18]

But did Ghislaine's father meet her new lover? Is the story true?

The source asserting that Robert Maxwell knew Jeffrey Epstein is Stephen Hoffenberg and, in turn, his source was 'Robert Maxwell's Israeli handler'.

When I interviewed Hoffenberg for the Hunting Ghislaine podcast I interrupted Hoffenberg's flow, right there.

> **Sweeney:** 'Who did? Sorry, say again?'
> **Hoffenberg:** 'Robert Maxwell's Israeli handler reported that substantially in his book that they did know each other and that Robert Maxwell was endorsing Jeffrey Epstein. That's been reported.'
> **Sweeney:** 'His handler is? Who is that? Not Ari Ben-Menashe?'
> **Hoffenberg:** 'Yes.'[19]

Attentive readers will recall that Ari Ben-Menashe claimed that Robert Maxwell was murdered by Mossad and that he himself saw George H. W. Bush in Paris meet with the Iranian government; this latter claim was found to be a fabrication. But what about Hoffenberg himself? How reliable is the word of the former CEO of Towers Financial? His company collapsed in 1993 and Hoffenberg pleaded guilty to cheating investors out of $475 million. He served eighteen years in prison for what the SEC called 'one of the largest Ponzi schemes in history'.[20] So the two people who openly claim that Robert Maxwell knew Jeffrey Epstein are a fantasist and a convicted fraudster. This being the land of Maxwelliana, that does not mean it is not true. It is possible that the two men did meet, as we shall see.

The common-sense argument against Epstein hiding Maxwell's pirate gold in a sunny place for shady people is that at the end of his life the media mogul was desperate to lay his hands on hard cash. If he had £60 million in an offshore bank account, he would have given it to the Swiss Bank Corporation to get them off his back. As we have seen, he told his Russian mistress at the fag-end of his life that he didn't care very much for Betty and most of his children, so the notion of leaving a pot of treasure for the kids is to misread Robert Maxwell.

There is a perfectly good explanation for Epstein's immense wealth from the early 1990s onwards and it has nothing to do with the House of Maxwell. Sometime in the late 1980s, Epstein met Les Wexner, the multi-billionaire owner of a fashion empire, its best-known brands being Abercrombie & Fitch, and lingerie chain Victoria's Secret. The two men became close friends. The precise nature of that relationship is disputed.

There are some cold hard facts here. In July 1991 Les Wexner, then just fifty-three years old, signed a power of attorney, granting Epstein the right to, quote, 'sign, seal, execute . . . such checks, drafts, deeds, leases, mortgages, bills, bonds, notes, receipts' as he saw fit.[21] Epstein ended up with power over Wexner's fortune. There was a ton of money to be made, right there, simply by taking a modest percentage of Wexner's billions for handling his affairs and reducing his tax bite by, as they say, astute wealth management. Epstein bought Wexner's plane for $10 million and his Manhattan mansion for $20 million. In the summer of 2019, Wexner issued a statement saying Epstein had 'misappropriated vast sums of money' from him and his family. His statement points to Wexner realising he had been ripped off in 2007. Tax records reportedly indicated that Epstein made a

$46 million transfer to a Wexner charitable fund in January 2008. What is striking, however, is that Wexner said nothing public about what appears to be the theft of $46 million for eleven years until Epstein was arrested a second time. It's almost as if Epstein still had a hold over Wexner. The multi-billionaire's statement continued: 'I am embarrassed that, like so many others, I was deceived by Mr. Epstein. I know now that my trust in him was grossly misplaced and I deeply regret having ever crossed his path.'[22]

Let's return to the moment in November 1992 when Ghislaine was photographed flying from London to New York on Concorde, causing howls of rage from *Mirror* pensioners. The *Mail on Sunday* had the story behind the story, that the tickets were most likely picked up not by her but by the rich man she was travelling with: Epstein. It was the first article to document the relationship between Ghislaine Maxwell and Jeffrey Epstein and the first article to profile the American. The story was written by Michael Robotham, now a thriller writer. He reported on the new man in her life: 'Jeffrey Epstein, a shadowy, almost maverick New York 'property developer'.[23] The article, dated 15 November 1992, implied that the couple had been an item for more than a year, so that places the relationship starting sometime roughly before her father's death and thus, again, restokes the possibility that Epstein and Robert Maxwell might have met and might have had a business relationship.

What is fascinating about Robotham's article is that it is extraordinarily well-informed about Epstein long before he was a household name. It is full of private detail, the kind of stuff that is never easy for a reporter to work out without inside information, for example that Epstein's telephone number is listed under the name 'Jeffrey Edwards'. Robotham links Epstein to the CIA and Mossad, suggests he had been a concert pianist and a maths teacher at an exclusive girls' school, and that he was a corporate spy hired by big businesses to uncover money that had been embezzled. That is the Epstein legend as Epstein or his familiar would have liked it. The other side of the story – that

Epstein was a creepy perv kicked out of a fancy private school, then kicked out of a big player on Wall Street for cooking the books, then working alongside a big Ponzi fraudster – doesn't get a look in. Fancy that.

There are persistent rumours that Epstein was involved in 'intelligence', both with the CIA and Mossad, but, contrariwise, if you are an upmarket debt collector, spreading those very rumours may be a smart thing to do. Real spooks stay in the shadows.

Like everyone else, Robotham was intrigued by the mystery of where Epstein's wealth came from, contrasting his inexhaustible supply of money, his Rolls Royce, his fabulous art collection, with the lack of public knowledge of its true source. Robotham clocked Epstein's key business relationship with Les Wexner.

Robotham refers obliquely to Ghislaine's previous lovers, before quoting a friend saying: 'Jeffrey is much more like her father.' You can say that again.

Robotham's source was very well placed, clearly close to Ghislaine, so much so that the thought occurred to me that she might have been source herself. After all, if Ghislaine and her family are being roundly abused because she was seen to be flying on Concorde but the man paying the bill was Epstein, then it could be in her interest and that of the wider Maxwell clan for the relationship to be out in the open. Puzzled, I got in touch with Robotham through two literary agencies that represent him. There was no reply.

This, then, is the third act of Ghislaine Maxwell's tragedy. She is so broken by her grief and the disgrace that dogged anyone bearing the Maxwell name, she makes the single greatest mistake of her life. She falls in love with Jeffrey Epstein.

The first video of the couple together is from 1992 and on it you can see Ghislaine's great skill at slipping into the shadows. Go to YouTube and dial in 'New Tape Shows Donald Trump and Jeffrey Epstein at Mar-a-Lago Party in 1992'.[24] It's an out-take from a 1992 NBC TV news package featuring president-to-be Donald Trump throwing a party at his Mar-a-Lago estate in Palm Beach. Viewer discretion is advised as the clip looks like a prequel to a down-scale porno: Trump the king of kitsch, the women all big hair, the men predatory, chops-a-slather. Trump is dressed for the boardroom in dark suit, white shirt and pink tie, sweaty and ogling the women when Epstein walks into the party. Epstein is prematurely grey, dressing down in a denim shirt, cool, looking like the defrocked maths teacher he once was. What's fascinating is that Trump, the great manipulator, fawns over Epstein, craving his good humour, seeking his blessing. It's quite a thing.

At twenty-three seconds in, a woman with dark hair cut in the style of Peter Pan and white blouse momentarily peeks out behind the president-to-be and the paedophile-to-be-convicted. She's camera-shy but for a moment the lens captures her dark eyes a-glitter: Ghislaine Maxwell. She disappears, reappears for a second, is then caught mid-frame for three whole seconds from thirty seconds in. And then she's gone. This is classic Ghislaine. You catch a glimpse of her in the background, you're intrigued, but by the time your mind registers her presence, she's vanished.

Early on, there is another person talking about Epstein's perverted lust for under-age women, the first being the roast performer Christopher Mason, the second being Donald Trump. Epstein and Donald Trump were big pals for a long time. It's clear from the NBC footage they were firm friends in 1992. Down the track, Trump went out of his way to diss his former buddy. In 2019 he told White House reporters, after Epstein had been arrested a second time: 'I had a falling out with him. I haven't spoken to him in 15 years. I was not a fan of his, that I can tell you.'[25]

But in 2002 Trump told *New York* magazine: 'I've known Jeff for 15 years' – placing the start of their friendship back to 1987. Trump continued: 'Terrific guy. He's a lot of fun to be with. It is even said that he likes beautiful women as much as I do, and many of them are on the younger side.'[26] What did the president-to-be know and when did he know it?

By the early 1990s, Ghislaine is running Epstein's diary, if not his life, for him. In 1993 the magazine *Yoga Journal* ran an advert for a yoga instructor for 'a private individual'. The telephone number given was for Epstein's office; the person to be asked for was 'Miss Maxwell'.[27]

She was his organiser, his uber-secretary and his some-time lover. Ghislaine, according to a friend of the writer Vanessa Grigoriadis, used to joke about keeping herself painfully thin because Epstein liked thin girls. 'She said, "I do it the way Nazis did it with the Jews, the Auschwitz diet. I just don't eat." '[28]

When it comes to the Holocaust, Ghislaine is as crass as her father.[29]

Ghislaine wanted Epstein to marry her, her friends say. But he was as much a monster as her father. In *Trash* Christina Oxenberg tells the story of how, in 1993, Epstein and Ghislaine conspired to bring Robert Kennedy Junior into their set by organising an exhibition to go dinosaur fossil-hunting out West on Epstein's plane. Christina's source is anonymous but someone she calls 'Tony'. But, Christina writes, 'the snag was that Kennedy showed up at the private airport with a bunch of kids – and they were not the sort of children Epstein had a predilection for.' Tony told Christina that when the plane landed in dinosaur country, everyone got out but Epstein who stayed put and Tony spotted this strange behaviour. The fossil-hunting was good fun and Bobby and the kids enjoyed it. But not Epstein. On the flight back, the plane landed at Chicago where a beautiful blonde woman appeared. Epstein disappeared with her for two hours, while Bobby and the kids waited and waited. Meanwhile, Ghislaine 'dissolved into a flood of tears. She was inconsolable. Tony remembers someone comforting her but she never stopped crying.' Eventually, Epstein reappeared without the blonde and the party returned home, Ghislaine's public humiliation absolute.[30]

Throughout this time Ghislaine never loses a foothold in London. She's there for at least some of the fraud trial of her brothers, which ends in January 1996, and gets to know and befriend Kevin's Anglo-American lawyer Leah Saffian, of whom we will hear more later. Ian only met Epstein once, on a trip to New York after the trial ended. There was little love lost between Ghislaine's older brother and the New York multi-millionaire: 'He was cold. He just didn't exude the warmth of someone who wanted to spend a lot of time with me.'[31]

In July 1996 coppers in London's Knightsbridge noted a car moving without any lights on at 4.30 a.m. and stopped it. The driver – Ghislaine Maxwell – was breathalysed and found to be well over the limit. Prosecutor Nazir Afzal – who later became the top officer for the Crown Prosecution Service in the north-west – told the court that Ghislaine had first explained to the arresting policemen that she 'was allergic to alcohol and had not had a drink for four and a half years'. The allergy alibi proved to be an easy lie.

For this book, researcher Daisy Bata emailed Nazir Afzal, who replied: 'She looked ashamed when I told the court that she had claimed at first to be allergic to alcohol, but nobody believed her. I remember her saying she was something big in the internet world, which given the infancy of the internet was quite something then. I can now claim to be the first person in the world to have successfully prosecuted Ghislaine Maxwell.'[32] She was banned for a year and the court, noting that she was a woman of 'modest means', fined her £1,000.[33]

In January 1997 Ghislaine – 'a woman of moderate means' – spent £290,000 buying a mews flat at Kinnerton Street in Belgravia, a flat that becomes infamous four years later when she is photographed in it standing next to Prince Andrew, the Duke of York, with his arm around the waist of seventeen-year-old Virginia Roberts.

Back in Manhattan, Ghislaine never shared a house with Epstein. Ian Maxwell told *The Sunday Times*: 'One important point is that they never lived together. He had his place, she had her place. If she was going to see him, she had to ask. This enabled him to lead his life, the life he wanted. This was a man who was highly compartmentalised.'[34]

Ghislaine was renting her own apartment in the Upper East Side, where she threw her own parties, pretty much like the one described by Nicola Glucksmann. *Vanity Fair* reported after her arrest on the 'boldface-name Ghislaine, who seemed to be everywhere at once, so socially connected and sexually self-assured that she once hosted a dinner for East Side socialites on the fine art of giving a blow job, with dildos at each place setting'.[35]

Epstein moved into Les Wexner's old home, Herbert N. Straus House on 9 East 71st Street in the Upper East Side of Manhattan, in 1995. It was a vast mansion, perhaps the biggest private home with its own front door in the whole of Manhattan, and had originally been a private school. By the turn of the millennium, Epstein was obscenely rich. His property portfolio was totted up by *Vanity Fair* and consisted of the Manhattan mansion, worth around $77 million at the time of his death; what was thought to be the biggest private ranch in New Mexico, an $18 million, 7,500-acre property named 'Zorro', which, said Epstein, 'makes the town house look like a shack'; a 70-acre island in the US Virgin Islands known as Little St James or, by its nickname, Little St Jeffs; and a $6.8 million house on El Brillo Way in Palm Beach, Florida, just down the beach from Donald Trump's Mar-a-Lago resort. To commute between New York, New Mexico, Florida and the US Virgin Islands, Epstein had a Gulfstream IV, a helicopter and a Boeing 727, complete with stock market trading room. His planes came to be collectively nicknamed the Lolita Express, but not by him.

When Epstein took over Les Wexner's home in Manhattan, he hung a life-size female doll from a chandelier, and decorated the mansion with snaps of his pals, Bill Clinton, Mohammed Bin Salman, Crown Prince of Saudi Arabia and Woody Allen, moral titans one and all.[36] He lined the vast entrance hall with row upon row of glass eyes manufactured for blinded Tommies in the First World War.[37] How you decorate your home tells you a lot about who you are. Any visitor to *chez* Epstein must have been disturbed by the rows and rows of glass eyes. Epstein may have been extremely rich, funny, charismatic. He was also sick. My sense of it is that he was a particular kind of sadist, not one of the flesh, but of the mind. He enjoyed, got some sexual gratification, out of watching people wrestle with anxiety. The younger and more innocent the girl, the more scared she was, the better the hit for him. He took pleasure in their fear. When

Vanity Fair reporter Vicky Ward visited the Epstein mansion in 2002, there was only one book on view: a paperback copy of the Marquis de Sade's *The Misfortunes of Virtue*.[38]

Maybe the glass eyes were a nod to Epstein's belief system: transhumanism. People who call themselves transhumanists believe that body and mind are perfectible, that man can evolve into a higher form of being. The brain is what really matters, the body being a sum of parts, hence, perhaps, his home décor preference for industrially manufactured eyeballs. Epstein reportedly wanted to use his Zorro ranch in New Mexico to impregnate women to further mankind on its upward trajectory. Epstein was also into cryonics, another branch of junk science where bodies are deep-frozen to be brought back to life in the future. According to the *New York Times*, Epstein told scientists that he wanted his brain and penis frozen.[39] Doesn't everyone?

Down the track Epstein gave $9 million to Harvard, most of that to set up the university's Program for Evolutionary Dynamics, which sounds like a front for transhumanist claptrap and was closed down in 2021 with some embarrassment when the most famous university in the United States did a reverse ferret. Back in the day, brainy folk were wined and dined at Epstein's mansion on Dom Pérignon bubbly and expensive vintages, even though Epstein did not drink. Some of the scientists were also flown to his private island, Little St Jeffs. The brainboxes courted by Epstein included the late, great astronomer Stephen Hawking; the Nobel Prize-winning physicist Murray Gell-Mann, he who discovered the quark; the palaeontologist and evolutionary biologist Stephen Jay Gould; the brain boffin and bestselling author Oliver Sacks; the MIT theoretical physicist Frank Wilczek; the theoretical physicist Lawrence Krauss; the cognitive psychologist Steven Pinker; Martin Nowak, a Harvard professor of mathematics and biology and George M. Church, a molecular engineer who has worked to identify genes that could be altered to create superior humans.

So what attracted these alpha brains to hanging out with Epstein? Was it the intellectual adventure? Or something else?

Much of Epstein's manipulative genius was down to bespoke packaging. He would offer a weekend in Little St Jeffs or a party in Manhattan discussing higher mathematics and future biology, but the nuts would be handed out by stunningly beautiful models out of a catalogue. Clever men can be rubbish about sex. Who knew? There is, of course, no suggestion that any of the stellar intellects committed any wrongdoing.

Some of the great minds are now doing their own reverse ferrets, having been clocked hanging out with Epstein. Professor Church once listed the non-profit Jeffrey Epstein VI entity (the VI stands for Virgin Islands) as a source of his funding. In his 2019 apology for 'poor awareness' of Epstein's sex offender status, Church said he had 'nerd tunnel vision'.[40] Steven Pinker told the *New York Times* that Epstein was an 'intellectual impostor ... He would abruptly change the subject, ADD-style, dismiss an observation with an adolescent wisecrack.'

Epstein shunned the limelight but on one of the few occasions he did allow himself to be taped, by Bloomberg News, his musings were on the interface between maths and biology: 'The idea that people receive pleasure when they get the right answer to a puzzle, when you say pleasure, does that mean there's a bit of dopamine released in the brain? What's going on in someone's head when they have what Duchamp referred to as the Aha! Moment?'[41]

Marcel Duchamp was a Dadaist, chess player and thinker who mucked around in the foggy bottom known as the philosophy of perception. But in reality what you have here is Epstein playing at being clever, not the substance of intellectual hard work. Pinker is right to smell a rat. But it was worse than that. Pinker said that at one session at Harvard, Epstein criticised efforts to reduce starvation and provide healthcare to the poor because doing so increased the risk of overpopulation.[42]

This smacks of what transhumanism bleeds into: eugenics. The fear is that Epstein's ideology ends up with its adherents playing God over ordinary, boring, lesser people with smaller brains, thinner wallets and unfrozen penises. Epstein, then, was a kind of genetic or cerebral supremacist. Why bother to worry about people poorer, less interesting, less well connected than you? As humanity evolves into a higher state of being, these specimens will be left behind. This kind of stuff never ends well. There is no record of Ghislaine ever questioning her boyfriend's philosophy. On this territory, Robert Maxwell was far better than Jeffrey Epstein. After all, Ghislaine's father did actually fight Adolf Hitler's soldiers whereas Epstein turned out to be a bit of a Nazi.

The first great missed opportunity to stop this particular tin god happened in the mid-1990s. Maria Farmer was a beautiful young artist in her early twenties when Epstein and Ghislaine met and took a shine to her. The *New York Times* reported on Maria's 'specialty, exploring figures of nudes and adolescents . . . One of her paintings was done in a voyeuristic style, showing a man in the frame of a doorway looking at a woman on a sofa – a painting she said was inspired by Edgar Degas's famous piece *Interior*, which is sometimes known as "The Rape".'[43] This was one of her paintings Epstein wanted to buy. In 1995 the couple set Maria up as the receptionist at his New York mansion. At first, Maria found Ghislaine very likeable. She told the *New York Times* podcast: 'She was most charming, most eloquent, she was delightful.' But then, as in a slow-to-develop horror movie, things happened that didn't add up or if they did they were dark. One summer evening, Maria said she got a call to go to Epstein's office. She had been running and her legs were bare and there was no one about: 'And Trump comes into the office, doesn't say anything to me, looks at me and kind of snickers and stares at my legs. And Epstein comes out at about that time, and Epstein looks at him and goes, "No, no. She's not here for you." That's what happened.'[44]

Beautiful women were very much a part of Jeffrey Epstein's life. But Maria could not help noticing that some of them were young, very young, and some even wearing school uniforms, some in braces. They would go upstairs to where Jeffrey Epstein was at the time. When she questioned what was going on, she was told that they were in the mansion to try out for modelling gigs for Victoria's Secret, the lingerie chain owned by Les Wexner whose personal finances Epstein was controlling. The host of the *NYT* podcast asked how many girls. She replied: 'Hundreds. Hundreds. Hundreds.' How old? 'Thirteen, fourteen, fifteen.'

Maria explained how she often witnessed Ghislaine leaving the house, on the hunt for the girls Epstein liked, all of them just out of puberty: 'She would turn like that. [Clicks fingers.] I've got to get the nubiles, I've got to get the nubiles . . . so several times I was in a car with her . . . She would ask the driver to stop the car, and she'd dash across to the school or the park or wherever she was going, and she'd write down her number for a child, a young girl. And then I'd see that child in the house.'

When Maria challenged her, Ghislaine explained: 'They're auditioning. I've found a model in the park.' Maria found it really strange because she saw a couple of girls in braces: 'I'd never seen a model in braces and all of them were completely flat-chested.' Sometimes they would be wearing school uniform. One day a girl came down crying, and Maria asked Ghislaine why she was crying, and she said 'She didn't get the job, she needs to toughen up.'[45]

So the picture that Maria Farmer paints is that Ghislaine worked hard, and successfully so, at deflecting her anxieties about what was going on, so much so that it is only with the benefit of hindsight that she gets the full horror of what was happening in front of her eyes. As ever, there was bait: Maria's parents had divorced, money was tight, Epstein was offering to buy and promote her art. In the summer of 1996 Maria said she was lured to Les Wexner's estate in home state of Ohio to work as 'artist-in-residence'. But there was a catch: big though the property was, it was aggressively guarded by Wexner's armed security people. If Maria wanted to leave the house or estate, she had to ask for permission: just the kind of thing that, some say, happens inside a cult like Scientology.

It was at the Wexner estate, Maria says, where she was sexually assaulted by Jeffrey Epstein and Ghislaine Maxwell working together: 'Ghislaine escorts me to Jeffrey's room and he's lying there . . . Ghislaine sits on the other side. And they began assaulting me.'[46]

Maria Farmer said she ran to another room and piled up

furniture against the door, barricading herself in. She said security would not let her go for twelve hours. She managed to call her father and he drove all the way from Kentucky to Ohio to rescue her. Maria then discovered that three nude photographs she had kept in a storage box were missing. The photos were of her younger sister Annie and a third Farmer sister, who was twelve at the time, modelling for Maria's figurative paintings.

Only after the attack on Maria did it come out that Annie – who was sixteen at the time – had also suffered unwelcome attention from Ghislaine and Epstein. In January 1996 Annie Farmer was invited to New York by the couple. Annie found Epstein 'kind', casually dressed in sweatpants, pouring champagne and talking about her college plans, she told the *New York Times*. They all went to see a movie. As the film progressed, Epstein began rubbing Annie's hand, and then her lower leg. Annie's diary for 25 January 1996 read: 'It was one of those things that just gave me a weird feeling but wasn't that weird + probably normal. The one thing that kind of weirded me out about it was he let go of my hand when he was talking to Maria.'

That April Annie Farmer was lured to Epstein's Zorro ranch in New Mexico on the false pretence that other students would be there too. Only at the ranch did the sixteen-year-old realise that the party consisted of just three people: Epstein, Ghislaine and her. She told the *NYT* podcast that Ghislaine gave her a massage. Annie undressed: 'She had me flip over to my back. And then she pulled the sheet down so that my breasts were exposed. This feels weird. This feels uncomfortable. I don't think this is probably right, but I don't know.' Then the sixteen-year-old becomes aware that there may be someone else in the room, close by, watching: Jeffrey Epstein. 'I could feel his presence, like, oh, I'm sure he can see me from where he is.'[47] Here, the allegation is that Ghislaine carried out a sexualised massage without Annie's consent while Epstein played voyeur.

Maria Farmer complained first to the New York City Police Department about the theft of her photo and what she says Jeffrey Epstein and Ghislaine Maxwell did to her and her sister. Nothing happened. Then she complained to the FBI. Again, nothing. But soon, she says, Ghislaine started harassing her, threatening to burn her paintings, burn her career, and for the next twenty years, both Maria and Annie Farmer lived in fear. They were poor; Epstein and Ghislaine rich and powerful.

Why would Ghislaine want to be with a man who was so very keen on having sex with other women, especially ones much younger than her? Ghislaine, I suspect, blinded herself to what was going on. Vassi Chamberlain reported one of Ghislaine's friends from New York setting it out bluntly: 'She would not have been unique in being someone who lives well and possesses a sexual peccadillo of sharing women with her boyfriend. Underlying all of this was her libertarian sexual appetite.'[48]

In 2002 there was a second great missed opportunity to stop Epstein. Reporter Vicky Ward was commissioned by *Vanity Fair* to write a piece about him by the magazine's editor, Graydon Carter. She set out to discover what lay at the bottom of the two things that obsessed Epstein: 'It was two-pronged: the mystery about Jeffrey Epstein was how he had made his money. It was also known that he would gather New York's rich and famous for dinner parties at his home but there would be these very young women, the women were always part of the Jeffrey Epstein story.'[49]

Vicky Ward discovered the story of the Farmer sisters and Maria's unsuccessful complaints to the NYPD and the FBI that she and her sister had been sexually abused by Epstein and Ghislaine Maxwell. Remember Maria said she had been abused in Ohio, her sister Annie in New Mexico: that was federal crime. Vicky, when she was researching her article in late 2002 and early 2003, was pregnant with twins. She said Epstein threatened her unborn babies, a threat she took so seriously that she hired security for the maternity clinic where they were born. Much to Vicky Ward's apparent dismay, all mention of Maria and Annie Farmer was removed from her article when it appeared in March 2003 because, she was told, she did not have enough evidence to meet the legal thresholds necessary at *Vanity Fair*.

On the day of publication, a live bullet was found on the door-step of Graydon Carter's home in Manhattan. Three years later, *Vanity Fair* had another go, with a reporter investigating claims of Epstein abusing under-age girls in Florida. This time, the head of a dead cat was found on the porch of Graydon Carter's home in the countryside.[50]

In her 2003 article Vicky Ward hinted deftly at some of this menace: 'One reporter, in fact, received three threats from Epstein while preparing a piece. They were delivered in a jocular tone, but the message was clear: There will be trouble for your family if I don't like the article.'[51] I suspect that the reporter in question was Ward herself. I have emailed her but have received no reply. The security team in the maternity clinic, the bullet on the doorstep and the dead cat on the porch suggest not just that Jeffrey Epstein was good at sums, but also that he was an uber-gangster, using not violence but the suggestion of it to intimi-date and knock flat his enemies. If so, then Ghislaine was the gangster's moll.

Writing about Epstein's mansion, she clocks the hall of glass eyes, its grandiosity, but also – and here's an echo of Headington Hill Hall – 'the house is curiously impersonal, the statement of someone who wants to be known for the scale of his possessions.' Epstein tells people he bought the house because he knew he 'could never live anywhere bigger'.[52]

Vicky Ward's *Vanity Fair* article suggests that she found Epstein charming but also a cold calculus: 'he doesn't let the charm slip into his eyes. They are steely and calculating, giving some hint at the steady whir of machinery running behind them.' She notes that he has made it so that the true source of his wealth remains a mystery.

Epstein secured a major victory by the pressure he placed on *Vanity Fair* to take out the evidence of Maria and Annie Farmer on his sexual abuse of them and Maria's wider testimony on the constant traffic of under-age girls, some in school uniforms, some with braces, to see him.

Graydon Carter has since said: 'If we had three people on the

record willing to stand up for us in court if Epstein had chosen to
sue, we would have run it. Period. End of story.'[53]

To be fair to *Vanity Fair* and Graydon Carter, three points. First:
I have spent large chunks of my forty-plus years as a reporter
watching expensively shod lawyers taking out the most interesting bits of my copy. Second: the piece that *Vanity Fair* did publish
was pretty tough on Epstein. Third, down the track Vicky Ward
posed for a photo with Ghislaine at New York's Gramercy Hotel
in 2009 and sang Ghislaine's praises and admired Epstein in a
blog written in 2011.

In that blog Ward conceded that she did 'hear stories about the
girls' in 2002, but not knowing quite whom to believe, she concen-
trated on the financial mystery instead. She goes on to explain
that she got to know 'Jeffrey' – note that use of the first name –
and Ghislaine much better after writing her 2002 article: 'The
truth is, Epstein does know a lot about a lot of things. Just a few
moments in his company and you know this to be true . . . And
Ghislaine? Full disclosure: I like her. Most people in New York do.
It's almost impossible not to. She is always the most interesting,
the most vivacious, the most unusual person in any room.'

Vicky Ward concludes: 'In this city, money makes up for all sorts
of blemishes.' In 2021 Vicky Ward hosted the 'Chasing Ghislaine'
podcast in which she reports on not the 'blemishes' but the pure
moral evil of Ghislaine and Epstein but somehow forgets her own,
spectacular reverse ferret, the 2011 blog she has since deleted. The
Wayback Machine prevents such airbrushing of history.

There is one more unexplored shadow to the mystery of Jeffrey
Epstein. In 1996 Epstein had escorted Maria Farmer, the receptionist at the big house in Manhattan, through a hidden door to
a secret media room, underneath the stairs, where she saw a bank
of stacked TV monitors overseen by male operators. On the multiple screens she saw: 'toilet, toilet, bed, bed, toilet, bed.' She resolved
never to sleep there: 'It was very obvious that they were, like, moni-
toring private moments.'[54]

What Maria Farmer saw looks very much like the machinery for
blackmail. The question is: who was on Jeffrey Epstein's sucker list?

chapter six

The Black Book

Ghislaine Maxwell's black book is actually two address books in one: hers comes first, the names are more obviously British, the selection that of a star-loving socialite who went to Oxford and knows her way around the knobs and nobs of the British Establishment. Jeffrey Epstein's book is shorter, orientated more to business, the names and numbers more exclusively American. Stapled together, there are roughly one and a half thousand names and five thousand phone numbers in the two books. The original belonged to Epstein's late butler, Alfredo Rodriguez, with 'P.B. 2004–2005' scribbled on the very first page, placing it from Epstein's home on El Brillo Way in P.B. – Palm Beach – in those years. Rodriguez sought to make $50,000 by selling it to a mystery buyer, who turned out to be an investigator. The naughty butler had kept his knowledge of the book back from law enforcement, so he was convicted, did jail time and died of natural causes shortly after his release. Someone, no one knows who for sure, has circled thirty-eight names in the book.[1]

In Epstein's second half you find names like Donald Trump – circled – lawyer Alan Dershowitz and Epstein's business partner Les Wexner. The late Dr Oliver Sacks, the great neurologist who wrote *The Man Who Mistook His Wife for a Hat*, is a rare exception to the men of money and power. Ghislaine's little black book is something else, providing a window into her soul. The picture that emerges is that she is both spectacularly successful and somehow empty.

On the very first page, there's a number for Charlie Althorp, also known as the ninth Earl Spencer, the brother of the late

Princess Diana. Then there's the actor Alec Baldwin who's so good at lampooning Trump on *Saturday Night Live*. There are pages and pages of it, the great and good or is it the not-so-great and the not-that-good? Tony Blair, Mike Bloomberg, Richard Branson, Alastair Campbell, Naomi Campbell, John Cleese, Phil Collins, Sophie Dahl, Jonathan Dimbleby. For the podcast *Hunting Ghislaine* I ring that number but it is no longer valid. Ghislaine has eighteen separate telephone numbers for Sarah Ferguson, Duchess of York, and her staff, and eighteen numbers for Sarah's ex-husband, Prince Andrew, the Duke of York, and his staff too.

Intelligence analysts call this traffic analysis: you can glean something, not from messages received and sent, but from the volume of traffic, the number of interactions or in this case phone numbers. The longer the list of numbers Ghislaine has of a contact, the more likely they're higher up in her circle of friends.

Bernie Ecclestone, Brian Ferry, Ralph Fiennes, the actor who plays 007's boss, M, in the Bond movies, Flik Mook – no idea who she is but what a fantastic name – Rocco Forte, His Royal Highness Prince Pavlos of Greece, Geordie Greig, the last but one editor of the *Daily Mail*.

I give him a ring.

> **Geordie Greig:** 'Hello?'
> **John Sweeney:** 'Hi Geordie, it's John Sweeney. I'm doing a podcast on Ghislaine Maxwell.'
> **Geordie Greig:** 'I'm probably not going to be quoted on it . . . Can I talk off the record?'
> **John Sweeney:** 'Yes, you can.'

A source close to the editor of the *Daily Mail* noted that he had known Ghislaine Maxwell for a long time and that was no secret, and he had nothing of substance to add.

Lloyd Grossman, Marie Helvin, Michael Heseltine, Dustin Hoffman, Liz Hurley, Mick Jagger, Peter Mandelson: ten numbers for him. I gave Peter, now Lord Mandelson, a ring too:

John Sweeney: 'Hello, I'm doing a podcast on
   Ghislaine . . .'
Peter Mandelson: 'Can't hear you . . . I'm on a Zoom
   call . . . Call back later . . .'

He never did. Andrew Neil, David Puttnam, Joan Rivers, Kevin Spacey, Koo Stark, Ivanka Trump, Chris Tucker, Toby Young . . .

The latter wrote a piece for *The Spectator* ruminating on the curse of *The Black Book*:

'Every time Jeffrey Epstein is in the news, I start getting calls from strangers wanting to scream abuse at me . . . My best guess is that, in reality, the address book belonged to Ghislaine, whom I do know slightly.' Young recalls that when he lived in New York between 1995 and 2000, he bumped into her occasionally at parties and the London address listed as his dates back to that period. He adds: 'Rather unhelpfully, the *Daily Mail* recently ran a picture spread showing Ghislaine out and about "in society" and including a photo of me saying something funny to her in a night-club, making her howl with laughter.'

Young bemoans how that photo has done the rounds on Twitter: 'It's guilt by association, although as I point out to the screamers on the other end of the phone, Ghislaine hasn't actually been found guilty of anything.'[2] His last point was correct when Young wrote his article.

Nicholas Coleridge, Ghislaine's old friend from Oxbridge days, recalled how, about twenty years ago when she became Jeffrey Epstein's gatekeeper, he received a fax from her Manhattan office, asking for 'the addresses and landlines for your principal residences, your weekend homes and ski chalets, and then the questions became yet more surreal – the mobile numbers of your pilot on your private jet, your yacht captain, your butler. It was dispiriting to have to write 'N/A' against so many of them.' The form was sent to around three hundred of Ghislaine's university friends. 'Now, of course, inclusion in Epstein's infamous little black book is an embarrassment, and many of us are regularly rung by newspapers to ask how often we frequented his parties and massage table.' Coleridge says that none of his set ever met Epstein or had really heard of him before the scandal erupted: 'Most of the people listed, Ghislaine's old mates, are now Lord Lieutenants and High Sheriffs of their respective counties.'[3]

Both Toby Young and Nicholas Coleridge are right to bemoan how some people have foolishly joined too many dots and linked the fact of being in someone's address book to knowledge of dark acts.

There is, of course, no suggestion that people in Ghislaine Maxwell's address book ever knew that they were hobnobbing with an alleged facilitator or pimp for a paedophile. But you cannot help but wonder whether Ghislaine Maxwell used her connections to provide a smokescreen for Epstein's sociopathy. And it is true to say that there are more than a hundred telephone numbers in Ghislaine's black book under the heading 'Massage' – the cover Epstein used to hide his crimes against young girls. So it's an address book. And it's a spider's web.

Before we move on, here's one last observation on what the Black Book might tell us about Ghislaine. Compare my contacts book with Ghislaine's – in 2004, I was a BBC reporter – and mine is a bit rubbish, frankly. Ghislaine's black book is extraordinarily detailed and well organised, pedantically so, to the point that makes me wonder whether Ghislaine is autistic or on the spectrum. Autism would appear to run in the family. Robert Maxwell's extraordinary, almost supernatural ability to juggle with languages and numbers while binge-eating and having zero emotional intelligence suggests that he might have been a very high-functioning autistic; his son Philip was so brilliant at maths he won a scholarship to Balliol at sixteen but found it difficult to prosper in life. Autism is held to be far more common in boys than girls, but that may be a problem of perception not fact. Autistic girls are better at masking the condition than boys. Three psychologists at Bournemouth University have studied autistic girls. They report that they 'struggle with managing conflict in relationships, and that social time is exhausting to them.' But autistic girls are far better than autistic boys at adapting. They are 'more likely to engage in pretend play than autistic boys and may appear to have rich inner lives which under closer scrutiny may be seen to be extraordinarily scripted and repetitive.'[4]

Psychologists record that among autistic females there is increased evidence of social anxiety, self-harm and anorexia. Ghislaine suffered from the latter condition at the age of three. This leads on to a related thought, inspired by a conversation I had with Cordelia Grossman who has studied this area, that autistic people can be far more sexually adventurous than the general population. Four German psychiatrists reported: 'Individuals with ASD' – Autism Spectrum Disorders – 'seem to have more hypersexual and paraphilic fantasies and behaviours than general-population studies suggest.'[5] Paraphilia is fancy talk for sexual deviancy. As the story of Ghislaine's conduct gets darker and darker, hold on to this thought: that there is quite a lot of evidence – her anorexia, her social anxiety masked by a strange intensity, even her own contacts book – that points to her being a high-functioning autistic, which can, in turn, lead to being hyper-sexed and sexually deviant. In short, there might be something far out of the ordinary in her genes that has been passed down to her.

That said, what is striking is how utterly unconnected were Epstein's victims, how they didn't have any powerful movers and shakers in their address books, how none of them ever wrote a piece in *The Spectator* though they all ended up in a different kind of black book. Take Virginia Roberts, after she got married, Virginia Roberts Giuffre. Poor, white, born in California but raised in Florida, she was molested by a family friend when she was seven. She ran away, was fostered, ran away again, lived on the streets. When she was thirteen, she was picked up by a sixty-five-year-old sex trafficker, Ron Eppinger. For months, she says, she was sexually abused, kept in an apartment and pimped out to paedophiles.[6] She lived with him for six months until he was busted by the FBI. Virginia was reunited with her father working as a janitor at Trump's Mar-a-Lago estate in Palm Beach. Her father got her a job as a spa attendant, handing out towels and the like to the rich people. Then in 2000 along came a woman in a chauffeur-driven car. She spotted Virginia and told the driver to stop. Virginia was very young-looking, blonde, wearing her uniform of white miniskirt and a skin-tight white polo top and reading a library book about massage therapy.

Virginia recalled: 'She was like this really bright Mary Poppins kind of a figure . . . And she goes "Oh, you know what, I know this guy, there's an opportunity actually if you wanna become a real massage therapist, we can get you trained, you can come for the interview tonight and if he likes you then you'll be a real masseuse."'

This is when the two worlds collide, when Ghislaine Maxwell meets Virginia Roberts Giuffre. It is not 'he meets her'. It is Mary Poppins – with lovely beautiful British accent – meets her. As the *New Yorker's* Ariel Levy put it in Broken, her podcast about the Epstein case, if you're a teenage girl and a man approaches you in a car, 'you know to keep on walking. But if it's another woman, and she sounds all fancy and well-educated, you're probably going to get in the car.'[7]

Virginia said she, blind-sided by Ghislaine, became Epstein's sex slave. She said she was paid $200 the first time she had sex with Epstein. And Ghislaine? Well, in 2000 she moved into a $5m-dollar townhouse on the Upper East Side ten blocks from Epstein's mansion. The New York home had been bought by an anonymous limited liability company with the same address as Epstein's main company and acting for the buyer was Darren Indyke, Epstein's then lawyer.[8]

Julie K. Brown in her brilliant investigative series for the *Miami Herald* in 2018, 'Perversion of Justice', quotes an affidavit from Virginia on Epstein: 'His appetite was insatiable. He wanted new girls, fresh, young faces every single day – that was just the sickness that he had.' Virginia told the *Herald* that Epstein had cameras throughout his homes and said he liked her to tell him about the sexual peccadilloes of various important men she had sex with. So that means there are two separate witnesses who speak to Epstein's machinery of blackmail, first Maria Farmer, second Virginia.

'Epstein and Maxwell,' said Virginia, 'also got girls for Epstein's friends and acquaintances. Epstein specifically told me that the reason for him doing this was so that they would "owe him," they

would "be in his pocket," and he would "have something on them,"'
Virginia said in a court affidavit. 'I understood him to mean that
when someone was in his pocket, they owed him favours.'[9]

Virginia highlighted Ghislaine's role when she was interviewed
by the *New Yorker*: 'Ghislaine would say, "We want you to please
these men in whatever way they want, I don't care how gross or
kinky it is."' Virginia said Epstein wanted her to report back about
what the men liked. She added that a video-recording system had
been installed in the New York mansion and she was convinced
that Epstein was gathering information to use for leverage on the
men. She told the *New Yorker*: 'I wasn't chained to a sink but they
had an invisible chain for me. I know he had power. He was
constantly telling me, "I own the police department. I have friends
that owe me favours."'[10] Virginia's sense of an 'invisible chain'
binding her to Epstein's and Ghislaine's grossly dysfunctional
family, that body and soul were locked in, is very cult-like.

The most famous of these important men Virginia claims she
was required to have sex with is Andrew Windsor, also known as
Prince Andrew, also known as the Duke of York, KG, GCVO, CD,
ADC. The second son of the Queen of England had served as an
anti-submarine helicopter pilot for the Royal Navy and was
awarded 'best pilot' by his father when he received his 'wings' in
1981. Famously, he did his bit during the Falklands War, becom-
ing a 'royal top gun'. He continued to fly after leaving the Navy,
though his helicopter heroism has been limited to more minor
crises, such as saving the late magician Paul Daniels from being
late for a show.[11] In 1986, Prince Andrew married Sarah Ferguson
and the couple had two daughters, Princesses Beatrice and
Eugenie. After they separated in 1992, photos appeared of her
financial adviser, John Bryan, sucking her toes. The couple
divorced in 1996 but stayed close.

Virginia claims that she had sex with Prince Andrew three times.
In a sworn affidavit, Virginia said the first time was in London when
she was seventeen. The age of consent in Britain is sixteen, so that
was legal, just. The second time was in New York, where state law on
consent is the same as Britain's. The third time was at an orgy on

Epstein's island. Both the duke and Ghislaine have separately denied Virginia's extraordinary allegations. After Jeffrey Epstein was arrested in 2019, Prince Andrew issued a press statement saying that he met Epstein in 1999, that he saw him infrequently, that he stayed in a number of his residences: 'At no stage during that limited time I spent with him did I see, witness or suspect any behaviour of the sort that subsequently led to his arrest and conviction.'[12]

He also issued a separate statement, 'categorically' denying any sexual contact with Ms Giuffre, which we shall go into in some detail.

After the *Mail on Sunday* first ran in 2011 Virginia's allegations that Ghislaine pimped her out for Prince Andrew years before, Ghislaine released a statement through Devonshires solicitors saying: 'the allegations made against me are abhorrent and entirely untrue and I ask that they stop. A number of newspapers have shown a complete lack of accuracy in their reporting of this story and a failure to carry out the most elementary investigation or any real due diligence. I am now taking action to clear my name.'[13]

That phrase commonly means that you are going to sue the newspapers you are complaining about. She did not.

Let's examine what Virginia says, what might back up her account, and the nature and strength of the denials of Prince Andrew and Ghislaine Maxwell.

Some circumstantial evidence is very strong, as when you find a trout in the milk,' wrote the American philosopher Thoreau, suggesting that that scenario is so unnatural that someone must have put the trout where it should not be. But no-one knows for sure how the fish got in the milk. Likewise, there is evidence that suggests that Virginia Roberts Giuffre is not a fantasist: the photograph of the prince holding the 17-year-old around the waist and her lawyers have witness statements putting the prince and Virginia in the same place and the same time on a number of occasions. But none of that proves Prince Andrew had sex with Virginia. For example, there is no audio or video tape of that. The prince denies ever having met her, denies having sex with her. She says she did have sex with him, three times; he denies it.

How well did Prince Andrew know Ghislaine and Epstein? Exhibit A is the flight logs of the 'Lolita Express' and the other aircraft belonging to Epstein. They show that in April 1988, Epstein met 'Princess Sarah Ferguson and kids' on the ground in Nassau in the Bahamas. The American pilot can be forgiven for getting the royal title wrong: it's Sarah Ferguson, Duchess of York. The Yorks had been divorced for some years but they were and are close, as we shall see. The flight logs then bring Prince Andrew into the picture in February 1999, when he is on the Gulf Stream flying from Teterboro airport in New Jersey to St Thomas in the US Virgin Islands to Little St Jeffs, Epstein's island, also with Epstein and Ghislaine.[14]

The island was staffed from 1999 to 2007 by a South African couple, Cathy and Miles Alexander, hired by Ghislaine Maxwell in Manhattan. The couple say they never saw proof of under-age sex. Miles found Epstein pleasant to deal with; Cathy did not like Ghislaine who referred to herself as 'Queen Bee'. She recalled Ghislaine setting down the rules of the island: 'She said we had to keep quiet about what we saw or heard on the island. She told us that although Mr Epstein and she were a couple, we would see lots of beautiful girls passing in and out, but that was his nature . . . Although she could be very friendly, I discovered that she was also rather arrogant.'[15]

In April 1999 Prince Andrew came to the island with a body-guard and a female escort who self-identified as a brain surgeon, as you do. Cathy told the *Daily Mail*: 'She was tall, bleached blonde and had big boobs.' One day the prince came back into the house in great mirth, explaining that his 'brain surgeon' guest had stepped on a sea urchin and he had urinated on her foot as a remedy. 'The royal member has done its duty,' he chuckled. Cathy said the prince 'was great fun and very undemanding.' The prince stayed for two weeks and left a tip of $350 (£220), which was unusual because most guests never tipped.[16]

In the summer of 1999 Andrew reportedly invited Epstein and Ghislaine to the Queen's Scottish castle at Balmoral. In February 2000 there's a photo taken at Trump's Mar-a-Lago resort showing Donald and Melania Trump, Prince Andrew, Epstein lurking in the shadows, and Ghislaine Maxwell photo-bombing the shot from the edge of frame on the right.[17] In June 2000 Epstein and Ghislaine attended the so-called party of the century, Prince Andrew's fortieth birthday party, Princess Anne's fiftieth, Princess Margaret's seventieth, and Prince William's eighteenth. That Halloween, there was a change in tone when Prince Andrew and Ghislaine – no sign of Epstein – attend a 'Pimps and Hookers' party thrown by Heidi Klum, who was a German supermodel working for Les Wexner's Victoria's Secret lingerie chain. Ghislaine came as a hooker in a bleach blonde wig, bare midriff top and gold pants, Prince Andrew came in a suit and didn't look very much like a pimp. In December 2000, just before Christmas, Andrew invited Ghislaine and Epstein to Sandringham for a pheasant shoot. To celebrate the New Year the happy trio of Prince Andrew, Epstein and Ghislaine all go to the Thai island of Phuket – pronounced not 'Fuck it' but 'Fookette' – where Andrew was snapped sunbathing on a yacht surrounded by a number of topless young women.

All of that evidence above just shows the prior connections between Epstein, Ghislaine and Prince Andrew. But in the spring of 2001 the flight logs show 'JE' (Epstein) and 'GM' (Ghislaine) took 'Virginia Roberts', as she was described in the logs, around half the world in six days, from Palm Beach to Canada, Paris, Grenada in Spain, Tangier in Morocco, and then, on 9 March, to Luton Airport.[18] American readers will not be aware of, in English eyes, the quintessential naffness of Luton Airport. This was baked in by a series of brilliant 1970s TV ads for Campari, starring former model Lorraine Chase enjoying drinks in exotic places with a posh playboy suitor. Smoothly, he asks, 'Were you truly wafted here from paradise?', whereupon Lorraine declares in her eel-pie Cockney accent: 'Nah, Luton Airport.'[19]

The trio, Epstein, Ghislaine and Virginia, hooked up with Prince Andrew for a night out on the town, ending up at Tramp night club in the West End, where Virginia claims Andrew asked her for a dance. Virginia told BBC *Panorama*: 'He is the most hideous dancer I've ever seen in my life. His sweat was like it was raining basically everywhere.' When they left Tramp, Virginia claimed

Ghislaine Maxwell gave her instructions: 'In the car Ghislaine tells me that I have to do for Andrew what I do for Jeffrey and that just made me sick.' Virginia then claimed that was when she had sex with Prince Andrew upstairs at Maxwell's house in Belgravia. 'I sat there in bed, horrified and ashamed and felt dirty.'[20]

There is a photograph of Prince Andrew with his arm around the bare waist of Virginia; next to them is Ghislaine Maxwell, smiling. The photo was reportedly taken by Epstein at Ghislaine's mews home in London in 2001. Freelance photographer Michael Thomas, then working for the *Mail on Sunday*, first copied the picture in 2011. Thomas told *Panorama* that he is convinced the picture is genuine because he found it in the middle of a bundle of photos that Virginia handed him from her travels with Epstein and Ghislaine: 'It was nothing sophisticated. These were 5×7 photos that looked like they had come from Boots the chemist. They were typical teenage snaps.' *Panorama* also found evidence that supported Virginia's claim that she gave the originals to the FBI. A redacted court document shows she gave twenty photos to the FBI in 2011 and they were scanned front and back. In the redacted public version, there are only nineteen photos shown. The BBC *Panorama* website article stated that the programme was 'told the Prince Andrew photo was removed from the public document to protect his privacy'.[21]

The prince defended himself on BBC *Newsnight* in 2019 in what is probably the worst royal car-crash interview, ever. It is an extraordinarily brilliant forensic examination by Emily Maitlis, like an anatomist dissecting a frog.

> **Prince Andrew:** 'I can absolutely, categorically tell you it never happened.'
> **Emily Maitlis:** 'She provided a photo of the two of you together. Your arm was around her waist. How do you explain that?'
> **Andrew:** 'I can't. I have absolutely no memory of that photo being taken.'

Virginia Roberts Giuffre stuck to her guns. She told *Panorama* what she thought of the prince's denial: 'He knows what happened. I know what happened. There is only one of us telling the truth and I know that's me.'

Credit must go to *Newsnight* producer Sam McAlister who managed to secure the interview, a story she tells brilliantly in her book, *Scoops*.[22] Prince Andrew told Emily Maitlis that 'there are a number of things that are wrong' with Virginia's story. He didn't have sex with Virginia because, first, he was at Pizza Express, Woking, Surrey, at a birthday party for his daughter: 'Going to Pizza Express in Woking is an unusual thing for me to do. I remember it weirdly distinctly.' That may be true, but the alibi only works if it's the Pizza Express in Aberdeen. The one in Woking is only an hour from London so it is perfectly possible to eat chicken wings, dough balls and a Sloppy Giuseppe then get to London for the night out with Epstein, Ghislaine and Virginia. Second, Prince Andrew noted that Virginia had claimed he bought her an alcoholic drink: 'I don't drink, I don't think I've ever bought a drink in Tramps whenever I was there.' That may be true also; Epstein could easily have picked up the bill; it doesn't knock out the sex allegation. Third, Prince Andrew admitted to Emily Maitlis a rare medical condition that, he said, put him in the clear. Defining a 'problem' with Virginia's story, he said he could not have been sweating: 'I didn't sweat at the time because I had suffered what I would describe as an overdose of adrenalin in the Falklands War when I was shot at.' He said he had only started to be able to sweat again 'in the recent past'.[23]

For the Hunting Ghislaine podcast, I asked my mate Ash whether Andrew's story, that he was in the Falklands War, was attacked by the Argentinians and had a tremendous adrenaline rush, and because of that, Prince Andrew can't sweat, was that kosher? Ash replied: 'That sounds a very bizarre story. An absence of sweating is a very rare finding. To my understanding, the only way that can occur is if you're born without sweat glands. So the concept that excessive stress would stop you sweating is not something I have come across.'

But Ash was just some geezer I had met in the pub, wasn't he? He replied: 'Well, yes, in a sense, I suppose that that part is true. I've got a few qualifications.' I asked him what they were. An O level or two? Ashley Grossman set out his stall: 'I'm currently Emeritus Professor from the University of Oxford and Senior Fellow at Green Templeton College and Professor of Neuro-endocrinology at Barts and the London School of Medicine. And I've been president of a variety of different national and international societies. And I've written in scientific publications a few chapters about sweating and flushing, too.'

I asked if he had written any papers on medicine: 'Approaching a thousand.' Had he got any letters after his name? 'Yeah, quite a few, but don't often use them.' Go on: 'B.A., BSc, MDFRCP. I got a very nice honorary PhD, which is the easiest thing I ever did, from the University of Athens, and I'm a Fellow of the Academy of Medical Science.' So I put it to Ash that when Prince Andrew says, 'Listen, it wasn't me because I can't sweat', that's just bollocks?

Professor Grossman, to give him his correct title, replied: 'I wouldn't use that precise terminology, but I've never come across a case where excessive stress, which I imagine came from PTSD after the Falklands War, would cause that problem. So that really is quite novel to me.' I said, you are professor of sweating at Oxford University? He replied: 'I have an interest in sweating amongst very many other things. I am not his personal physician, but to the best of my knowledge, I'm not aware of any endocrine condition that might account for this claim.'[24] To be clear, Ashley's comments are based on scientific evidence in the public domain, not personal knowledge of the prince's health. But who do you reckon is the expert, Ashley Grossman, professor of sweating at Oxford University, or the Duke of York?

Prince Andrew's general demeanour throughout the interview was comically unconvincing. That does not necessarily mean he is lying. He has a history of being so cocksure in his own entitlement that he comes across as inherently unlikeable and unpleasant; that does not equal dishonesty. Vassi Chamberlain profiled him for *The Sunday Times*: 'I have met Andrew several times over the years, and his reputation as a blundering and arrogant buffoon is not without foundation. One of my friends described him as a man with "all the airs and graces of royalty, but none of their superiority – he lacks Eton charm."'

Vassi Chamberlain witnessed what she calls his 'boorishness' first-hand at a lunch she attended in his honour in the mid-2000s in Condé Nast UK's Vogue House boardroom, hosted by the division's then head, Nicholas Coleridge. 'Andrew was awkward and uneasy in a group conversation', but then he went on to give a half-hour lecture to the eight editors present on reversing a tanker into port: 'he was so clearly used to being heard that he never learnt to listen or to read the room'.

Vassi goes on to write that Andrew's sexual appetite, or, more precisely, his desire to be wanted, is his blind spot. She recounts a dinner party in London in the 1990s when all the guests bowed and scraped when the duke showed up. Then a bunch of sexy young women, models, joined the party, flying their arms around him, crying out, 'Andy, darling!' Vassi recalls: 'what I remember above all about this most unusual experience was the look on his face. It wasn't that of a creepy, sex-obsessed man – he looked more like a dumbfounded adolescent.'

Vassi spoke to several of his friends for her profile of the duke, the most perceptive I have read. She found two firmly held opinions, first, that Andrew would have had no idea that the girls he met through Jeffrey Epstein were being trafficked and ordered to sleep with him. The second, that Andrew almost certainly did sleep with Virginia Roberts – he denies it. 'He has always chased a shag,' said one female mutual friend, who, Vassi adds, 'should know, because she once shagged him herself.'

One ex-lover, 'Lucy', told Vassi that he had a total lack of emotional intelligence. 'Lucy' recalled his annoying habit of introducing himself to her pals as 'the Duke of York', even when they were dancing on tables at two in the morning at Momo [a popular Moroccan restaurant in London with a basement club]. 'Every joke always ended with ". . . because I'm the Duke of York!" He tells the most pathetic jokes. He finds poo cushions funny.'

Sexually he was a bit keen, said Lucy, 'but perfectly straightfor-
ward. There was a bit of chasing around the sofa, but not in an aggres-
sive way. I remember, one day, looking out of his Buckingham Palace
bedroom window and thinking, "What a sad life." People were standing outside the gates 24/7.' Lucy says Andrew would eat popcorn but
shunned garlic and alcohol, and his email at the time was invisible-
man@—.com. Vassi writes that despite all this, Lucy still describes
him as 'always gentlemanly' and that there was 'nothing awful or
sneaky about him', except when it came to paying the bill, which he
and his entourage conspicuously avoided. One evening she suggested
that they go to the cinema, and planned to buy two tickets. He needed
seven for his security team and she had to pay up. Lucy ended up
chucking him, but Andrew didn't seem to be bothered. Lucy
suspected that he was still in love with Fergie but he told her that he
would never get married again. She concluded that he was a loner,
with no true friends, and not close to his brothers and sister.[25]

How strong is Virginia's evidence that she had to have sex with
Prince Andrew in New York and on Little St Jeffs? Bradley Edwards
tells a story in his book, *Relentless Pursuit: My Fight for the Victims of
Jeffrey Epstein*, citing the evidence of a victim, now known to be
Johanna Sjoberg, one of Epstein's former sex slaves. She described
Virginia sitting in New York on one of Prince Andrew's knees and
herself sitting on the other, Edwards writes. 'While the two girls
were in his lap, Ghislaine took out a puppet figure of Prince
Andrew and placed the puppet's hand on Virginia's breast, at
which point Prince Andrew placed his hand on Johanna's breast.
Everyone laughed.'[26] It was a glove puppet of the Prince Andrew
character from ITV's *Spitting Image*.

In 2003 Prince Andrew met puppeteer Steve Wright at a reception at Buckingham Palace and when Steve showed him a photo
of one of his creations, the prince said, 'Oh my God, puppets!
Spitting Image – do you know that my friend bought my *Spitting
Image* puppet and you'll never believe it, he played a trick on me.'
The prince told Steve that he went to an apartment in New York
and saw the 'bloody thing' sitting up on the sofa and that he
'nearly had a bloody heart attack' as he was there looking at

himself. On hearing the allegations made by Virginia Roberts Giuffre, Steve told the *Daily Mail*: 'Why would she [Ms Roberts] make up a story about puppets? It all just clicked.' The newspaper contacted the Duke's PR people but he declined to comment.[27]

Satire is so very dead. The puppet story is not proof that the shenanigans led to sex but it does place Virginia and the duke under the same roof, spy-hole cameras and all.

Once again, Prince Andrew denies ever having sex with Virginia, and Ghislaine Maxwell denies pimping her out to him. But neither has ever sued Virginia.

By the turn of the millennium, Ghislaine and Jeffrey Epstein were no longer lovers but good friends. She was still running his life, still his introduction to money and power and rank. But nature abhors a vacuum. In April 2000 the *New York Post* caught Prince Andrew dining with Ghislaine Maxwell during an intimate lunch at Nello's restaurant on Madison Avenue. The prince held hands with his new love, the tabloid reported breathlessly, but the couple seemed keen to keep the romance under wraps. Lunch over, Ghislaine left first, leaving Andrew to settle the bill. When the prince walked out, he immediately pulled a cell phone from his jacket. Ghislaine was window-shopping down the street, a witness said. When the prince spotted the *Post*'s photographer, Ghislaine vanished into a shop, occasionally playing peep-bo, checking to see if the coast was clear.[28]

Prince Andrew and Ghislaine are not easy people to sympathise with, but this story suggests that swimming inside the royal gold-fish bowl was never much fun.

chapter seven

Out of Africa, etc.

New Year's Day 2002 saw Ghislaine Maxwell at the height of her astonishing recovery from her wretched state after her father's death eleven years before. She is rich, owning two homes, one in Manhattan, one in London, fabulously well connected, the ultimate socialite and extraordinarily busy too, running ragged around the world. To give the reader a flavour of just how bonkers her lifestyle was, researcher Bertie Harrison-Broninski, the poor sod, tracked her movements from 2002 to 2013 for this book. Let us just flag her travels in January 2002. The flight logs show that on 6 January, after New Year's Eve, a party of six people flew into Newark, New Jersey, from St Thomas in the United States Virgin Islands. On board were Epstein, Ghislaine, Cindy Lopez, Alexia Wallert, 'AP' – possibly but not certainly Prince Andrew – and 'SK'.[1]

'SK' is Sarah Kellen, who appears in 350 logs of Epstein flights and was one of Ghislaine's most long-serving assistants. Sarah had been raised in North Carolina as a Jehovah's Witness, which some ex-members suggest is an Armageddon cult. When she was still in her teens, she married another member of the church, Noa Bonk. The new Mrs Bonk moved to Hawaii but the marriage broke up and Sarah parted from the church for the sin, in their eyes, of leading 'an immoral lifestyle'. She had modelled nude for art classes and fashion magazines. She ended up, again called Sarah Kellen, working in Manhattan for Jeffrey Epstein, and also as yet another entry in Ghislaine's black book: address on East 66th Street, cell and home numbers, email.[2]

After five days in New York, Epstein and Ghislaine flew on 11 January from Newark to Palm Beach with three others. Two days later Epstein and Ghislaine flew to Provo, in the Turks and Caicos Islands, and back to Palm Beach. The next day they were on the move again, flying to New York. Three days later, on 17 January, Epstein, Ghislaine Maxwell, Sarah Kellen, Cindy Lopez, 'Joanne', AP – possibly Prince Andrew – and '1 female' flew from Westchester, New York – it's a small airport serving private jets, due north of Manhattan – to the US Virgin Islands, and presumably by heli-copter on to Little St Jeffs. Three days later, on 20 January, Epstein, Ghislaine, Sarah, 'AP', Cindy Lopez, Kathy Alexander and Stacey Teelucksingh flew to Palm Beach. Two days later, on 22 January, Epstein, Ghislaine, Sarah, AP, Cindy Lopez and 'Joanne' (no surname) flew from Palm Beach to Westchester, New York. Three days later, on 25 January, Epstein, Ghislaine, Sean Koo, 'AP', Cindy Lopez, Alberto Pinto, Yves Pickardt, Steve Sherman and '3 females' flew from Westchester, New York, to Palm Beach. Two days later, on 27 January, Epstein, Ghislaine, Sarah Kellen, Ed Tuttle and '1 female' and '1 male' flew from Palm Beach to the US Virgin Islands. On 30 January a party, comprising Epstein, Ghislaine, Sarah Kellen, Cindy Lopez, Ed Tuttle, 'AP' and former president Bill Clinton flew from the US Virgin Islands to JFK. Clinton had left office in January 2001 but was to play a big role in Ghislaine's life for the next few years: quite how big is open to conjecture.

Ghislaine and Clinton were close. *New York* magazine, when profiling Epstein in 2002, touched on the friendship between them, reporting that she was recently seen dining with Clinton at Nello's on Madison Avenue, the same restaurant where Ghislaine was spot-ted holding hands with Prince Andrew just two years before.

David Seymour, the former deputy leader writer on the *Daily Mirror*, bumped into Ghislaine in 2004 at the London launch of Clinton's biography, *My Life*, a huge gig, two thousand guests thronging The Guildhall. The two old friends from *Mirror* days were chatting when Clinton appeared. Seymour describes Clinton as the most charismatic person he's ever been in a room with apart from Princess Diana. Clinton 'comes over to us and looks at

Ghislaine, his eyebrows going up and says, "Well, hi?" in that sort of way. "How are you?" And then Ghislaine just vanished. She turned tail and went. One knows what Clinton's reputation is. And I thought maybe they'd had some sort of a fling.'[3]

Clinton and Ghislaine 'were getting it on', write the authors of *A Convenient Death: The Mysterious Demise of Jeffrey Epstein*. They quote a source telling them: 'That's why he [Clinton] was around Epstein – to be with her.'[4] The flight logs show that in the first six months of 2002 Clinton spent time with Epstein and Ghislaine in January, February, March – not April – May and June. For example, the logs tell us that in May 2002 Clinton went on a four-day tour of Asia with Epstein, Ghislaine and some of their young women associates, visiting Japan, Hong Kong, mainland China, Singapore and Thailand. Clinton's spokesman has denied the story and Ghislaine's lawyers have previously not responded to questions about the alleged affair.

Since the death of her father, she'd learnt to fly. Back in the 1980s, she had earned the nickname 'Good Times Ghislaine' for taking her pals on terrifying helicopter rides in the 1980s. Once, she told the pilot to put her father's helicopter into a dive to 'give her friend a scare'. She was proud of her 'licences to pilot submarines, pilot helicopters, pilot ROVs and AUVs', fancy talk for mini-subs.

Transporting Epstein's guests by helicopter from the Cyril E. King airport in St Thomas to his private island, Little St Jeffs, could have been one factor driving her ambition. That way, who they might be would be Ghislaine's little secret. Her first great beau, the Turbo Count, loved to fly. As well as paying for Ghislaine's pilot's licence, Epstein bought her two helicopters, both registered to 'Air Ghislaine Inc.', and named the first after her with the tail number 'N491GM'. Court documents from 2016 show Ghislaine claimed to have earned her pilot's licence 'in 1998 or 1999',[5] but according to Federal Aviation Authority records, she was not legally allowed to pilot helicopters until 2007.[6] Flight records show she had been piloting helicopters for Epstein for years before this: very naughty.[7]

Quite the most extraordinary incident involving her skill at flying may or may not have taken place in the summer of 2002 when Colombia's narco-wars were at their height. It's the kind of story that makes you gasp. As usual in the fabled land of Maxwelliana, the source is an utter disgrace. His name is Vikram Chatwal, an American rich kid of Indian Sikh heritage, whose family are hotel money, and who was a bit-part actor, landing a role in the movie *Zoolander*. In 2013, Chatwal was arrested at Fort Lauderdale International Airport in Florida while trying to board an aircraft with cocaine, marijuana and prescription pills. In 2016, he was arrested again, this time by the New York City police for setting fire to two dogs. He had squirted an aerosol can holding flammable liquid at the dogs and ignited the jet with a lighter. One eyewitness said: 'It was like a fire-breathing dragon, shooting out flames two to three feet long. This isn't OK. You can't walk the streets setting dogs on fire.' Chatwal was booked for torturing an animal, reckless endangerment and arson and got five days' community service.[8]

Vikram the Dog Torturer was, back in the day, a friend of Ghislaine Maxwell, and in an interview with the *New York Observer* in November 2002, he discussed a party he had recently attended at Ghislaine's home in Manhattan. The guest of honour, Chatwal said, was Prince Andrew, who told a 'quite humorous' joke involving diarrhoea and his brother Prince Charles' girlfriend, Camilla Parker Bowles. One can only shudder at the thought of the punchline to that one. Then Ghislaine told a story about how she flew a Blackhawk helicopter in Colombia and fired a rocket into a supposed terrorist stronghold. 'Ghislaine is just the most rocking babe I've ever met. I said, "You have to be the coolest person alive." . . . She blew up a tank.'[9]

Even with her family history, the tale that Ghislaine Maxwell blew up a tank sounds too over-the-top to be true, but this is Maxwelliana. Researcher Bertie Harrison-Broninski got stuck in. In 2000, in one of the last acts of his presidency, Clinton approved Plan Colombia, helping President Pastrana's government fight 'narco-terrorists', FARC, a group with Marxist ideology and tons of cocaine, with $1.3 billion in aid, $400 million of which went towards thirty Sikorsky UH-60 Black Hawk helicopters, but the scheme got blocked in Congress.

In June 2002 Pastrana met Clinton, Epstein and Ghislaine in Dublin at an 'Achievement Summit'.[10] The foursome became pals. Clinton, out of office, was still lobbying Congress to lift the block on Colombia's use of the $1.6 billion aid money.

The Black Hawk Arpía III is fitted with eight machine-guns, two rocket launchers and, crucially for the dog torturer's story to work, AGM-114 Hellfire missiles. They destroy tanks. FARC did buy thousands of AK-47s from the Russian mafia in the 1980s, but there is no record of them ever buying tanks from abroad. However, FARC regularly overpowered small police units in Colombia and they were equipped with both armoured vehicles and Buffalo anti-riot vehicles: not true tanks, but that's what civilians often call them. Congress approved the freeing up of the US Colombian aid package, allowing the Black Hawks to be used against FARC, on 24 July. President Pastrana's term ended on 6 August.

In early July Ghislaine and Epstein flew from Nice, France, to Salé, Morocco, where Bill and Chelsea Clinton had been attending the royal wedding of King Mohammed VI and Princess Lalla Salma. Leaving Chelsea behind to make her own travel plans, Bill Clinton flew with Epstein and Ghislaine to the Azores, then on to New York, arriving on 13 July.

From that date to 17 August, bracketing Pastrana's final weeks in office, Ghislaine disappears from Epstein's flight logs. There's no mention of her, too, in the New York gossip magazines where her name normally pops up in write-ups of art gallery exhibitions, dinner parties and restaurant openings. Bill Clinton spent the latter half of July doing fundraisers in the States. But his first five days after arriving in New York with Epstein and Ghislaine seem blank. Ghislaine next pops up on the flight logs in Santa Fe, New Mexico, on 17 August.

So there is a time-slot, just shy of a month long, from when Ghislaine Maxwell arrives in New York on 13 July to 6 August, when President Pastrana steps down. During that time, Ghislaine steps into a void, vanishing from the New York and London gossip columns and the Lolita Express flight logs. Is it possible that Vikram the Dog Torturer got the story right that Ghislaine did indeed fly a Black Hawk in Colombia and blew up a tank? That, like her father, she too is a killer? I wrote to her PR man Brian Basham and he replied: 'I believe that G has a helicopter license but I've never heard the Blackhawk story and it's so dramatic, I guess I surely would have heard. Sounds untrue to me.'

On 21 September 2002, the flight logs tell us the Lolita Express flew from New York to the Azores; on board were Epstein; Ghislaine; Sarah Kellen; Cindy Lopez; Bill Clinton; the actor Kevin Spacey, the comedian Chris Tucker; and a host of others: Rodey Swater; Eric Nonacs, a PR and policy wonk; Gayle Smith; Andrea Mitrovich; Ron Durkle; Casey Wasserman; Doug Band, then a Clinton adviser; Laura Wasserman; Jim Kennez; Ira Magaziner; David Slang; and Chauntae Davies, acting stewardess, who had been a massage therapist from LA when she was recruited by Ghislaine.

They're on a tour of Africa to highlight the fight against AIDS, taking a spin through Ghana, Nigeria, Rwanda, Mozambique and South Africa during the five-day trip. Chauntae Davies told the *Daily Mail* that she was shocked when Clinton boarded the plane in New York, saying he was 'charming and sweet'. Clinton was photographed being given a neck massage at the stopover in the Azores by Chauntae. She explained: 'Although the image looks bizarre, President Clinton was a perfect gentleman during the trip and I saw absolutely no foul play involving him.' She explained the massage happened when they had a stopover for the jet to refuel and while they were in the terminal the ex-president complained of stiffness after falling asleep in his seat. 'Ghislaine chimed in to be funny and said that I could give him a massage. Everyone had a little chuckle but Ghislaine in her prim British accent insisted and said "I was good". The president then asked me, "Would you mind giving it a crack?"'

She did and nothing untoward happened between her and Clinton, she said.[11]

Clinton told *New York* magazine after the trip: 'Jeffrey is both a highly successful financier and a committed philanthropist . . . I especially appreciated his insights and generosity during the recent trip to Africa to work on democratization, empowering the poor, citizen service and combating H.I.V./AIDS.'[12]

Yadda yadda.

Chauntae Davies has far darker memories of Epstein and Ghislaine. She told National Public Radio in the USA in 2019 that she was twenty-one years old and studying massage in LA when she treated Ghislaine in the Four Seasons Hotel in Beverley Hills, and that led to an immediate invitation to come to Palm Beach. Ghislaine told her that Donald Trump was a neighbour, that her partner was 'a sort of . . . Ralph Lauren type . . . and did I like that type?'

Chauntae remembers thinking that the comment was strange but she didn't get its true significance until too late. Once she arrived in Epstein's home in Palm Beach, an assistant knocked on her door, saying that Jeffrey was ready for his massage. She showed Chauntae to their room, and there was a massage table already set up. Enter Jeffery Epstein: 'before I knew it – I mean, he was pretty quick into it – he flipped over onto his back and asked if I minded if he touched himself'. Chauntae had been sexually abused before and, in her words, 'been taught to just look the other way, really, and not say anything. And I gave him the OK to touch himself.'

Epstein finished, jumped off the table and got in the shower and she was dismissed.

Chauntae did not tell anybody because she felt that he was doing this behind Ghislaine's back: 'so there was another layer of deceit that I felt, like, I felt like it was my fault. And here's a woman who had shown an interest in me in a motherly sort of way, almost.'

Ghislaine paid Chauntae and put her on a commercial flight home. Over the next couple of months, Ghislaine came out to LA and booked separate appointments with Chauntae on her own: 'at that point, I really still believed that she had no clue what was happening, and I felt a certain amount of loyalty to her'.

Chauntae spent at least two years serving Epstein and liking

Ghislaine, Africa trip and all. Asked why did she keep so silent for so long, she told NPR: 'This is something I had intended to take to the grave. I was never going to come forward with this. I really wasn't. I kept it a secret because I was just so ashamed.'[13]

Another reason she didn't articulate, perhaps, might have been that she knew she was poor and they were rich, and when the poor take on the rich it never turns out well. After Epstein, Ghislaine and Clinton had done Africa, they dropped in on London. Clinton, with Spacey in tow, went on to visit the Labour Party Conference in Blackpool where he was the guest of honour. Peckish after a long day, Clinton and Spacey went out to eat at McDonald's, Clinton ordering a steak burger with large fries and coke, Spacey plumping for a burger, while the pair shared Chicken McNuggets.[14] That made front-page news. What they had got up to in London didn't hit the papers for all but two decades.

They had invaded the throne room in Buckingham Palace. It is a holy of holies for the British monarchy. Someone snapped a photo and it appeared on the front page of the *Daily Telegraph* in 2020, and it's an extraordinary image. In place of the Duke of Edinburgh there is Kevin Spacey and sitting on the throne of the Queen of England is Ghislaine Maxwell. The paper explained that Prince Andrew had arranged the tour of the Palace for Bill Clinton and his guest, Spacey, while Ghislaine came along as a friend of the duke. 'They were larking about on the thrones, doing regal waves,' said the source.[15]

This is *Game of Thrones* for real. Ghislaine's ambition and arrogance led her to play at being the Queen of England. Perhaps, in doing that, nemesis lies. Bill Clinton's first appearance on the Lolita Express in late January 2002 signalled the zenith of Ghislaine's social success. It also heralds her Icarus moment, too. From the Africa trip onwards, who exactly Epstein is and where did he get his money from is a proper subject of public interest. And that, down the track, will come to haunt them all. Clinton is shamed, Spacey disgraced, Prince Andrew a pariah, Epstein dead and Ghislaine's future more bleak than the saying of it.

chapter eight

The Fresh Child Factory

Michelle Licata was sixteen years old and had just got rid of her braces. White, poor, troubled, flat-chested, sexually inexperienced, Michelle lived on the wrong side of the tracks in West Palm Beach. Some idea of the geography is useful here. Palm Beach proper is an island that faces east, looking out to the ocean. In 2004 it is home to Donald Trump's Mar-a-Lago estate and Jeffrey Epstein's house on El Brillo Way. The island is where the billionaires live. West Palm Beach is on the mainland; the further from the ocean you go, the poorer it gets. Pretty soon you're driving past trailer parks. You can drive from American dream to junk reality in twenty minutes. That's where Michelle came from. She wasn't connected. Nor did she write for *The Spectator*.

These days she lives in Tennessee with a small boy who is, as all small boys are, a bit of a handful. Being poor and on her own, she couldn't talk to me via Zoom until her boy had gone to bed. That meant I got up at five o'clock in the morning, London time, to record the interview for the podcast, Hunting Ghislaine. I was half-dead with lack of sleep until she got going. This conversation with Michelle remains one of the most haunting, one of the most tragic, interviews I have done, and I have been a reporter for a long time.

Michelle's mind went back to that day in November 2004: 'We drove over the bridge. I saw the beautiful fountain that was like made out of horses.' The fountain sits at the entrance of Palm Beach, signalling 'Here be rich people.' Michelle was with a girl-friend who was roughly the same age, who had floated the idea of giving this old guy a massage. Michelle didn't understand that her friend was being paid and paid well for pimping her out. Nor did she realise that this was going to be a sex massage. She was then, she now knows, hopelessly naive about the world.

'We pulled into his driveway and I was kind of like, you know, like, where are we? And she' – her schoolfriend – 'said "Oh, well, you know, this is where we have to go." There were two ladies that had walked in after us and one had a clipboard. They were laughing, smiling. They looked so pretty.'

The woman with the clipboard, Michelle discovered years later, was Sarah Kellen. They climbed a winding staircase, past photographs of naked girls. At the top of the stairwell was a big bed, a bath and a massage table. The light was dim, the temperature very cold:[1]

> She was telling me 'Jeffrey is going to be coming in. He's going to be making some phone calls. All you need to do is to massage him and do what he asks.' She walked out of the room. He walked in, he introduced himself and he asked me what my name was. And then he told me he was going to be on the phone making some business phone calls. And that's what he did.

Epstein played the busy man. He had a timer with him and set it to forty-five minutes; from then on, Michelle recalled, 'there's that ticking that you can hear in your mind. And so most it's almost like you're just sitting there waiting and listening to the clock just tick away.'

Epstein was wearing just a towel covering up his bottom half. Once he got off the phone, she became a little bit more concerned because she still didn't know who he was or what the lady that walked her up there had meant. Michelle had been kept deliberately in the dark. She didn't know her friend was going to leave her to be on her own. She didn't know she was going to be the only person there: 'There were a lot of factors just to be blindsided with, only to be led into the lion's den.'

Epstein got off the phone, told Michelle to get undressed to her underwear and then he started talking to her about her sex life. At the time, Michelle had only had sex with two people. With them, embarrassed about how she looked, how flat-chested she was, she had kept her shirt on. 'There's this older man that is telling me to take off my clothes and looking at me up and down like lip-licking his lips pretty much. So he grabbed me, touched me, did some things to my body and he told me to touch all over him. Told me to pinch his nipples. He was masturbating himself while he was doing things to me and telling me how beautiful I was.'

Michelle says that, to this day, she doesn't know how to take a compliment: 'Like when people tell me those things, I get flash-backs. I just see myself as pretty much like a man's play toy because that's all that I was ever told I would ever be worth.'[2]

The ticking stopped, the unknown man had a shower and Michelle was dismissed.

Some months passed, then came the men in black. Michelle told me: 'At first I didn't know what they were talking about. There were just two men in black suits. And my brother answered the door and he asked me, "Why are the men in black here to talk to you?"'

Michelle had no idea. They were police officers and came up with a name. 'And I was like, "Jeffrey Epstein? I don't know who that is." I thought that a kid had died in school and they were asking me questions about it. As soon as they said the words "Palm Beach", it all started rushing back to me.'

Michelle was scared. She had forgotten that the beautiful ladies had written down her name. The police officers said that since she was under the age of eighteen, they had to have parent's consent to talk to her. So she had to tell her mother and Michelle asked her not to tell anyone else in the family. She was unhappy that the police officer asking the questions was male and worried sick: 'I was like, "Oh, my God, I did something wrong. I'm going to be going to jail. I'm in trouble."'

Michelle Licata had fallen into Ghislaine's spider's web without even knowing Jeffrey Epstein's name, still less hers.

Spencer Kuvin is a lawyer in West Palm Beach. The first Epstein case he handled was in 2006 when a fourteen-year-old girl came with her parents into his office. They told him a story about a young girl coming and recruiting her to go over to a large mansion on Palm Beach Island where she would be giving an older man a massage and get $200. The man was without clothes during the massage: 'He had pleasured himself during the massage while reaching out and trying to touch this young girl whom he had asked to get undressed. She was essentially locked in a massage room with him and scared out of her wits.'

The Palm Beach Police Department investigation began in March 2005 after a fourteen-year-old had got into a fight at school. When a teacher investigated, she found more than $300 in the girl's purse. The girl cried as she told detectives that she had got the money after she had gone to Epstein's mansion to give him a massage. He had ordered her to take off her clothes; she said she stripped to her underwear and massaged him as he masturbated and used a vibrator on her. The cops traced the student who had recruited the first girl, who told them that Epstein paid her to pimp for girls, telling her 'the younger the better'.

Detective Joe Recarey of the Palm Beach Police Department recorded the testimony of some of Epstein's many victims. The stories are bleakly similar.

> He asked me to take off my skirt.

> And then he asked me to take off my shirt.

> He masturbated, he ejaculated.

> I thought I was going to die.

> And then when he started pleasing himself he got up and he went over to a draw and he pulled out this vibrator thing and then he pulled down my panties and he started, it was just like this stick with a knob thing on it.

He didn't stick it inside me or anything, but he, you know, put it on me. And that was it and a couple of minutes later it was over and he left and I put my clothes on and I went downstairs.

Cuz when I heard it was just a massage, I was like, you know, I'm like, are you sure there's nothing else? She's like, 'Yes, I'm sure.' I'm like, 'Is there anything weird about this guy that I need to know?' She's like 'no'. And ever since, like I felt she lied to me and betrayed me. You know, even though you know, being stupid, I had just met this girl.[3]

When I discussed this testimony with my producer Ruth Barnes for the Hunting Ghislaine podcast, she said: 'That's just so hard to listen to. They just sound so young.' I replied: 'I hated doing the research for this. I physically didn't like listening to this stuff because you've got to wade through it and it's dark.'

To protect Michelle Licata, the cops called her 'Jane Doe'. Julie K. Brown in her brilliant investigative series for the *Miami Herald* noted: 'There would be many Jane Does to follow: Jane Doe No. 3, Jane Doe No. 4, Jane Does 5, 6, 7, 8 – and as the years went by – Jane Does 102 and 103.'[4]

As the Palm Beach Police Department came across case after case of under-age girls being sexually abused by Epstein, word came back to them that private investigators were being hired to intimidate the witnesses. That could only mean one thing, that someone or some people on their team or in Florida state prosecutor's office was betraying their investigation to Epstein's people. Joe Recarey realised he was being followed. He told Julie K. Brown of the *Miami Herald*: 'At some point it became like a cat-and-mouse game. I would stop at a red light and go. I knew they were there, and they knew I knew they were there. I was concerned about my kids because I didn't know if it was someone that they hired just out of prison that would hurt me or my family.'[5]

When Palm Beach Police Department raided Epstein's place on 20 October 2005, they found the digital birds had flown: Epstein's computer hard drives, surveillance cameras and videos had gone, leaving loose, dangling wires. There is a possibility that some of this missing evidence may have ended up in Russia.

John Mark Dougan was a cop working for the Palm Beach Police Department when the raid took place. He wasn't on the case and fell out with his bosses, leaving the force in 2009. In his muddily written and self-published book, *Bad Volf* (sic), he claims that the force was corrupt and badly led. Although he claims he tried to blow the whistle, he was frustrated and fled to Russia in 2016 with the FBI chasing him. But long before that he claims that Joe Recarey, the head of the Epstein investigation, had given him a cache of files for safe-keeping, which he took with him to his new home. The *Daily Mail* got in touch with him to check out what information he had.

> I was acting as Joe Recarey's computer 'safety deposit box'. It also means that the FBI has the same exact data that I possess and are in a position to know everyone who is implicated in the videos, recordings, and documents . . . Do I have dirt on Prince Andrew? I have lots of things. But I'm not a Kremlin agent and I did not share any materials with the Russian Government. I don't intend to blackmail anyone with my information. It's against my principles.[6]

The idea that anyone who cannot return to the West for fear of being locked up, and who is therefore stuck in Russia for good, is 'not a Kremlin agent' is nonsense. The Russian secret state has no interest in Dougan's principles. That leads one ex-MI6 officer I know to conclude that the Russians will have seen everything Dougan has got. But what this is, exactly, remains as muddy as Dougan's prose. Reportedly, he posted what he claimed was one of Epstein's blackmail tapes but online sleuths discovered that it was from a porn site generated long after the 2005 raid on El Brillo Way. In 2022 he popped up in Russian-occupied Ukraine, spurting conspiracy theories about Ukrainian bio-labs. Dougan is employed in some fashion by the Kremlin lie factory and his story of securing a cache of Epstein's tapes is yet another of his dark fantasies.

The iron law of forensic investigation remains true: contact leaves trace. Epstein's people had hoovered up most of the digital evidence. But they missed the old tech stuff including hundreds of messages scribbled on a pad, some from Donald Trump and magician David Copperfield, some from phone numbers that matched the under-age girl victims Recarey had already interviewed. They read: 'Courtney called, she can come at 4', or 'Tanya can't come at 7 p.m. tomorrow because she has soccer practice'.[7] Other messages were directly damning, one reading: 'She is wondering if 2.30 ok cuz she needs to stay in school.' That had been left in February 2005. Another note shows that 'Colleen' phoned to tell the Epstein child abuse factory: 'Going into class – will be out in 45 min.'[8]

None of these messages arranging massages for Epstein mention Ghislaine. But other, ordinary business messages were left for Ghislaine, suggesting she was in the El Brillo house at the same time as the under-age girls were coming and going. Lawyer Brad Edwards writes in his book, *Relentless Pursuit*, 'From the messages that had been confiscated in the infamous trash pulls, we learned that callers were leaving messages for Maxwell as if she lived in the house during a time when high-school girls were regularly being shuttled there.'[9]

Recarey told Julie K. Brown that they also found naked photographs of under-age girls amid Epstein's possessions. Recarey, a good cop, flipped two of Epstein's butlers, who testified on the trafficking of under-age girls, finding sex toys when cleaning up after Epstein's sex sessions and paying off the victims. Rodriguez told Recarey that he was 'a human ATM machine' because he was ordered by Epstein to keep $2,000 on him at all times.[10]

Down the track it gets nasty for many of Epstein's victims. Private investigators go through their lives, turn up at their homes, sit outside in dark cars, waiting, waiting. I have been spied on by the Church of Scientology's private eyes and it's horrible. Epstein's lawyers go for the victims, making them out to be untrustworthy trash. Michelle Licata told Julie K. Brown that Epstein's lawyers tried to turn her life inside out, asking if she had had a baby, an abortion, had she slept with thirty different guys?[11]

Michelle Licata never heard mention of Ghislaine Maxwell when she was sexually abused by Epstein. That is common: the vast majority of Epstein's Palm Beach victims never meet Ghislaine, never hear that name. But from at least 1992 to March 2005 when the Palm Beach Police Department investigation gets going, Ghislaine controls Epstein's schedule. Throughout those thirteen years she's organising his diary and that is super complicated because he's got all these fancy people, like former president Bill Clinton, Donald Trump and Prince Andrew, Duke of York, captains of finance and the Nobel-winning scientists coming and going. Epstein and Ghislaine are moving between four points of the compass, his mansion in Manhattan, his ranch in New Mexico, the place in Palm Beach, the island in the US Virgin Islands. And for much of that time he's having three massages from under-age girls a day.

The last known photograph of Ghislaine and Epstein together is taken on 15 March 2005, in New York, at a Rod Stewart gig at Cipriani Wall Street.[12] Epstein grabs her in arm-lock, signalling 'she's mine' to the photographer. Ghislaine is smiling but, as the saying goes, the smile does not reach her eyes. That's the month that Detective Recarey gets going. So that's also the month when Epstein is in trouble. But don't forget the power of his money to buy fancy lawyers, his connections to important people, some of whom – who knows – he could even have a hold over.

March 2005 is, it just so happens, when Epstein does something entirely out of character. He gives an on-the-record interview to the *Chicago Tribune* citing just how extraordinarily generous he can be. Epstein told the paper that he paid the three women who worked for him $200,000 a year, an extraordinary sum if all that was expected of them was secretarial work. The *Tribune* reported on how very well-paid Epstein's assistants were: 'Citing scientific studies, he calls them a "social prosthesis", whereby their intuitive knowledge of his needs and their 24-hour presence make them virtually indispensable to his success. "They are an extension of my brain," said Epstein, who rarely talks publicly.' This smacks of his weirdo belief in transhumanism, whose adepts think they are on the path to a higher form of being. The paper continued that Epstein 'does not stint in compensating them. In addition to the rich payday, he also ladles on the perks' – a charge account at Frederic Fekkai, the society hair dresser, all food eaten during his lengthy business hours, trips on his Boeing 727, etc., etc.[13]

Epstein loved to lurk in the shadows. It strikes me that by brazenly telling a paper that he pays his staff top dollar, that he could have been signalling to his victims, keep mum, play along with me and you, too, will see some of my money.

One of those assistants on $200,000 a year was Sarah Kellen, the pretty woman with the clipboard Michelle Licata met before Epstein abused her, the former Jehovah's Witness, the same Sarah Kellen who had flown multiple times on the Lolita Express, very often with Ghislaine, sometimes, too, with Prince Andrew and Bill Clinton. *Mail Online* tracked down Sarah's parents, still Jehovah's Witnesses, in North Carolina. Sarah's mum got a few emails hinting at unease at her new way of life. She emailed her mother in June 2000. 'I just feel so confused. It's hard to express what I feel because half the time I'm not even sure.' Sarah's mother, Mary, now in her seventies, told the *Mail*: 'I think it shows that she was very vulnerable, she sounded desperate, confused, not knowing what to do. What happened to all those girls is horrendous but I do feel that Sarah was also a victim. I'm not a psychologist or a psychiatrist but I can see that she was manoeuvred or brainwashed.'[14]

Brainwashed. Log that word.

chapter nine

Blackmail

In April 2005, a man called Jean-Luc left a telephone message for Jeffrey Epstein at his Palm Beach house about a Russian teacher. The message written down on the pad and later read by Palm Beach Police Department went as follows: 'He has a teacher for you to teach you how to speak Russian. She is 2×8 years old, not blonde. Lessons are free and you can have your 1st today if you call.' Do the sums: 2 times 8 equals 16, which is two years below the legal age of consent in Florida. A second message from the same Jean-Luc reads: 'He just did a good one – 18 years – she spoke to me and said "I love Jeffrey."'

Even by the standards of the major characters in this book, Jean-Luc Brunel is a truly disgusting human being, someone who has been accused of the sexual abuse of young women, especially aspiring models, for three decades; who currently faces charges of the rape of minors in France; who was bankrolled by Jeffrey Epstein. A French model scout who found Sharon Stone, Christy Turlington and Milla Jovovich, Brunel is or was also a close friend of Ghislaine Maxwell. There is a photograph of the two of them, 2003, in Little St Jeffs, she giggling helplessly while he holds her in a head-lock, grinning wolfishly at the camera.

The flight logs nail the friendship, telling us that Brunel took twenty-plus flights on Epstein's private jet over the space of four years, travelling to the Bahamas, the US Virgin Islands and elsewhere.

Researcher Jaysim Hanspal went through Brunel's appearances in the logs and the French newspapers for this book with the finest of tooth-combs. Early on in the logs, Brunel's full name was entered in the manifest alongside the initials of regulars such as 'GM' for Ghislaine. But soon he was familiar enough to the pilots to go by 'JLB'. The earliest flight was in 2000, when Jean-Luc flew on the Lolita Express between the US Virgin Islands and New Jersey. In June 2002 'JLB' is recorded on flight #1570 between Palm Beach Florida and the Bahamas, with Virginia Roberts, Epstein, Sarah Kellen, Cindy Lopez and Ghislaine Maxwell. The last flight for the trio is on 24 August 2005: Epstein, Ghislaine and Brunel flew to Ecuador to attend the Models New Generation contest. One can only imagine what these three people got up to at a beauty pageant in one of South America's poorest countries.

Brunel was first exposed as a sexual abuser of multiple young women back in 1988 when *CBS 60 Minutes* reporter Diane Sawyer investigated 'American Models in Paris'. Several American models who worked with Brunel explained how they had been routinely drugged and sexually abused. In his book, *Model: The Ugly Business of Beautiful Women*, published in 1995, Michael Gross discusses accusations against Brunel, most notably by Jérôme Bonnouvrier, who used to own a rival model agency. He said, 'Jean-Luc is considered a danger. He likes drugs and silent rape. It excites him.' Gross went on to accuse Brunel of being a cocaine addict. Brunel's response was that he did not have a drug problem since he refrained from using cocaine during the day.[1]

Doesn't everyone?

Brunel survived the CBS investigation and went on to create Karin Models of America in 1995. In 1999 he was turned over in a BBC *MacIntyre Undercover* film and banned from his own modelling agency in Europe. In the early 2000s, Brunel moved to the United States. Ghislaine, according to Bradley J. Edwards, a lawyer for some of the victims, had first met Brunel in the 1980s and it was she who introduced Brunel to Epstein. In 2004 Epstein gave the Frenchman $1 million in seed capital to set up a modelling agency, written MC2 but pronounced MC Squared. It's a joke based on Einstein's famous equation, E=MC2, the missing E standing not for energy but Epstein. Virginia Roberts Giuffre alleged in a 2015 affidavit that Epstein boasted to her that he had 'slept with over 1,000 of Brunel's girls'. Virginia also accused Ghislaine and Epstein of pimping her out to Brunel, along with Prince Andrew. Brunel responded by denying involvement in any illegal activities with Epstein, saying: 'I strongly deny having committed any illicit act or any wrongdoing in the course of my work as a scouter or model agencies manager.'

The third man Virginia Roberts Giuffre claims that she was required to have sex with by Epstein and Ghislaine is Alan Dershowitz, one of the most famous lawyers in the United States. Virginia first made the claim in a 2015 affidavit and then repeated it in the 2020 Netflix documentary, *Filthy Secrets*. Virginia had sex with Dershowitz, she said, 'at least six times, in Epstein's various residences, on his island, in a car, and on his plane'.

Dershowitz denies Virginia's allegations against him vehemently. The lawyer has called Virginia a 'serial liar', a 'prostitute', and a 'bad mother', and has written a book setting out his evidence, *Guilt By Accusation: The Challenge of Proving Innocence in the Age of #MeToo*. A former Harvard law professor, Dershowitz had spent some of his life championing ignoble causes. One such was defending Claus von Bulow, a Danish-German socialite who was accused of the attempted murder of his wife in 1982 by injecting her with insulin, leaving her in a coma. Tried and convicted, he was freed on appeal and at a second trial he was found not guilty. There were serious flaws in the prosecution's evidence but widespread suspicion remains that Dershowitz's brilliant legal mind helped free a guilty man. Von Bulow died in 2019, partially mourned.

Dershowitz's great claim to fame is being one part of the legal 'dream team' who helped OJ Simpson walk free from court after being tried for the murder of his wife, Nicole Brown Smith, in 1995. The essence of the defence case was that OJ didn't kill his wife because the cop who arrested him was a racist who used the 'N' word, denied it and was proven to be a liar because he had said the word on tape.

In his book, Dershowitz tries to discredit Virginia. He claims that on 7 April 2011, Virginia told a lawyer that she was born on

9 August 1983, and that she first met Epstein 'around June of 1998', which have put her age at fourteen years, ten months. Dershowitz writes: 'That was a lie. She didn't meet him until – at the earliest – mid-summer 2000, when she turned 17 . . . Her own employment records conclusively proved she was 17 when she first met Epstein.'

Virginia later claimed she made an honest mistake rather than told a lie. Dershowitz wasn't buying that: 'Nevertheless, the media continues to refer to her as under age and to anyone who she claims had sex with her as a paedophile.' The age of sexual consent varies from country to country and in the USA from state to state. In Britain it is sixteen, in New York state seventeen, in Florida eighteen. Virginia, then seventeen and living in Florida, describes having sex with Epstein from very early on. Virginia had sex with Epstein when she was under age: fact.

Dershowitz continues that Virginia's own statements show that she was close to nineteen when she claimed Epstein started to ask her to 'entertain' his friends. He argues: 'The combined evidence of my innocence and her history of lying about her accusations and her age totally discredited her accusation against me.'[2]

Virginia accepts that she got some of the details wrong: 'When you are abused, you know your abuser. I might not have my dates right, I might not have my times right . . . but I know their faces and I know what they've done to me.'[3]

Dershowitz denied ever meeting Virginia on BBC *Newsnight* in 2019: 'Let me be very clear. I never met Virginia Roberts. I never heard of her. And she never met me or heard of me . . . She told the FBI that she did not have sex with me, she told her best friend she did not have sex with me, she told her boyfriend she did not have sex with me.'[4]

There is no corroborating evidence that Virginia ever met Dershowitz, no photograph – unlike Prince Andrew – no flight logs pinning him and her on the same plane ride, no witnesses coming forward.

The FBI did interview Virginia in 2011. The *New Yorker* got hold of a copy of the FBI agents' report; much of it is blacked out, including the men Virginia identified. So one cannot make a firm judgement on what Virginia told the FBI. The magazine also set out the long friendship between the two men, dating from 1996; how Epstein's philanthropy benefited Dershowitz's university, Harvard, and how Epstein stepped in when Dershowitz lost several hundred thousand dollars in an investment that tanked. Dershowitz had sunk his money into a fund run by Orin Kramer, the founder of the hedge fund Boston Provident. When the fund sustained enormous losses, Epstein contacted Kramer and said, 'One of us is going to make Alan whole — and if I have to do it, that is an outcome you will regret.' Kramer made Alan, as it were, whole. Epstein's action is not something you do for a casual acquaintance. Dershowitz said that he never heard that Epstein had made this call and that he understood Kramer had restored his money because he felt a 'moral obligation'.[5]

Dershowitz has been called upon in his professional life, too, to discredit young women making allegations of abuse against his clients. One victim, known to the police as 'A.H.', was a key witness against Epstein. A.H. told Palm Beach cop Recarey that she had started going to Epstein's house in 2003 when she was sixteen, and she had become his 'favourite'. He sent roses when she starred in her high-school play. Epstein photographed her naked. She had set a rule with Epstein that they wouldn't have intercourse, but one day he pushed her down and forcibly penetrated her. She kept on coming to see him because he had told her he would pay for her to go to NYU: 'Cause my dream was like right in front of me, you know?'

Dershowitz told the *Mail on Sunday* that Epstein had passed a lie-detector test showing he was innocent of all allegations. The financier had paid for massages, but had not engaged in sex or erotic massages with any minors, the lawyer insisted. Dershowitz said that the girl who accused Epstein of forcible sex 'had a long record of lying, theft and blaming others for her crimes'.[6]

She told the Palm Beach detective Joe Recarey that she had sex massages with Epstein multiple times:

Victim: 'Towards the end I just got naked.'
Police: 'Would he perform oral?'
Victim: 'Sometimes.'
Police: 'Oral sex on you?'
Victim: 'Sometimes.'

The *New Yorker* reported that Dershowitz sent Recarey a letter about A.H. pointing to evidence suggesting 'troublesome and telling illustration of her character'. Dershowitz said he sent two private investigators to see her 'because we feared that she, an accomplished drama student, might try to mislead them as successfully as she had misled others'. The PIs were, Dershowitz said, 'quite shocked at the overwhelming, non-stop barrage of profanity ... from what initially appeared only to be a young woman of slight build and soft demeanour'. He also enclosed snippets from A.H.'s presence on social media, detailing her 'apparent fascination with marijuana'.

The *New Yorker* put all this to Dershowitz, who replied, denying gathering information from social media. He said that the letter was composed by someone else in his office, although, the *New Yorker* pointed out, it bears his signature and is written in the first person. The magazine headlined its piece on Dershowitz 'The Devil's Advocate'.[7]

The year 2005 had been difficult for Epstein, what with the Palm Beach Police Department raid on his house on El Brillo Way and their seizure of what evidence was left, the phone-call log, pointing to a string of schoolgirls arranging massages with his team. The good news was that for at least some part of the Christmas break one of Ghislaine's best friends, Peter, Lord Mandelson, was on hand in the Caribbean to cheer him up. Mandelson was captured trying on a white belt in an upmarket boutique on the island of St Barts, roughly 140 miles due east from Little St Jeffs, with Epstein looking on. The photograph was discovered by the *Daily Mail* who reported that the hitherto unknown shopping trip by Epstein and Mandelson took place on 27 December 2005.[8] I contacted Lord Mandelson's office for a reaction to this story but received no reply.

By the back end of 2005 going into 2006, the Palm Beach cops thought they had the goods on Epstein. They had interviewed numerous under-age victims, they had the messages, they had witness statements from Epstein's staff. Police chief Michael Reiter said in a deposition that when he discussed the investigation with Florida state attorney, Barry Krischer, 'he said, "Let's go for it, this is an adult male in his fifties who's had sexual contact with children."' Once Dershowitz started acting for Epstein, Reiter said, 'the tone and tenor of the discussions of this case with Mr Krischer changed completely'.

In June 2006, a grand jury charged Epstein with one count of soliciting prostitution. There was no mention of under-age girls; no requirement that he register as a sex offender; no mandatory jail time. Reiter, a tough cookie infuriated by the soft soap treatment for a serial paedophile, called in the Feds. The FBI cast their net wider, interviewed almost forty girls, some as young as fourteen, who said Epstein had sexually abused them.

In the meantime, there was yet another royal bash to go to. In July 2006 – that is one month after he had been charged with a sex crime – Jeffrey Epstein was invited to a masked ball at Windsor Castle to celebrate the eighteenth birthday of Princess Beatrice, Prince Andrew's elder daughter. Guests donned period costumes, marking the theme 1888. The duke later explained Epstein had been invited via Ghislaine and that he wasn't aware at the time the invitation was sent out 'what was going on in the United States'. He said Epstein never mentioned that he was under investigation.[9]

From the Palm Beach Police Department raid in 2005, the story changes, a little. Evidence of abuse of under-age girls in Palm Beach dries up. But stories of abuse, more often of vulnerable women of age, continue. The locations are Little St Jeffs and New York; Palm Beach had become too hot for the child sex factory.

Sarah Ransome was in 2006 a young woman in her very early twenties, exquisitely beautiful, and unlike most of the victims of Epstein and Ghislaine in being originally upper class, her mother's father being Lord James Gordon Macpherson, 2nd

Baron of Drumochter. But, like all the other principal victims, Sarah was from a broken home, her mother an alcoholic, her father absent in South Africa. In one word, she was vulnerable: you get the pattern. At twenty-two, she had dropped out of Edinburgh University and had resorted to being a prostitute to get by. She left Britain for New York in September 2006 and fell into the world of Ghislaine and Epstein. In her book, *Silenced No More: Surviving My Journey to Hell and Back*, she paints an entirely convincing picture of Little St Jeffs as a rotten paradise. She writes that Epstein took sadistic pleasure in his sexual abuse: 'With one hand he began masturbating . . . with his other hand, he pressed the massager onto my clitoris as I half-sobbed, half-screamed, "Stop . . . please stop!" . . . "Just breathe," he leaned towards me and whispered, as if my nurturer, not torturer.'[10]

Sarah Ransome writes that she was repeatedly raped on Little St Jeffs, but as she was about to leave, Epstein offered her a beautiful flat in New York City and, far more precious, an offer to pay her way through the Fashion Institute of Technology, FIT, which was Sarah's impossible dream come true. She took the carrot, knowing it to be poisoned. She became a sex slave for the money but perhaps more crucially for the fantasy of the alternative life she so wanted for herself. What is so saddening is that she now understands the depth of the dark tricks played against her and the other beautiful and vulnerable women entombed in Epstein's amber. She was put up in an apartment building in New York and began to suspect that other young and beautiful women were there on Epstein's dime, too. As ever with personality cults, isolation was the key to the operation. She saw many pretty young women walk in and out of building, 'tall, pimple-sized breasts, emaciated, white' – Epstein's type. But they all remained locked in their own private worlds, scared to challenge Epstein and Ghislaine even in their absence.[11]

Sarah Ransome's chapter 'Ghislaine's Inferno' is a hideously fascinating read. She writes that she can see how Ian Maxwell and others – Donald Trump, Bill Clinton, Prince Andrew, Boris Johnson; I'm plucking four names at random – were confused about who Ghislaine really is. Blowing hot and cold, switching between madam boss lady and nurturing mother figure, Ghislaine was, for Sarah Ransome, a chameleon: 'Which face she displayed depended on who was in the room or on the phone – the human rubbish she regarded me as, or the high-society guests she and Jeffrey hosted. The posh people got the "Gracious Ghislaine". We got the conniving tyrant.'[12]

Like the Farmer sisters, Maria and Annie, Sarah Ransome identifies a critical factor: that Epstein and Ghislaine's own personal cruelties reinforced each other. Like Lord and Lady Macbeth, their joint darkness was all the more powerful because it was entwined. He was the sexual sadist; she was artful at psychological torture. There is also a sense that Ghislaine smelt Sarah Ransome's old money, that she understood Sarah's fall from grace, and that meant she was subjected to a heightened degree of cruelty, to underscore the reality that they were masters and she was a minion. Ghislaine and Epstein deemed Sarah obese. She wasn't, of course, but the fun in being at the top of a kind of cult is in unhinging reality and then making the lesser beings genuflect to the lie. Ghislaine told her that she if gave up eating for a month, she'd still be 'over-weight and disgusting'. When Ghislaine looked at her, she would go 'Oink! Oink!' She would call her a piglet and a heifer. For her first two trips to Little St Jeffs, Sarah enjoyed the same food as everyone else, omelettes, breakfast burritos, fresh fish, chicken, salads. Then she was put on a starvation diet of cucumbers, tomatoes and a sliver of beef so small it was something you would feed a child. Sarah weighed 146 pounds; Ghislaine demanded that she should cut down to 114 pounds, or else the flat and her chance at studying at fashion college would disappear. Sarah did not know that Ghislaine has first been diagnosed anorexic at the age of three.

Sarah spent New Year of 2006 going into 2007 on Little St Jeffs. Sarah slipped off to South Africa for a couple of months and then returned to New York to be greeted by Ghislaine: 'Look who's back . . . the fat cunt.'[13] There's her father's daughter, right there.

Sarah Ransome didn't last much longer. She was too much of her own person and she came to realise that, for Jeffrey, she was too old. She exited Maxwelliana in May 2007, more broken than before.

Around this time a photograph pops up of Epstein celebrating his birthday in Paris by blowing out the candles on the cake along with his chum, Peter Mandelson, or, at least, that is what the *Sun* claims. The date is not stated in the article but the context suggests it is either January 2007 or January 2008.[14] I contacted Peter Mandelson's office about this photograph and did not receive a reply.

Meanwhile, the FBI had taken over the investigation into Epstein started by the Palm Beach Police Department. The agents unearthed yet more victims. But despite the mass of evidence that Epstein was being serviced by a fresh child factory, in 2008 Epstein's lawyers, including Dershowitz, secured a sweetheart deal. Epstein coughed to two counts, one of soliciting a prostitute, one of procuring an under-age girl for prostitution in Florida. He served thirteen months but benefited from a clause so that he could leave the jail during the day to go to his office, six days a week for up to sixteen hours a day.

Epstein, for the rest of his life, never accepted that he had done anything bad, later telling the *New York Post*: 'I'm not a sexual predator, I'm an "offender". It's the difference between a murderer and a person who steals a bagel.'[15]

Spencer Kuvin, a lawyer for several of the victims, told me: 'It was unbelievable that the US attorney's office would enter into such a deal. We know that Mr Epstein got a deal that no other person I have ever seen in twenty-six years of practise get. The FBI had interviewed over forty victims, forty young girls, and he gets a deal; it's a get-out-of-jail-free card.'[16]

But that was not the only thing that stuck in Spencer Kuvin's craw: 'The deal gave full immunity to Jeffrey Epstein for crimes in the past with respect to the victims. And it gave immunity to, at least by name, those he considered his co-conspirators. But it also mentions "and any other co-conspirators that may have been involved" in a general phrase.'

The alleged co-conspirators were Epstein's executive assistants Adriana Ross, Lesley Groff, Nadia Marcinkova and Sarah Kellen, the former Jehovah's Witness. She invoked the Fifth Amendment when questioned by investigators. Nadia Marcinkova was allegedly brought from the former Yugoslavia to live with Epstein. Marcinkova 'encouraged and engaged in acts' with victims while Epstein played voyeur, according to written testimony by several alleged victims. Adriana Ross, also known as Adriana Mucinska, originally from Poland, was a model who also helped organise Epstein's massage sessions. She moved to Florida in 2002 and often popped up on the Lolita Express flight logs. When questioned by police, Adriana exercised her right to remain silent. Lesley Groff was claimed to have coordinated the travel plans of his victims and scheduled massages. When Groff announced she was pregnant and tried to leave in 2004, Epstein bought her a Mercedes to make her commute less taxing.[17] It's worth noting that while Ross and Marcinkova have stayed silent, Groff has since denied having anything to do with any of Epstein's sexual misconduct, but Sarah Kellen is 'aware of the pain and damage Epstein caused and deeply regrets that she had any part in it'.[18] If, as that suggests, the Feds have succeeded in flipping Sarah Kellen, then Ghislaine's old fellow traveller on the Lolita Express could cause trouble, not just for her but for others in Epstein's circle too.

The sweetheart deal also granted immunity to any 'known or unknown co-conspirators', and that catch-all would have embraced Ghislaine Maxwell. Epstein got a soft sentence, Ghislaine got immunity. Nice work Professor Dershowitz, some might say.

So why did the then US Federal Attorney for Florida, Alex Acosta, who went on to become President Trump's Transport Secretary, okay the sweetheart deal? One of the prosecutors wrote that it was better to secure a conviction than aim high and lose and that some victims were so scared of Epstein they hired lawyers to avoid appearing before a grand jury. That raises the possibility that Epstein used his vast wall of money to pay off some of the victims, to buy their silence. Spencer Kuvin, a lawyer for some of the victims, told me: 'We know that Epstein was paying a number of young girls to keep quiet . . .' There's always a but: 'But a few came forward and the ones that came forward told a story of vide-otapes and cameras that were hidden within both the Palm Beach mansion as well as the New York mansion.'[19]

The Epstein blackmail tapes, if they exist, have never surfaced, never popped up in the mass of evidence thrown up in a slew of court cases against Epstein, Ghislaine and, after his death, his estate. However, there are some tantalising pieces of evidence suggesting that Epstein was indeed a blackmailer – and he did so with the sanction of the deep state. Vicky Ward wrote a story for the *Daily Beast* in 2019 that set out why America's spyocrats, led by the CIA, might have reason to protect Epstein. Vicky wrote that when she was interviewing an unnamed but senior figure in the White House, the name Jeffrey Epstein came up. Her source told her that Epstein was: 'A charming guy. Useful, too. He knew a lot of rich Arabs, including the crown prince of Saudi Arabia.'

That is Crown Prince Mohammed bin Salman, also known after the slaughter of dissident Jamal Khashoggi in the Saudi consulate in Istanbul in 2018 as Mr Bone Saw. The crown prince denies any wrongdoing. Vicky's source continued to reflect on Epstein: 'OK, so he has a girl problem,' but this wasn't, in her source's judgement, that big a problem. Vicky went to report that Team Trump, before moving into the White House, prepped Acosta for his nomination hearings and worried about his role in the sweetheart deal back in 2008. 'Is the Epstein case going to cause a problem?' Acosta later explained he'd cut the non-prosecution deal with one of Epstein's attorneys because he had 'been told' to back off, that Epstein was above his pay grade. 'I was told Epstein "belonged to intelligence" and to leave it alone.'[20]

Epstein had a Slovakian bodyguard called Igor who told lawyer for the victims, Bradley J. Edwards, to back off more than once. When Epstein was convicted in 2008, Igor spread the word that he was sent on a course run by the CIA in Washington where he was given secret communications to pass on to Epstein. Edwards did not know whether to believe Igor or not.[21] This hint that Epstein was working for intelligence is an echo of the *Mail on Sunday* piece from 1992, which first outed the love affair between Ghislaine and Epstein. It is hard to tell but it smells like a con to me.

But there are credible witnesses who can corroborate that Epstein had powerful friends that the CIA would most definitely be interested in. In 2013 Epstein got back in touch with the reporter Edward Jay (EJ) Epstein because, decades before, EJ had worked with Vladimir Nabokov, the author of *Lolita*, a novel about an older man molesting his twelve-year-old step-daughter. EJ was wary but intrigued. The huckster, who in the 1980s used to hand out fake first-class upgrade tickets, had made it big time: a mansion that filled a whole block in Manhattan, the homes in Palm Beach, New Mexico, Little St Jeffs. When EJ asked Jeffrey about his business, he replied: 'I manage money for a few select clients.' On the walls were photos of Epstein with Saudi Crown Prince Mohammed Bin Salman, MBS, and Emirate Prince Mohammed Bin Zayed, MBZ. In the Arab world, there is no better alphabet spaghetti to bag.

'Are these clients?' asked JE. Some were, said Jeffrey, cryptically.

'What about Russia? Any clients there?' He shrugged, telling JE that he often flew to Moscow to see Vladimir Putin. JE reflected on this in his piece on Jeffrey Epstein for the *Mail*: 'I found this hard to swallow.'[22] In the absence of any other supporting evidence, so do I.

Remember that fake Austrian passport the Feds found in Epstein's safe in 2019? Remember the address in that passport inside Saudi Arabia. Remember his connections with Adnan Khashoggi, the Saudi arms dealer uncle of Jamal Khashoggi? The picture here is murky – but could Epstein have done such a big favour for the CIA in the past that the agency helped secure the sweetheart deal?

James B. Stewart of the *New York Times* reported that he'd picked up a story that Epstein was advising Elon Musk, the billionaire behind Tesla, and wanted to check it out. Both Epstein and Elon Musk denied it. There is a photograph from 2014 from an Oscar party ball with Elon Musk grinning at the camera and Ghislaine Maxwell immediately behind him. Elon Musk's PR says that

Ghislaine photo-bombed the billionaire: nothing to see here folks. Epstein showed Stewart, the *New York Times* reporter, around his Manhattan mansion, pointing to a full-length shot of a man in traditional Arab dress. 'That's MBS,' said Epstein. So was Epstein and also Ghislaine protected because he was spying for the CIA?

The song 'Stool Pigeon' by Kit Creole and the Coconuts sums up this hypothesis: 'if you wanna squeal . . . we can make a deal'.

Really clever bad people hook the authorities, turning the power of the state's agencies created to protect the common interest into a private insurance policy. They turn stool pigeon. For example, fraudster Allen Stanford became an informer for the US Drugs Enforcement Agency, throwing them sprats, while he himself was a whale, hiding a $7 billion Ponzi scheme in plain sight. The gangster 'Whitey' Bulger based in Boston had nineteen people murdered while informing for the FBI, a massive con against law enforcement brought to celluloid by Martin Scorsese with Jack Nicolson playing Bulger in the 2006 film, *The Departed*.

The best book about blackmail ever written is Raymond Chandler's *The Big Sleep*. In it, the blackmailer Arthur Geiger sends the gambling debts to General Sternwood run up by his wild daughter, Carmen, acknowledging their 'legal uncollectibility'. Smart blackmailers don't show their hand. They wear a mask when they threaten shame on you. Consider, once again, the fact that to date not a single tape, audio or visual, of Epstein's sex factory – both child and adult – at work has emerged into the public domain. It's possible that the tapes exist but have been hidden by the embarrassed authorities. A second possibility is that Epstein deleted everything. There is a third option, one that I favour, that Epstein never once pressed the record button but that his targets, rich and powerful men having sex with young and possibly under-age women, did not know that. Epstein would still have a hold over them, but, because he never pressed record, he himself had not committed a criminal offence. As I have said before, this is a dark fairy story.

chapter ten

Submerging

The last photograph of Ghislaine Maxwell with Jeffrey Epstein that we know about was taken in March 2005. The last time they were seen together in posh society was, as far as we can tell, in July 2006 at Windsor Castle for Princess Beatrice's '1888' party. The last time the flight logs suggest that they flew together was on 2 November 2006 from Massachusetts to New Jersey.

It's hard to know exactly when, but from late 2006 or early 2007 Ghislaine cuts Epstein out of her life and quietly submerges, slipping away from the public eye. She resurfaces from time to time, with different rich or powerful men on her arm, at a charity event here, at a book launch in 2013 in New York for Geordie Greig's *Breakfast with Lucian* with friend Piers Morgan captured in an excruciatingly cheesy photo. Morgan tweeted on New Year's Eve, 2021: 'I met Ghislaine Maxwell . . . We spoke for 5 minutes about her father Bob who once owned the *Daily Mirror*. She seemed nice. Obviously, she's a monster. Sadly, I'm not a psychic.'

True, but you don't have to be psychic to note the following: that Ghislaine's love affair with Epstein over several years, first published in the *Mail on Sunday* in 1992, was widely known to many in the media, especially in the circle where Morgan struts his stuff; that Epstein's paedophile conviction in 2008 was widely reported; that the *Mail on Sunday* photograph of Prince Andrew with his arm around Virginia Roberts Giuffre's waist with Ghislaine standing next to them was published in 2011; that Ghislaine's threat to sue the *Mail on Sunday* came to naught; that Piers Morgan writes columns for the *Mail on Sunday*. So, by 2013, people without powers of premonition knew that Ghislaine Maxwell had been close to a convicted paedophile.

Greig's profile of the artist paints Freud as 'selfish, secretive and sexually sadistic', according to the *Financial Times*, so Ghislaine may have found some food for thought there.

Post-Epstein, Ghislaine is out of the limelight and no one ever accuses her of taking part or orchestrating sexual abuse after 2006. But for more than a decade, from 2006 onwards, Ghislaine carried out a discreet but determined campaign to deny her part in Jeffrey Epstein's fresh child factory, to deny its existence and to call out anyone who insisted that she had questions to answer. The key person she effectively assisted in her denial was, of course, Jeffrey Epstein. And, in return, he paid some of her mounting legal bills.

Throughout these years from 2006 onwards, sightings of Ghislaine are rare. Tim Willis, a writer for *Tatler*, met Ghislaine in 2009 in New York when he and a friend went round to her 'enormous brownstone on the Upper East Side' for tea. 'We were shown to the first-floor drawing-room by an inscrutable maid, who told us that "madam" would be with us shortly. The decoration was kind of brash: a big cream carpet, a colour-scheme of royal blue, red and black, ornamental china everywhere and a couple of samurai armour-suits on the wall.' This sounds a bit like the décor in Headington Hill Hall.

Tim and his friend waited in the oppressive silence: 'If there wasn't a clock ticking too loudly, there should have been. The minutes passed, my friend grew increasingly cheesed off ("So rude!") . . .' When Ghislaine appeared – polo neck, dangly earrings, trousers – she explained that she'd been writing an important email in her study upstairs.

Shades of her father.

Ghislaine, Tim Willis continues, 'sat down in her high-backed armchair and she was imperious, a little bit like Gladstone addressing Queen Victoria as though she were at a public meeting. You certainly wouldn't call her engaging.'

Ghislaine banged on about the parlous state of the oceans, told her guests how she'd been on several expeditions to discover the extent of their degradation and, with a laugh, told us that she now had a pilot's licence for deep ocean submersibles. Tim met her again at Christmas 2013, at a party in Hampstead, handing out cards for the foundation she'd started that year, the TerraMar Project, which aimed to gain legal protection for the open high seas unclaimed by nation states. One wag looked at the card and said something like, 'You Maxwells seem to love it underwater', and, Tim recalls, 'she guffawed like the rest of us'.

Tim seized the moment and asked if she'd write a free article about TerraMar for a website he was editing, and she said, 'Sure, mail me in the New Year.' He did, and she delivered a well-composed piece, leavened with a few personal revelations. As a child, she'd been a Donny Osmond fan until she switched her affections to Jacques Cousteau. She began diving aged nine when she would collect shells and 'discover imaginary islands'.

Tim liked the draft piece but thought it would be improved by the 'underwater Maxwells' joke. 'So,' Willis writes, 'I asked if she'd pop it into the text. Big mistake. She swiftly sent a stiff missive to the effect that I could forget the whole thing if there was any reference to her father.'[1]

Jeffrey Epstein enjoyed, by all accounts, an easy time for his thirteen months in prison, from halfway through 2008 onwards, commuting to his office where his activities, whatever they were, were unchecked by the prison guards whom he was paying by prior agreement with the authorities to stand outside his office complex.

Convicted paedophile though Epstein was, he was still open for business with money and power. In January 2009 while still serving his sentence, Epstein was in his office when an associate was present. The associate claims: 'While I was there, he [Epstein] received a call and said, "Hello, Petie". And Petie wanted to meet Jamie Dimon of J. P. Morgan. He [Epstein] said: "yes, I'll sort it out".'

'Petie' was, allegedly, the then British Secretary of the Board of Trade, Peter Mandelson and a key adviser to then prime minister, Gordon Brown.

The story appeared in a Channel Four *Dispatches* investigation and was written up in the *Sun*. The paper carried a statement from Mandelson's lawyers: 'Our client has no recollection of a telephone conversation with Mr Epstein in January 2009. He talked to bank CEOs on a regular basis, including Mr Dimon. These contacts were arranged through his office.'

Banker Jes Staley, then with J.P. Morgan, popped by his prison-cell-cum-office to pay his respects. Staley, who ran a private bank inside J. P. Morgan, got to know Epstein in 2000 and stayed loyal. Investigators found that between 2008 and 2012 the banker and the paedophile exchanged 1,200 emails. One referred mysteriously to 'Snow White'. In late 2021 Staley stepped down as head of Barclays Bank because of the British bank regulator's concerns about his relationship with Epstein. The *Daily Mail* quoted his lawyer, saying that their client had no involvement in any of the alleged crimes committed by Epstein and codewords were never used by Staley in any communications with Epstein. Staley, it was reported, was going to contest the regulator in proceedings.[2]

Another long-time loyalist was billionaire hedge funder Leon Black, who first made Epstein a trustee of his charity doo-dah back in 1997. Black, one of the founders of Apollo Global Management, which controls some $455 billion in funds, is seriously rich, worth several billion dollars in his own right, and he's a mover and shaker in the art world. In 2012 he bought one of four versions of Edvard Munch's *The Scream* for $120 million. When news broke of the relationship between him and the paedophile, Apollo called in a law firm to investigate. It found that from 2012 to 2017, Black had paid Epstein some $158 million in fees for advice on tax matters and philanthropy, potentially saving him $1.3 billion in taxes. Black has never been accused of any wrongdoing related to his association with Epstein. He stepped down as CEO of Apollo in 2021, saying that he 'deeply regrets' his relationship with Epstein.[3]

By December 2010 Epstein is out of jail, free, back in New York, albeit as a registered sex offender with one count of paedophilia. But he's got a visitor, Prince Andrew, the Duke of York.

And Ghislaine? She has disappeared from public view but there are a few traces of evidence – an unredacted email here, a chance admission of a meeting there – that suggest, although behind the scenes, she is still intimately involved in denying the existence of the fresh child factory.

By 2009 both Prince Andrew and Ghislaine Maxwell could not affect ignorance of Jeffrey Epstein's paedophilia. He had been convicted the year before, served time in prison, and in September 2009 fell into a very public elephant trap set for him by Spencer Kuvin, the lawyer from West Palm Beach representing three under-age girls sexually abused by the multi-millionaire.

> **Deposition clerk:** 'Do you solemnly swear the testi-
> mony you are about to give will be the truth the
> whole truth and nothing but the truth so help you
> God?'
> **Jeffrey Epstein:** 'Yes I do.'
> **Spencer Kuvin:** 'Could you please give us your name?'
> **Epstein:** 'Jeffrey Epstein.'
> **Kuvin:** 'Is it true, sir, that you have what's been
> described as an egg-shaped penis?'

There is a clunking sound as Epstein takes off his mike.

> **Kuvin:** 'Sir, according to the police department's prob-
> able cause affidavit, one witness described your
> penis as oval-shaped and claimed when erect it was
> thick towards the bottom but was thin and small
> towards the head portion and called it egg-shaped.
> Those are not my words, I apologize.'
> **Judge:** 'This court is now adjourned.'

The deposition was part of a civil case brought by the under-age victims against Epstein and not disclosable to the public. However, once Epstein had walked out, Kuvin was legally entitled to file an appeal and part of his evidence to the court that Epstein should answer the deposition was the video – and that appeal evidence was publicly disclosable. Someone phoned a local paper, and the video of Epstein walking out of a depo having been asked if he had an egg-shaped penis was up on YouTube. It still is.[4]

One year later, in December 2010, Prince Andrew flies to New York and stays at Epstein's mansion for four days and is photographed walking in Central Park with the convicted paedophile. It's cold and the sequence of photos show the two men talking with sombre faces. Looking at the photos with my podcast producer Ruth Barnes, I said: 'It looks like a setup, like a bad movie, where you've told two not very good extras to go for a walk in the park and look as though they're discussing something serious. It looks staged as hell to me.'[5] For the Hunting Ghislaine podcast I got in touch with the photographer who took the photos through his website, but he did not get back to me.

Emily Maitlis of BBC *Newsnight* challenged Prince Andrew on why he stayed at Epstein's New York mansion. He replied that he had wanted to break off his friendship with Epstein and that it was best to do that in person: 'I thought that doing it over the telephone was the chicken's way of doing it . . . it was definitely the wrong thing to do but at the time I felt it was the honourable and right thing to do . . . I admit fully that my judgement was probably coloured by my tendency to be too honourable, but that's just the way it is.'[6]

A surfeit of honour is one explanation for the duke to stay at Epstein's. Prince Andrew could have paid for a hotel in New York as ordinary folk do. Or, perhaps, he could have stayed at the British Consul-General's home in Manhattan, which is funded by the British taxpayer for the exact purpose of putting up visiting government ministers and members of the royal family when they pass through New York. But the central issue is why – if Epstein was a casual acquaintance of the duke's, originally a plus-one for Ghislaine – was it necessary to end the friendship in person? If you want to break off a friendship with somebody, you can split with them by phone or email. You don't go for a walk in the park with them. Prince Andrew and Epstein were not lovers.

Royal biographer Andrew Morton told me: 'Like all the royals, if Prince Andrew falls out with somebody, he just doesn't get in touch with them. As simple as that. You're out.'

Prince Andrew is, then, either a fool or a knave. If the latter, he had good reason to do what he did, though he might not wish to share it with the rest of us. The idea that Prince Andrew is a fool is extremely tempting. There is an abundance of evidence that his sense of entitlement blinds him to what ordinary people feel and think, that he has no empathy and no common sense. This view was put in coruscating prose by Vassi Chamberlain, the woman who knew Ghislaine in London back in the day and had come across the duke on a number of occasions. She wrote: 'Andrew's lifelong incarceration within the rigidly observed confines of the royal family, coupled with a lack of self-awareness, a constant entourage of fawning yes-men, not to mention a reduced position as second son, meant he was disadvantaged from the start. He is a man without a point, and I suspect no one feels that quite as keenly as he does.'[7]

The second explanation for the walk in the park is that he is a knave, worried about money or rather the lack of it. Prince Andrew is very close to his ex-wife, Sarah Ferguson. They divorced in 1996 but from 2008 onwards have been living together in the same house, the Royal Lodge in Windsor, and they work in tandem to support their two daughters. Andrew Morton commented on how the Yorks handle cash: badly. 'She in particular, she's a fool with money. I've got a cartoon that's in my office which shows Fergie looking at a £5 note and she's saying to herself, "I'm sure I came out with £50,000 this morning." Fergie is a shocker when it comes to money. She's notorious. And that, quite frankly, has been her downfall.'[8]

And, perhaps, the duke's downfall too. In May 2010, the so-called 'Fake Sheikh', the crooked *News of the World* reporter Mazher Mahmood, secretly filmed Sarah Ferguson offering access to Prince Andrew for half a million quid. She was filmed taking a briefcase containing $40,000 in cash in part pre-payment. That August the *Sunday Telegraph* reported Sarah Ferguson had debts of £5 million and that Prince Andrew was masterminding a 'rescue plan' to avoid the embarrassment of her filing for bankruptcy.[9] The next day the *Guardian* reported Fergie's debts had been exaggerated. They were only £2 million.[10]

Four years later in 2014 the Yorks buy a skiing chalet in Verbier in Switzerland for £18 million, £4 million to follow and £14 million on a mortgage. I asked Iain Campbell, who is both an accountant and an investigative journalist, to look into the Yorks' books: 'Officially, he receives a £20,000 pension from the Royal Navy and £250,000 as a grant for the maintenance of his personal office from the Queen. So if he is on £270,000 a year, they ought to be able to borrow five times that, but that only adds up to £1.3 million.' So how come they can afford a mortgage of £14 million? Campbell replied: 'Well, it's confusing and certainly outside of the normal parameters of bank lending. It's a head scratcher.'[11]

The sequence of events is important here. In February 2011 the *Mail on Sunday* broke the story alleging Prince Andrew had sex with Virginia Roberts Giuffre, complete with a photo of his arm around seventeen-year-old Virginia. There's a hue and cry against the prince and people start to call for him to resign as Britain's trade envoy. A few days later Sarah Ferguson gave an exclusive interview to Geordie Greig, then editor at the *Evening Standard*, and an old friend of Ghislaine Maxwell. Sarah Ferguson said: 'I abhor paedophilia and any sexual abuse of children and know that this was a gigantic error of judgment on my behalf. I am just so contrite I cannot say. Whenever I can I will repay the money and will have nothing ever to do with Jeffrey Epstein ever again.'[12]

What money? Sarah Ferguson admitted accepting £15,000 from Epstein to help her pay down the debt. One of the people Sarah Ferguson felt badly about was her former personal assistant, Johnny O'Sullivan, owed £78,000 in unpaid wages and other bills. Epstein helped out with £15,000 in January 2011, a few weeks after he and Prince Andrew went for their walk in the park. That payment helped enable a restructuring of Sarah Ferguson's debts, the whole process overseen by the Duke of York. Andrew Morton told me: 'When Fergie said, yes, she owed Epstein some money, that's when the penny dropped. I think that Andrew was going along to help out his ex-wife and to help her to renegotiate this debt. So they were obviously at that time hard up. And Epstein, inveigled his way into many people's lives. He had the money in order to support them or to at least give them an advance.'[13]

This then is the other possible explanation for the walk in the park: that Epstein's money helped sort out the Yorks. We don't know whether it was just £15,000. Or a bigger sum. Within four years they can afford to buy a chalet in one of the most expensive ski resorts in the world. And the theory goes that, in return for that earlier favour, Prince Andrew takes a walk with a paedophile in the park. So, running with this theory, could this have been reputation-laundering? That Epstein is a social pariah and he's paying Prince Andrew indirectly by reducing Sarah Ferguson's indebtedness. And in return the prince whitens Epstein's dirty image. We'll never know for sure.

Emily Maitlis's interview with Prince Andrew for BBC *Newsnight* was extraordinarily good. But one question was missing: Prince Andrew, were you paid for the walk in the park? What's the going rate for a duke? Sorry, I'm being vulgar. I put a series of questions to the duke, one of which asked him to put all moneys flowing between Epstein, Sarah Ferguson and himself into the public domain. That didn't happen. But a public relations firm working for Prince Andrew's lawyers did issue this statement: 'It would be entirely wrong to characterise the duke and duchess as having shared financial responsibilities following their divorce in 1996. They share a household at Royal Lodge which they have done in order to co-parent the princesses during their childhood and into young adulthood.'

Boiled down, the statement says that Prince Andrew and Sarah Ferguson weren't a financial unit after they got divorced. But the fact they have lived together since 2008 seems to suggest to me that they had interests in common when Epstein paid down £15,000 of Sarah Ferguson's debts in 2011, had so when they jointly bought a £18 million ski chalet in 2014, and do so now at the time of writing in 2022. So the charge against Prince Andrew – that he effectively benefited from Epstein's money after the walk in the park – stands. While Prince Andrew has never commented

on many of these specific allegations, he has always strongly
denied any impropriety.

The evidence that Prince Andrew met Epstein after his conviction for being a paedophile is strong. New York literary agent
John Brockman sent an email to a friend about the last time he
visited Epstein's house where he met a British guy getting foot
massages from two young well-dressed Russian women, one of
whom was called Irina. The Brit was named Andy. After a time,
the penny with his mum's head on it dropped. The recipient of
Irina's foot massage was His Royal Highness, Prince Andrew, the
Duke of York.

'Lucy', the duke's former girlfriend, told Vassi Chamberlain:
'[Andrew] said he was particularly fond of four-handed [massages],
where two women work on you at the same time. When mention
of a foot massage came up . . . I immediately thought, "Yes, that's
him." '14

One week later, the *New York Post* ran a front-page photo of
Jeffrey Epstein and the Duke of York walking in Central Park
under the headline: 'The Prince and the Perv'.15

None of this could have happened without Ghislaine originally
playing go-between for the prince and the paedophile. The Duke
of York invited Ghislaine and Epstein to Balmoral, Buckingham
Palace, Sandringham and Windsor thanks to her. The tricky thing
with favours between friends is that they are often subtle and
under the radar. So hats off to the brilliant researchers at *Panorama*
who dug through a bundle of thousands of pages of legal documents and found gold. It's an email from 2015 from Prince Andrew
to Ghislaine: 'Let me know when we can talk. Got some specific
questions to ask you about Virginia Roberts.' Ghislaine replies:
'Have some info – call me when you have a moment.'16

The prince and the socialite appear to be trading favours at the
expense of Virginia, someone who says that she was a sex slave for
Epstein and the Duke of York at the age of seventeen.

Ghislaine also stays mum about what she knew about Epstein.
He is paying her legal fees all the way up to 2017, but there are no
walks in the park. Prince Andrew is seen with Epstein in 2010. But

not Ghislaine. Lawyer Brad Edwards was working on behalf of some of the victims suing Epstein for damages, and he was on Ghislaine's case from 2009. He heard gossip that Ghislaine was thick with the Clintons. So that year he sent along some private eyes to the Clinton Global Initiative annual meeting in the New York Sheraton. They publicly served Ghislaine with orders to turn up for the deposition: 'To say she was upset about being publicly served at this function is an understatement,' Edwards wrote.[17] Come July 2010, Ghislaine skipped out of planned deposition hearing, explaining that she had got to go home because her mother, Betty, was ill. That wasn't the whole truth. A couple of days later, she was seen at Chelsea Clinton's wedding in the United States. Eventually, in 2016, Ghislaine has to turn up in a legal hearing in the civil case; in American legal jargon, she was deposed. Throughout, she flatly denies knowledge of Epstein the predator, protested her innocence repeatedly and at one point she banged her fists on the table. The deposition happened behind closed doors, but in 2020 a 400-page transcript was released. However, some passages and the names of several well-connected men whom Virginia Roberts Giuffre said were involved in Epstein's activities were blacked out because of privacy issues. What remains is both grimly fascinating and just plain grim.

> **Lawyer:** 'Have you ever said to anybody that you recruit girls to take the pressure off you, so you won't have to have sex with Jeffrey; have you said that?'
>
> **Ghislaine Maxwell:** 'You don't ask me questions like that. First of all, you are trying to trap me, I will not be trapped. You are asking me if I recruit, I told you no . . .'
>
> **Lawyer:** 'Do you recall ever giving [redacted] a gift of a puppet that was in the same – that looked like him?'

This seems to be a reference to the *Spitting Image* puppet of Prince Andrew. NPR noted Ghislaine was initially reluctant to identify the object as a puppet, preferring to call it a 'caricature'. She was then asked if the puppet was used in a game where the man – unidentified in the transcript but elsewhere identified by Virginia as Prince Andrew – mimicked the puppet's groping of a woman.

> **Ghislaine:** 'I never gave him a gift of a puppet . . . I recollect the puppet but I don't recollect anything around the puppet . . . I characterize it as, I don't know, as a characterization of [redacted].'
> **Lawyer:** 'Do you recollect asking Virginia Roberts to sit on [redacted] lap with the caricature of [redacted]?'
> **Ghislaine:** 'I do not recollect that.'[18]

Virginia wrote in the manuscript of her unpublished memoir that she and another young woman had been told to sit on the duke's knees, along with the puppet. 'Ghislaine wanted to take a picture of the bizarre scene and even got Johanna, another one of Jeffrey's so-called personal assistants, to come sit on his other knee for the snapshot, giving the impression girls couldn't stay away from Randy Andy.' The deposition continued:

> **Lawyer:** 'Did Jeffrey Epstein have a scheme to recruit underage girls for sexual massages?'
> **Ghislaine:** 'I don't know what you're talking about.'
> **Lawyer:** 'Were you aware of the presence of sex toys or devices used in sexual activities in Mr Epstein's Palm Beach House?'
> **Ghislaine:** 'No, not that I recall. I was not aware of anybody that I interacted with, other than obviously the plaintiff who was 17 at this point.'[19]

Anna Pasternak, Ghislaine's old acquaintance from Oxford, was struck by her aggression under deposition. Anna told me: 'Given her sort of haughty arrogance in the deposition, it didn't seem to me that this is a woman who is absolutely full of remorse and self-loathing and shame and who feels that she's been brought to her knees by her own corruption. You don't get that sense at all. I'm sure she still is fighting on. But underneath it all, she feels that she's a victim, too.'[20]

The deposition also threw some light on when Ghislaine stopped working for Epstein. Lawyer Brad Edwards had placed Ghislaine's submerging act with the Palm Beach Police inquiry, which started in March 2005: 'As soon as the criminal investigation began, however, she became a ghost. She completely distanced herself from Epstein. This looked like someone with a guilty conscience.'[21] In the 2016 deposition she said her work for Epstein lessened considerably after 2002–03. When questioned about the last date she worked for him, she replied that she continued to work for Epstein in a 'very nominal way, maybe an hour or two a year, at sometime during 2008 or 2009' – by which latter date he had been convicted and was serving time in prison.[22] The significance of Ghislaine's admission has been drowned by noise. She continued to work, and therefore, one assumes, being paid, by Epstein after he was a convicted paedophile. That, it strikes me, makes her stance of ignorance of the fresh child factory all the more improbable. Rather, it suggests that for a very long time she just didn't get it. Perhaps she still doesn't.

That said, the evidence suggests that Ghislaine is not a whole person but fragmented and conflicted. So there is denial, anger – banging her fists against the table in the deposition – contempt, but also, perhaps, some sense of shame. And fear that a reckoning might one day happen. There were some clues to that in a series of emails going between her and Epstein that were released in a slew of court cases against Epstein. In January 2015 Epstein forwarded to Ghislaine a draft statement for her denying everything: 'I have been the target of outright lies, innuendo, slander, defamation and salacious gossip and harassment.'

Three days later, Ghislaine emailed Epstein, trying to distance herself from a sense of a long-lasting romance. She wrote: 'I would appreciate it if Shelley would come out and say she was your girl-friend – I think she was from the end of '99 to 2002.'

Epstein writes back a day later that this is 'OK, with me'.

The Shelley may be Shelley Lewis, the British daughter of a pawnbroker turned billionaire, Brian Lewis. A Shelley Lewis flew on the Lolita Express forty-one times. She hasn't responded to calls from reporters. Back to the email to and fro. Epstein then urged Ghislaine to cheer up: 'You have done nothing wrong and i woudl (sic) urge you to start acting like it. go outside, head high, not as an esacping (sic) convict. go to parties. deal with it.'[23]

Let's take that 'deal with it' email from Epstein. It suggests that Ghislaine is having a hard time doing exactly that, that she's hiding from the world, shunning society and she can't hold her head high. Around this time she did a talk for her TerraMar project, her green initiative to save the oceans and the fishes. Researcher Emily O'Sullivan for this book took a deep dive into TerraMar and came away thinking Ghislaine's knowledge of the big deep started and ending with her time spent on the kind of superyacht her father fell off. Ghislaine told her audience in 2014: 'Now, I know I speak with a funny accent, so yes, I did say country, not company [silence]. So, with that ... Why is the ocean so important to us, outside of the fact that under there lie millions of dollars – or billions of dollars – of assets, and the fish?'

It made Emily laugh as Ghislaine started going on about the 'assets' there were to be had and added 'and the fish' as a footnote. The audience applause for Ghislaine was sparse, her jokes fell flat, her delivery was faltering, almost pitiful.[24] TerraMar was a confidence trick, poorly done, aimed more at 'reputation management' than saving the fishes in the view of Euan Rellie, a British investment banker who had known Ghislaine for decades, according to the *New York Times*.[25] Ghislaine 'was not dealing with it' as Epstein had advised her. One reason might be that she knows what happened when she worked with Epstein was bad and she can't escape its shadow.

Sometime after slipping away from Epstein's tractor beam Ghislaine had found new love in the shape of American billionaire Ted Waitt. Ian Maxwell approved of his sister's new catch: 'I was entirely satisfied that the man who she then went on to spend time with really provided her with love and affection she needed after Epstein,' he told Rosie Kinchen of *The Sunday Times*. Rosie wrote that Ian was 'referring to the seven-year relationship she went on to have with Ted Waitt, an American billionaire and philanthropist'.[26] Waitt is by all accounts a decent man and so rich that he bought a superyacht for Ghislaine to mess about in, called *Plan B*. But that relationship hit the rocks and the word on the ocean wave is that the reason for the split was Waitt's unhappiness as the horror stories about Epstein and her started to seep out.

Ghislaine found a fresh new man, not as rich as Waitt, but one who was willing to marry her – albeit in secret so that no one in the world knew about it. His name is Scott Borgerson, forty-three, and they got hitched in 2016. Rosie Kinchen asked Ian Maxwell when the family first found out about Scott. 'At the same time you did, when it was in the papers,' he said, meaning in 2020 when it came out in a bail application. Ghislaine cut her family out of her wedding. If you think the Maxwells are a happy family, think again.

Throughout this saga, Ghislaine has never said a bad word about Epstein. That is also true of what she has said about Prince Andrew, the Duke of York: nothing bad about him, period. Nicola Glucksmann, the psychotherapist who ducked out of Ghislaine's sex game at Headington Hill Hall three months before Robert Maxwell fell off his yacht, feels that the British ruling class take their *omerta* seriously: 'The real aristocracy were as appalled by Diana's BBC interview as they were by Meghan's Oprah exposé. It's simply not done to talk. Ever.'

In holding her tongue about what she might know about Prince Andrew, Ghislaine, in Nicola's view, is obeying that law of upper-class *omerta*. Despite the massive pressure on her, she is being extraordinarily discreet: 'Ghislaine's refusal to talk, thus far, is really interesting. It might be borne of fear but it could also be the one reason why she might conceivably escape being a social pariah. But if, going to trial, she still protects those who've distanced themselves, they may feel both grateful and guilty about their own disloyalty. Her silence would, for the first time, show real class.'[27]

Or a kind of sickness.

chapter eleven

The Lady Vanishes

Every now and then a good reporter gets a break. In 2018 Julie K. Brown of the *Miami Herald* gets her hands on story gold, a police report, more than a hundred pages long, citing over a hundred Jane Does abused by Jeffrey Epstein. Much of it is blacked out. She combs through the document for numbers, bits of information, pieces that will help her complete the jigsaw. Julie tracks down more than eighty women who say that when they were very young, they were sexually assaulted by Jeffrey Epstein, and that with the 2008 plea bargain the authorities gave Epstein 'the deal of a lifetime'. The worst thing for Julie, she says of the victims, is 'They blame themselves. That was actually the hardest thing for me to deal with.'[1]

Goaded by Julie's heroic journalism, the authorities start to wake up to what they have done. More, lawyers for the victims get a court ruling overthrowing the sweetheart deal because the victims of the crime were not told of the deal in advance. In July 2019 Jeffrey Epstein's private jet returns from France, landing at the private airport in New Jersey he uses, where he's busted by the FBI. They lock him up and raid his mansion in Manhattan, seize hundreds of items of evidence, photos of naked girls, and there are reports of tapes labelled 'Young X and Mr X'. So far, these reported tapes have not shown up.

One month later Epstein is found dead in prison. Suicide, say the authorities. But very quickly a meme builds on social media: 'Jeffrey Epstein did not kill himself'. The theory goes like this. One, Epstein was a suicide risk but the prison guards didn't check up on him as they should have done. Two, CCTV cameras weren't working. Three, he should have been sharing with a cell-mate but he wasn't. Four, the hyoid bone – it sits roughly behind the Adam's apple – was broken and that's suspicious, some say, very.

Forensic pathologist Dr Michael Baden was hired by Mark Epstein, Jeffrey Epstein's brother, to attend the post mortem. Dr Baden popped up on Fox News, saying: 'I think that the evidence points towards homicide rather than suicide . . . because there are multiple, three, fractures in the hyoid bone, the thyroid cartilage. That is very unusual for suicide and more indicative of strangulation, homicidal strangulation.'[2]

President Donald Trump fuelled doubts in an interview with Jonathan Swan of Axios in the summer of 2020. Challenged by Swan for wishing Ghislaine well, Trump retorted:

'Well, her friend or boyfriend Epstein was either killed or committed suicide in jail . . . She's now in jail. Yeah, I wish her well . . . People are still trying to figure out how did it happen? Was it suicide? Was he killed?'[3]

Donald Trump was happy to echo the conspiracy theory that Epstein did not kill himself. He hasn't served time inside prison. At least, not yet. But someone who has is Chris Atkins, a former freelance BBC *Panorama* producer who got done for tax fraud. His book, *A Bit of a Stretch*, is a very funny diary of his grim time in Wandsworth nick in south London. I asked Atkins how surprising it was that Epstein's cell was not checked every thirty minutes, that he should not have been in a cell in his own, that the CCTV was not working. He replied: 'No, I find that wholly believable. It doesn't surprise me the safeguards that were there designed to prevent suicide failed.'

The physical context was set out in the *New York Times*. The wing where Epstein was held was infested with cockroaches. There were pools of stagnant water, piss and shit. One lawyer said mice would often eat his clients' paperwork.[4] And the human factor?

Chris Atkins explained the reality of prison culture on both sides of the Atlantic: 'He was a convicted paedophile. So he's not going to have a high level of sympathy. So you can see a situation where the officers don't give a shit, they're thinking to themselves, why should I stop a paedophile killing themselves? I'm going to go on my lunch break. So for that reason, I don't suspect that there was foul play. In a sense, he was allowed to kill himself.'

What about the failure of the CCTV cameras? Isn't that suspicious? I asked Atkins.

'Nothing works in prison. That's why I'm very much a believer in cock-up, rather than conspiracy. Having said that, I certainly saw situations in a British prison where the officers wouldn't do their suicide checks on certain prisoners, because of what that prisoner had done.'[5]

What about the pathology? Dr Baden said on Fox News that when the hyoid bone is broken, that points to murder, not suicide. One study of 175 cases of suicidal hangings found hyoid bones were broken in 68 per cent of cases and the chances of it happening grew the older the deceased.[6] The theory that someone murdered Jeffery Epstein is – and now I'm going to use a complicated medico-legal term – conspiracy bollocks. Sorry, that was plain English.

What about Epstein's former lover, Ghislaine? When Epstein is arrested in July 2019, she vanishes. Hunting Ghislaine is not going to be easy. She's got three passports – British, French and American – a fortune of roughly $20 million, a kaleidoscope of bank accounts, and she has pilot's licences for helicopters and submersibles. But the FBI are on the case. Their *modus operandi* is pretty simple. They go back to a missing person's last known contacts, their family and friends, and spy on their emails, phone calls, messages and meetings in the flesh. Oooh, that's awkward.

> **Emily Maitlis:** 'When was your last contact with her?'
> **Prince Andrew:** 'It was earlier this year funnily
> enough in the summer, in the spring, summer.'

Prince Andrew, the Duke of York, explained his last catch-up with Ghislaine to Emily Maitlis of BBC *Newsnight*.

Emily Maitlis: 'About what?'
Prince Andrew: 'She was here doing some rally.'

Emily Maitlis pushed Prince Andrew on the wisdom of meeting the close friend of Jeffrey Epstein.

> **EM:** 'So even though he had by then been arrested and was facing charges of sex trafficking?'
> **Prince Andrew:** 'No, no, no, no, no, no, no, this was . . . this was early spring I think, it was long . . . because . . . When was he arrested?'
> **EM:** 'July.'
> **Prince Andrew:** 'No, it was before July.'
> **EM:** 'And that was the last time?'
> **Prince Andrew:** 'Yeah, yeah.'
> **EM:** 'Did you discuss Epstein at all?'
> **Prince Andrew:** 'No, actually funnily enough no not at all, there wasn't anything to discuss about him because he wasn't in the news, you know, it was just . . . we had moved on.'[7]

Or had we? The FBI certainly hadn't.

The rally Prince Andrew referred to was the Cash & Rocket rally from London to Monaco. Ghislaine was in car number 28 with Nettie Mason, the wife of the Pink Floyd drummer, Nick Mason. And after the rally is over, Ghislaine disappears off the face of the earth. The papers have a field day, speculating she was in South America, Russia, France or Israel. My guess was that she would have ended up in a posh bit of Tel Aviv – Israel has no extradition treaty with the United States – and I was, like virtually everybody else, dead wrong.

The papers tracked down where she had been living for the past few years: Manchester-by-the-Sea in Massachusetts. It's posh, swanky and the neighbours say that she was hanging around with a guy called Scott Borgerson, who was the bloke she met while she was running her TerraMar project and had secretly married. The neighbours remember she had a vizsla, a Hungarian hunting dog, and didn't call herself Ghislaine Maxwell but Jennifer Elmax or simply 'G'. She was often seen running on the beach. Immediately, the best reporters in New York are running around Manchester-by-the-Sea when a photo pops up of Ghislaine in Los Angeles eating a burger and drinking a shake. The *Daily Mail*'s editor Geordie Greig puts his sleuths onto it and they dig up a whole series of strange things about the photo. There's something wrong about it.

There's a dog in the photograph with Ghislaine, but it's not Ghislaine's dog. It's not the big visla. It's a little dog, and the little dog is called Dexter and he's some kind of cockapoo. And that dog does not belong to Ghislaine Maxwell at all. It belongs to Leah Saffian, who's the British-American lawyer who defended Kevin Maxwell, Ghislaine's brother, at his fraud trial in 1996. That's not all. At the back of the photo showing Ghislaine in LA is an advertising poster for the film *Good Boys*. The *Mail* asked the ad agency who manages the posters and they said they had never ever put that poster there.[8]

However, just before the trial it came out that after Epstein's death Kevin Maxwell had hired a security company to keep Ghislaine from the prying eyes of the media. Former Paratrooper Matt Hellyer told the *Mail on Sunday* that he and his team had spirited Ghislaine from Manchester-by-the-Sea, that she had spent time in LA and that they had even hired a Ghislaine looka-like to pop up in Paris. 'Ghislaine was not running from the authorities, she was running from the media,' said Hellyer.[9]

If so, the tactic was extremely stupid, because the authorities misread it and assumed that she was running from them.

This, then, is the fourth act in the tragedy of Ghislaine Maxwell. The death of Epstein was the single best moment for Ghislaine to come clean, to say that she had been in thrall to and in fear of the second monster in her life, but now that he was gone she could admit to doing wrong. She could put forward the psychological abuse she suffered at the hands of her father and ask people to forgive her. This would not have been a get-out-of-jail-free card, but it would have lessened her prison time. However, Ghislaine does not face the music. Instead, she goes into hiding. The FBI has many faults, but it is the most powerful detecting machine in human history in a data-driven age when playing hide-and-seek from the Bureau is a mug's game.

One year later, on 2 July 2019, the inevitable happened: 'Good morning, my name is Audrey Strauss, I'm acting US Attorney for the Southern District of New York. Today we announce charges against Ghislaine Maxwell for helping Jeffrey Epstein sexually exploit and abuse multiple minor girls from 1994 to 1997. Maxwell has been taken into custody early this morning . . .'

'Victim 1' met Ghislaine when she was fourteen in 1994, the indictment reads. Ghislaine allegedly groomed her by taking her to the movies and on shopping trips, asking her about school, her classes, her family and other aspects of her life: 'She then sought to normalize inappropriate and abusive conduct by, among other things, undressing in front of her and being present when she undressed in front of Epstein.' Ghislaine, Epstein and Victim 1 then engaged in 'group sexualized massages' on more than one occasion. The victim was encouraged to travel to the financier's homes in New York and Florida 'for the purpose of sexual encounters with Epstein'.

'Victim 2' met Ghislaine in 1996 and was allegedly groomed by her at Epstein's New Mexico ranch. The indictment claims that Ghislaine gave her a topless massage and 'encouraged [her] to massage Epstein'.

'Victim 3' met Ghislaine in London in 1994 and was groomed 'knowing that Epstein would engage in sex acts' as she did so, prosecutors claim. The indictment alleges that Maxwell knew the three women were underage at the time. Acting US Attorney Audrey Strauss said that Ghislaine Maxwell enticed minor girls, got them to trust her, then delivered them into the trap that she and Epstein had set for them: 'She pretended to be a woman they could trust, all the while she was setting them up to be sexually abused by Epstein in some cases, by Maxwell herself. Today after many years, Ghislaine Maxwell finally stands charged for her role in these crimes.'[10]

The first indictments focussed on three victims, from 1994 to 1997, so nothing that directly touched on Virginia Roberts Giuffre – first encountered in 2000 – and therefore Prince Andrew or Alan Dershowitz or the Palm Beach Police Department inquiry from 2005 onwards. There were also two perjury charges. A fresh indictment came in April 2021, alleging that a fourteen-year-old girl between 2001 and 2004 was groomed by Ghislaine Maxwell, who gave her gifts to engage in sex acts with Epstein at the house on El Brillo Way in Palm Beach.[11] That widens the time-bracket up to 2004, before the Palm Beach Police Department investigation that led to the immunity deal. One view is that the prosecutors were anxious to avoid a legal argy-bargy over that and were seeking to refine their charges so that their witnesses speak to alleged crimes before the immunity deal bit.

The FBI had tracked the fugitive down by hoovering her phone traffic. When close, they then used an electronic 'stingray device', which pings at her phone, so it pops up on their radar, so to speak. She had been hiding in a swanky million-dollar hideaway in the middle of New Hampshire. Ghislaine had gone to earth in a place called 'Tucked Away', 156 acres of oak and pine forest with views of Mount Sunapee, a ski resort. It really is in the boonies, quiet, remote, the perfect place to disappear. But you can't be too careful. The papers said that when the Feds raided it, they found a phone wrapped in tinfoil, like you do. Ghislaine had paid cash for the secluded mansion through an anonymous shell company in December 2019.[12] Reportedly, she had used ex-British special forces to guard her. The mystery is not that the FBI found her. Rather, it is how she managed to stay hidden for almost a year.

Still, the cat was in the bag.

What the Butler Said

The lady in the white mask looks so good it's as if she's just stepped off a yacht. The hair is dark and glossy, the eyes alight, the figure trim, the movements liquid and lithe, quick-silver, those of someone younger than her fifty-nine years. She's quite the gracious host, mwah-mwahing her pals, hugs-a-go-go, passing them thoughtful little Post-it® notes, blessing her set with her exclusive attention. Only this is not a gathering of socialites over champagne and canapés, but a child sexual abuse trial, and her friends are her fancy defence lawyers; and the people who once served and allegedly serviced her and her ex-lover Jeffrey Epstein, body and soul, are in no mood for mwah-mwah.

Welcome to the cocktail party from hell, or to give the proceedings their proper name, the trial of the United States of America v. Ghislaine Maxwell. Staged in the grand US federal courthouse in a half-empty Manhattan, it is from the start a grimly fascinating study, if you side with the defence, in false memory syndrome and gold-digging. Or, if you favour the prosecution, how power and money robbed a whole series of victims – each more child than woman – of their innocence and pretty much got away with it.

For someone who has spent the last 500 days-plus in prison awaiting trial in a cell 6 foot by 9 foot, the lights on, the peephole clicking open every fifteen minutes or so and no one at all with whom to mwah-mwah, Ghislaine looks so sparkling that one wonders whether her older brother Ian Maxwell has over-sold her plight in the remand prison. The disconnect between how someone should appear having lived through his description of the dire conditions in the lock-up and the reality of how breezy she was in court is stark. He told the BBC in March 2021 that 'she is losing her hair'.[1] But watching her in court, her hair was thick. No sign of hair loss.

The lead defence super-lawyer is Bobbi Sternheim, a tough, short-haired woman with a real presence. She always wore a jacket with the collar flipped up high. The moodiness, the way she glowered at the world, that upturned collar gave me flashbacks of glam rock star Alvin Stardust but there the similarities end. Sternheim pooh-poohed the prosecution as nonsense from the get-go, grabbing the best zinger of the opening bout: 'Ever since Eve has been blamed for tempting Adam with an apple, women have been blamed for things men have done . . . She is not Jeffrey Epstein. She is not anything like Jeffrey Epstein.' The defence argument goes that only when Epstein died did the alleged victims claim that Ghislaine Maxwell had abused them. They were – the suggestion was not articulated but hung in the air – gold-diggers.

Ghislaine's lawyers are good: they swagger well for the big money she is paying them. In her affidavit to the court before the trial, she disclosed that she was setting aside $7 million for her defence. The prosecution team, led by Maurene Comey, the daughter of former FBI director James Comey, has less pzazz. They are younger, thinner, paler; they spend less time in the sun; their prose is flatter. In terms of rhetoric, posture, cutting throats, the defence is in a different league than the prosecution or, in US legal parlance, the government. That said, the defence's case is markedly weaker than the skill with which it is proclaimed. In essence, their argument is that Ghislaine was, too, a victim of Jeffrey Epstein; that she had no idea what was happening; that it never happened at all; that what was really happening was that the so-called victims were painting Ghislaine guilty to unlock more dollars in compensation for the gold-diggers in the witness stand. A moment's reflection tells you that these different propositions do not stand comfortably together. The defence's case is so conflicted as to seem childish, an example of wanting to have one's cake and eat it, reflecting, some might say, the entitled woman-child in the dock. Then again, it is up to the prosecution to prove guilt, not the other way around. Note, too, that the defence was being paid a lot more money than the prosecution and, all around the world, but especially in the United States, money bites and the more money you have the harder the bite.

The prosecution case is almost understated, their underlying argument simple: that no fourteen-year-old girl would ever get into a car with a man like Jeffrey Epstein. But if the first contact is with a woman, a bright, attractive, charming one, then that's the proof of Ghislaine Maxwell's guilt, right there. Prosecutor Lara Pomerantz said in her opening statement: 'the cover of massage was the primary way the defendant and Epstein lured girls into sexual abuse. The defendant massaged Epstein in front of the girls, then she encouraged the girls to massage Epstein . . . The defendant was trafficking kids for sex. That's what this trial is about.' She described Ghislaine as Epstein's 'lady of the house', luring young girls into Epstein's orbit, and in return she enjoyed the lifestyle to which she was accustomed.

Proceedings for someone who has spent far too long in British courts being bored to tears are much crisper, less fusty, on the money. That's partly down to Judge Alison Nathan, tough, fast, hard but not hard-bitten. Once a special assistant to President Obama, Nathan is the second openly gay judge on the federal bench. Her hair is worn short, her language clipped and to the point, her black judge's gown occasionally shimmering rainbow colours as she turns, a starling's wing caught in sunlight. Whenever an attorney pongs 'Objection!' she pings 'Sustained' or 'Overruled' instantly. What was striking is the very few times when she slowed down the trial to think through the objection. Throughout the proceedings, she was on top of pretty much everything, reminding me of the captain of the *Compass Rose* in *The Cruel Sea* played by Jack Hawkins.

When OJ was tried for killing his ex-wife and her lover, the trial was televised. But that trial was at a state level and happened in California where TV cameras are allowed in court. The charges against Ghislaine are that she groomed, molested and trafficked young women for Epstein in New York, New Mexico, Florida and the US Virgin Islands, and that makes her alleged crimes federal, and this being a federal court, the trial is not televised.

The courthouse was knocked up in 1932, big Corinthian columns out the front, ponderous, projecting the power of the American century from its imperial city. Critic Lewis Mumford called it a 'supreme example of pretentiousness, mediocrity, bad design and fake grandeur' and he never visited the canteen. Thanks to Covid, seats for reporters in the actual courtroom are limited to six with a bit of a bias towards New York-based court reporters. Most of the time most of the reporters watch the show from overflow court-rooms via a live CCTV feed. You can queue up for the seats in the court proper by standing in the freezing December cold before sunrise. Vicky Ward, who, attentive readers will recall, once blogged: 'Ghislaine? Full disclosure: I like her. Most people in New York do', paid a New Yorker $50 an hour to stand in the dark from 2 a.m. to bag a seat for her. One cold morning I got up too early, missed breakfast and stood in line so that I could get into the court proper and put my peepers on Ghislaine and drink in the atmosphere.

The courtroom is impressively high-ceilinged, kitted out in wood, with two new see-through glass boxes, one for the attorney addressing the court, one for the witness on the stand. There is some kind of extractor device on top of the glass box so that attor-ney and witness can speak without a mask. As you enter the court, the benches for the media and the public are to the bottom left. Top left is a bench for family of the accused and each day Ghislaine's brother Kevin, her sister Isabel and her friend, Leah Saffian, the one who appears to have photographed or photo-shopped her in LA, sat there. When the evidence was over, Ian Maxwell and Isabel's twin, Christine, joined the other two siblings to listen to submissions from the prosecution and defence. One no-show was Ghislaine's husband, Scott Borgerson. Before the trial, he told her in a bleak phone call to her prison wing that he had moved on. The papers reported that he had started a new rela-tionship with a yoga teacher.[2]

To the right are the seats for the jury and the alternative jurors.

The prosecution sit front centre; then the glass box for the attorney on his or her feet; then to the left sit the defence with Ghislaine at the very far left. On a dais sits the judge and to the right is the second glass box housing the witness.

What of the most important people in the court: the jury? The #MeToo generation of young white women does not appear to be represented at all, a result, perhaps, of the defence gaming the jury selection process. The jurors appear to be largely young men and women of colour with a few middle-aged not-well-off white men and women thrown in – the kind of people I see on my subway train on my commute to court. You can see the trick the defence has played, but then you reflect that these are exactly the kind of people who have spent their whole lives cleaning up rich people's shit. If so, I begin to wonder whether that might not bode well for the mwah-mwah princess in the dock.

Ghislaine Maxwell faced six charges of sex trafficking and two extra charges of perjury, but those counts were due to be tried after her sex trafficking trial. The perjury charges bite on sworn testimony she gave in a 2016 defamation case filed against her by Virginia Roberts Giuffre. The nitty-gritty of the trafficking charges read as follows:

> conspiracy to entice minors to travel to engage in illegal sex acts, carrying a maximum sentence of five years; enticement of a minor to travel to engage in illegal sex acts, maximum sentence 20 years; conspiracy to transport minors with intent to engage in criminal sexual activity, maximum sentence 20 years; transportation of a minor with intent to engage in criminal sexual activity, 10 years minimum, life maximum; sex trafficking conspiracy; sex trafficking of a minor.

If found guilty on all counts, that's the rest of her life in prison.

Given that jeopardy, the first thing Ghislaine did during the pre-trial jury selection process in November 2021 was more than a little mad. When a courtroom sketch artist drew her, Ghislaine picked up her pen, opened a notebook and started drawing her straight back.

We all understand the role of the courtroom artist: that because cameras are banned from US federal trials – and jury trials in Britain – someone goes to court with pencil and paper and gives the public a likeness of the key figures at court. Ghislaine was not just mocking a minion who had showed her an unbecoming lack of deference; she was also mocking the tradition of open justice that has been the rock of English common law since the eighth century. What was she playing at? Did she think the trial some bizarre version of Pin the Tail on the Donkey? On reading the story about her drawing the court artist I felt, again, that the person in the dock was more child than adult, and that cannot end well.

The first witness in the case for the prosecution was one of two of Epstein's pilots, Larry Visoski, a deep-voiced come-fly-with-me who recalled high-profile passengers such as Prince Andrew, Bill Clinton, Donald Trump, the astronaut John Glenn and actor Kevin Spacey. He never saw any sexual abuse of minors or any possible signs of it whatsoever. Seth Stevenson in his wryly written piece on the pilot's evidence for *Slate* quoted the American lefty trouble-maker Upton Sinclair: 'It is difficult to get a man to understand something when his salary depends on his not understanding it.'[3] Later, it came out that Epstein had paid for both Visoski's daughters to go through college and that he had given him 40 acres of land in New Mexico.

But the man who flew the Boeing nicknamed the 'Lolita Express' did say that he saw two very young women in the company of Epstein and Maxwell, one of them being Virginia Roberts. He clocked her in 2001. The second very young woman the pilot identified was the next witness, granted anonymity as 'Jane'. That is not her real name. A well-known actor in a big US soap opera, she explained why she had chosen anonymity because she feared public disgrace and so being shunned in Hollywood: 'I've always just wanted to put this past me. I moved on with my life. I work in the entertainment industry and victim shaming is still very present to this day.'

Visoski told the court: 'Mr Epstein brought her to the cockpit. She had piercing powder blue eyes.'[4]

Cross-examining, defence attorney Christian Everdell asked: 'And beyond the striking blue eyes, you have said she had large breasts, right?' Everdell is no Atticus Finch in *To Kill a Mockingbird*.

Visoski replied that Jane was 'a mature woman'.

Nearly right. When Jane, a woman of stunning beauty to this day, took the stand she explained that when she met Ghislaine and Epstein, when she flew on his planes, when she was befriended by Ghislaine, when she was required to have sex with him, she was fourteen.

The spell of the trial is that the focus widens from time to time to reveal a stark landscape of real America and its cruelty to the poor, to the wretched, to the unlucky. Jane told the jury that she was 'twelve, going on thirteen' and living in West (poor) Palm Beach when her father, a composer, died of leukaemia. His employers had cancelled his health insurance and when he died the family went into complete bankruptcy, lost everything and had to move out of the family home. The following summer, relatives clubbed together to pay for her and her brothers to go to Interlochen, a summer arts camp in Michigan. Had Jane's father not died, or had his employers not cancelled his health insurance, then none of what happened would have taken place.

Nine months after her father died, Jane vividly remembered that one day she and her classmates were eating ice cream when a tall, thin woman approached her and her gang. The woman was walking a 'cute little Yorkie and we asked if we could pet the dog. We started chit-chatting and the rest of my classmates had to go to class.'

Introduction secured, along came a man who seemed very interested to know what Jane thought of the camp: 'They said they were big benefactors of this camp and gave out different kinds of scholarships and wanted to know the students' perspective.'

The dog was called Max; the woman Ghislaine; the man Epstein. When Jane said she was from Palm Beach, Epstein replied: 'What a coincidence! We live there too. What are your parent's names?'

Jane explained that her father had just died. Around a month later, somebody from Epstein's office invited her and her mother round for tea at his mansion in Palm Beach. The first phase of grooming out of the way, Ghislaine worked on the next.

One day Jane went out to the pool area at the house on El Brillo Way and saw Ghislaine mucking about with four other women, all topless. Jane hadn't seen that before. She described Ghislaine as a bit odd, quirky. Ghislaine would tease her but the fourteen-year-old found her nice. At one point, Ghislaine told Jane that she was like an older sister to her. After each visit, Epstein would give Jane money, explaining that her mother was having a hard time and the money was not a big deal.

Sexual boundaries removed; money changing hands; the third stage of the grooming process followed soon after. Ghislaine gave Jane advice about her boyfriends, once telling her: 'If you fuck them once you can fuck them again because they are grandfathered in.'

Jane said: 'I giggled because I didn't understand what grand-fathered meant.'

Epstein and Ghislaine took her to Victoria's Secret to buy her underwear. Jane chose the basic white stuff. In the meantime, the couple would drop into the conversation that they were buddies with Donald Trump and Bill Clinton. Soon Epstein made his move:

> He pulled his pants down, he pulled me on top of himself and he proceeded to masturbate on me. Then he just got up and went into the bathroom and cleaned himself up and acted as if nothing had happened. I was frozen in fear. I had never seen a penis before let alone something like this. I was terrified and I felt gross. I felt ashamed.

She was still only fourteen.

Once induced into what, to me, sounds like a child sex cult, Jane did as she was told. She said that Ghislaine and Epstein once led her up the circular stairwell in their Palm Beach home.

'They came into the bedroom and took their clothes off. They started sort of fondling each other and kind of casually giggling. I was just standing there and he asked me to take my top off and then their hands [were] everywhere and Jeffrey proceeded to masturbate and Ghislaine was rubbing him and kissing him and fondling.'

Did Maxwell touch her body, asked the prosecutor.

'Yes,' Jane said, adding the sexual abuse happened 'every time I visited his house'.

Jane spoke out in her strong, well-modulated voice, which only wobbled when she was required to get into the detail of the sexual abuse. She wore a black high-neck top and grey cardigan and had a tissue in her hand. When she was upset she would dab her nose with the tissue.

Did Epstein touch her?

'Yes. Everywhere.'

On recalling this, her voice began to shake. She shuffled in her seat and took off her cardigan. Her discomfort was plain for all to see. In short breaks, while the lawyers got into their argy-bargy or the usher was slow to upload something to the monitor in the witness box, Jane avoided any eye contact with Ghislaine; for her part, the accused looked askance, avoiding the witness box.

Ghislaine would instruct her on how to massage Epstein, Jane said: 'He liked it very hard, like rubbing his shoulders very hard, twisting his nipples hard.'

What was Ghislaine's demeanour like during this?

'It seemed very casual, it was very normal. It's not a big deal.' Jane said it made her feel 'confused because that did not feel normal to me because I had never seen anything like that and it was very embarrassing . . . when you're fourteen you have no idea what's going on'.

Jane said that Epstein touched her 'breasts, vagina'.

Prosecutor Alison Moe asked if Epstein used sex toys, telling her: 'I'm sorry to ask you this but could you please describe what happened.'

'He liked vibrators, they were different sizes, even a back

massager. He'd put it on my vagina, even if I said it hurt.' At this point, she seemed close to tears.

The prosecutor asked if other people took part in the sex. Jane said yes, usually in the massage room or the bedroom in El Brillo Way. She said that Ghislaine would encourage others to 'start taking their clothes off, Jeffrey would get on the massage table and it would turn into this orgy ... kissing, oral sex with each other, oral sex with Jeffrey, full on intercourse'.

The others were women, older than her, but as she was fourteen when it started, they would not have been very much older. One of the women, Jane remembered, was called Eva.

Jane said she travelled to Epstein's other homes in New York and New Mexico, observing 'Art, sculptures. Pictures of famous people, presidents. I thought some of the art was odd – naked women, creepy animals.'

Recalling one trip to Epstein's Zorro ranch in New Mexico, Jane correctly placed it in the middle of nowhere. One of Epstein's aides entered her guest room, she remembered, and said Epstein wanted her in his bedroom: 'I felt my heart sink. I didn't want to go see him.'

The prosecution probed Jane about her mother's attitude to the attention she was getting from the couple. 'My mother seemed very impressed and enamoured with the wealth, the affluence. She thought they' – Epstein and Ghislaine – 'seemed very generous and they must think I'm special and that I should be grateful for the attention that I received.'

Did Jane ever tell her mother about the sexual abuse?

'No.'

Why didn't she tell her mother during those years?

'Because I felt very ashamed, I felt very disgusted, I was confused, I didn't know if it was my fault, and my mother and I did not have that kind of a relationship. We didn't talk about our feelings. We weren't allowed to. I was raised in a household where you were sort of spoken to, and you don't speak unless you're spoken to, and I would be afraid that I would be in trouble if I said something.'

Did she tell her brothers or her friends about the sexual abuse by Maxwell and Epstein in those years?

'No.'

Why not?

'Because how do you tell or describe any of this to any one of your peers or your siblings when all you feel is shame and disgust and confusion and you don't even know how you ended up there.'

When Jane was in the seventh grade at school, roughly when she was thirteen years old, a guidance counsellor got in touch to see how she and her family were coping with the loss of her father.

'She asked me what was going on at home, if we had been or I had been in grief counselling and how my mother was doing. So I told her how I was feeling and how sad I was and, you know, how unavailable my mother was and how unsupportive and there was really no one for me to talk to. So I spoke to her and she was . . .' – she paused, struggling to find the words, to contain her emotion – 'she was lovely and she would . . .' – she paused again – '. . . when she would see me. She would say if you need a place to go, just come to my office and sit there and we'll talk.'

The guidance counsellor got in touch with her mother but that spelt trouble for Jane.

> I came home from school one day and my mother said that the guidance counsellor had called her and had said that she wanted to see her because she was very worried about me. My mother proceeded to berate me and scream at me and slap me and tell me how dare I talk about myself and our family and that it was an embarrassment, and that you don't tell people about your feelings or what's going on at home.

One could understand completely why Jane felt it impossible to tell her mother when she was sexually abused by Epstein and Ghislaine.

As Jane spoke, Ghislaine, restless, would put on and take off her reading glasses, lean forward and pass Post-it® notes to her lawyers. Then it was their turn to pull the wings off this awkward butterfly. Defence attorney Laura Menninger – a chilly blonde, her voice soft, her language hard, sometime brutal – pointed out that Jane and other accusers received big money from a $121m (£90m) fund set up by Epstein's estate to compensate victims, implying that the more the victims squeal, the more money they get.

Menninger asked Jane if it was correct that she waited twenty years to speak to law enforcement. Jane said that was correct. 'The first time you spoke to law enforcement was after Epstein was dead.' Jane said: 'Yes.'

The defence lawyer swooped, saying that in the last twenty years Jane had never mentioned that Ghislaine Maxwell had sexually assaulted her to friends and family.

> **Jane (weakly):** 'I don't know. I was reluctant to go into details about embarrassing, shameful and despicable things . . . I didn't want to share it with them in the first place.'
>
> **Menninger (coldly):** 'Did you tell them about Epstein?'
>
> **Jane:** 'Yes I did.'
>
> **Menninger:** 'Did you talk to them about Ghislaine Maxwell?'
>
> **Jane:** 'I don't know.'

Earlier on, Jane had put down an anomaly in her evidence to a 'typo' in the write-up of her interview with the FBI. This would not be the first time that the guardians of truth and justice in the United States had made a mistake. Menninger reminded Jane that when she had spoken to the FBI in February 2020 she said there were other women involved the first time she had sexual activity with Ghislaine – and that was another departure from her direct evidence in the current trial.

> **Menninger (brutally):** 'Another typo by the government?'
>
> **Jane:** 'Yes.'

In a previous interview with the FBI in 2019, Jane had said that Epstein or his office would call her home.

The prosecutor set up her trap:

> **Menninger** 'Two years later, you remember that Ghislaine used to call your home to make appointments?'
> **Jane:** 'Right.'

'That memory has come back to you in the last two years?' asked the defence lawyer.

'Memory is not linear,' replied Jane, which, given the attrition she was under, was a rather good answer. The truth, of course, is that memory is not a slide-rule but a river that surges, then ebbs, with powerful eddies often whirring away in the wrong direction. It's human to see a moment in time indelibly scratched on your mind's eye but also to forget dates, to mis-order events, to scramble sequence. Nevertheless, if Menninger's job was to cast doubt on the essence of Jane's testimony by getting her to mangle the order in which things happened, she did well.

Then the defence turned on what Jane did for a living, working in Hollywood as a star in a big US soap. Menninger asked Jane: is an actor 'someone who plays the role of a fictional character . . . someone who takes lines borrowed from a writer?'

'Yes,' said Jane.

Menninger asked if Jane had played someone stalked by serial killers, an overly protective mother, a car-crash victim. Yes, she said.

And a prostitute? 'Not my favourite story line,' replied Jane bleakly.

Towards the end of several hours of cross-examination, Jane retired into herself. She kept on saying, 'I don't recall', as if she were being tortured and she just wanted it to be over. At the very end she was challenged once again about the $5m she got from Epstein's estate. She replied: 'I wish I would have never received that money in the first place.' She was crying.

Jane's story struck every reporter I spoke to as compelling, as that of somebody who did not tell the authorities until it was too late because she feared falling out with her mother over bringing the family name into disrepute. It does not mean what she was saying was not true but that she had a very good reason not to go there. Still, her withdrawal into herself on the second day would have been seen by the defence as a 'win'. Also, the defence needle that she was an actor, that she was just reading out someone else's script, resonated with some of my reporter colleagues. They didn't buy it themselves but they could imagine it cutting through to some of the jury.

The prosecution had planned to call one of Jane's brothers later on in the trial, but Jane had told her brother that Menninger was a c-word that rhymed with brunt. It's against the rules for witnesses to speak to each other, to cross-contaminate their evidence, even though it's very human, and that meant that the defence knocked out the word of the brother of a woman who claims she was first sexually violated by Epstein and Ghislaine when she was fourteen years old. It's nice work if you can get it, some say.

The next witness was 'Matt', another false name to protect his privacy. He, too, was extremely good-looking, an actor and had been Jane's boyfriend from 2006 to 2014. They remain friends. The couple both worked on the same US soap opera. Matt explained that Jane had told him about her 'godfather' figure who'd funded her family after her father died and they'd been left bankrupt. When Epstein was arrested in 2008, Jane told Matt that he was the 'godfather', adding: 'The money wasn't fucking free.' When Matt pressed her for more, she would only say, 'It wasn't pretty.'

Matt also said that Jane told him there had been a woman at Epstein's house who'd 'made Jane comfortable' notwithstanding the abuse. When Ghislaine was arrested in 2020, Matt contacted Jane to ask if this was the woman, and Jane had said yes, it was.

The problem for the prosecution was that this was subtle stuff, not direct evidence that Jane had Ghislaine front-of-mind as an abuser for twenty years, but somebody she had been extremely reluctant to talk about until her 'godfather' was dead and his woman was in handcuffs.

A fourth witness backed Jane's claim to have met Epstein at the Interlochen Arts Camp when she was fourteen, providing documents that Epstein had indeed been at the camp on the day stated by Jane. He'd given the camp $250,000 to build the Jeffrey Epstein Scholarship Lodge. 'It's since been renamed,' the witness said, drily. That was a home-run for the prosecution.

Next up was an expert witness, forensic psychologist Lisa Rocchio, who said there were a number of stages of grooming, starting with identifying vulnerable targets. The scene in *Jurassic Park* when the velociraptor sniffs the children hiding in the kitchen came to mind. Next comes establishing 'a false sense of familiarity . . . gift-giving can certainly be a very powerful inducement'. Then 'normalising touch' by sitting very close or by giving a massage. Abusers who sought to maintain a relationship meant their victims were 'far less likely to disclose' abuse, and the younger they were, the longer they would take to speak up.

Abuse of minors, said the psychologist, was 'one of the most underreported crimes'.

Prosecutor Lara Pomerantz asked: 'Is the person doing the grooming always the recipient of the sexual gratification?' Rocchio replied 'No', but the judge told the jury to disregard the exchange, explaining that it infringed prior limits she had placed on Rocchio's testimony. The defence have argued in court papers that prosecutors are accusing Ghislaine of 'grooming by proxy', saying there is no scientific research to support it.

Perhaps they had not heard of the psychiatrist Anthony Storr and his argument set out earlier in this book that some depressives have so little sense of self that they can over-serve their dominating partners.

The next witness to take the stand was the Palm Beach house butler, Juan Alessi. A squat, thick-set rubber ball of a man, in a black suit and yellow tie, he worked at the Palm Beach house from 1990 to 2002. He identified Virginia Roberts Giuffre and Jane as being at the house and scores of other very young women over the years. He said that Ghislaine told him: 'Mr Epstein doesn't like to be looked at in the eyes. Never look at his eyes, look in another part of the room and answer him.'

Alessi said Ghislaine introduced a fifty-eight-page booklet titled 'Household Manual', a book on etiquette. The rubric read: 'This manual is designed to give you the proper guidance and assistance to perform your duties to the best of your ability, while ensuring a consistently high level of service. By using your communications skills, listening and observing, you will be able to anticipate the needs of Mr Epstein, Ms Maxwell and their guests.'

Back in the day as a kid I used to read the *Beano*, and Ghislaine's etiquette book reminded me very much of the comic's character, Lord Snooty. Staff were warned to avoid wearing strong aftershave or perfume and to refrain from keeping items that 'bulged' in their pockets. 'Do not eat or drink in front of Mr Epstein, Ms Maxwell and their guests. Do not chew gum', the manual said.

In the master bedroom, staff were to ensure a gun was placed in a bedside table drawer, shutters were closed, and that reading glasses, eye masks and 'Jeffrey Epstein large and small notepads' were on both bedside tables. Ghislaine required the staff to use 'proper language' with a list of things not to say: 'Yeah', 'Sure', 'No problem', 'You bet', 'Gotcha', 'Right' and 'I dunno' were all out of bounds. When complimented, according to the manual, they should respond: 'You are very kind' and 'Thank, you, Ms ____. I enjoy doing it.'

Alessi's other duties were to make breakfast at five o'clock in the morning and bathe Maxwell's dog, Max.

One bit read: 'Remember that you see nothing, hear nothing, say nothing except to answer a question direct to you. Respect their privacy.' For the prosecution, this was evidence of a culture of silence deliberately engineered by Ghislaine so that the child sex abuse could happen unchallenged.

Prosecutor Maurene Comey asked what Alessi understood by the rulebook: 'I was supposed to be blind, deaf, to say nothing,' he replied.

Starting the cross-examination was Jeffrey Pagliuca, one of Maxwell's defence lawyers and someone who, with his curly grey hair and lean chops, looks like another great or not-so-great American, the TV lowlife host Jerry Springer. He pointed to prior testimony Alessi had given in a separate proceeding, in which he said that he answered to Epstein rather than Ghislaine. Alessi insisted that he answered to Ms Maxwell: 'She was my immediate superior.'

Later on, the jury heard from an FBI agent who had dug out some of Ghislaine's emails complaining to Alessi's line manager in Palm Beach about the butler. For fun, Ghislaine and Epstein called him John, not Juan. Ghislaine had complained by email in May 2001: 'I need to know what if any list John is using and he needs to understand that he is doing a truly awful job.' Among the major grievances were the following: Alessi had failed to supply bottles of water for the Mercedes; the colour printing card in the computer hadn't been changed; the massage creams 'in J.E.'s bathroom were a mess'.

Returning to Alessi's evidence, the Palm Beach etiquette manual came up again. The prosecution got it entered into the court record and it is a thing of madness. Toothpaste and shaving cream to be kept more than half full, tissues replaced when they fell below one-third, the razor blade swapped out after every use. The massage lotion was to be Burberry Baby Touch Soothing Massage Oil; the shaving cream, lip balm, and face moisturisers Kiehl's; the sunscreen, Peter Thomas Roth; the hairbrush, Mason Pearson. Personally, I've no idea what this crap is but I guess that's the whole point.

What was working for Ghislaine like? 'It was slavery,' said Alessi. On reflecting on that, Sarah Ransome's line about the posh people getting Gracious Ghislaine while the rest had to suffer the conniving tyrant echoed here.

Pagliuca told the court that Ghislaine had not written the house rules manual. 'You know they hired a countess to write the book?' he asked Alessi.

'I don't know that, sir,' Alessi replied.

Who is the likeliest contender to be the countess? Step forward

Clare Hazell, now the Countess of Iveagh, after she bagged an heir to the Guinness family fortune, Edward, the 4th Earl of Iveagh. The countess pops up in Ghislaine's black book as 'Clare Hazell-Iveagh' and seems to have flown on the Lolita Express thirty-two times between 1998 and 2000, including trips to his homes in New York, Florida, the Caribbean and New Mexico. The countess has not replied to enquiries from reporters.[5]

Call me thick – as Donald Trump once did – but I wrestle to understand where on earth Pagliuca was going with this countess claptrap. At the jury selection process, he was part of a defence team that had seemed to wipe out any juror who looked as though they had serious money. So rubbing posh snot into the face of some poor Hispanic wage slave struck me as being stupid and, in front of a poor, blue-collar jury, the very opposite of gaining their vote. One can only surmise that the lawyer was pushed into bringing up the countess by his client. If so, it's another spectacular example of Ghislaine failing to read the (jury) room.

Reflecting on the role of social ranking in the evidence, a reporter colleague from the *Financial Times*, Josh Chaffin, wrote that the defence have

> tried to use class to their advantage during the trial. In her opening statement, attorney Bobbi Sternheim claimed the accusers were money-grabbers who had twisted the truth in hopes of a financial 'jackpot'. It was reminiscent of political strategist James Carville dismissing former President Bill Clinton's sexual assault accusers in 1994 by remarking: 'Drag a hundred-dollar bill through a trailer park, you never know what you'll find.'[6]

Some sense of the defence team's grand strategy came up next: that Ghislaine was also a victim of Epstein's deceit. Pagliuca said that, on occasion, Epstein would arrive at Palm Beach without Ghislaine and when that happened he would order Alessi to take down pictures of Maxwell. 'You understand the reason for removing the pictures was that Mr Epstein was interested in the other women, correct?' said Pagliuca.

'I have no idea,' Alessi replied.

He confirmed he first met Jane in 1994. 'I don't know exactly how old she was but she appeared to be young. I would say fourteen, fifteen ... She was a strikingly beautiful girl, beautiful eyes ... long brunette hair, tall.' (Jane had said she was picked up and driven to Epstein's house by a chauffeur, a sweet Latin-American man. Alessi is from Ecuador.)

What the butler saw on Epstein's massage table was 'a large dildo. It looked like a huge man's penis with two heads.'

During some of the arcane legal to-and-fro, quite a few members of the jury looked as though they might have been asleep, but they were wide awake when they listened to the butler. When Pagliuca tried to rip his wings off, Alessi fought back, hard. Challenged that he had stolen $6,000 from the house after he quit, he admitted it, but he stuck firmly to his guns that he never arranged sex massages for Epstein, only under order drove girls to and from the house on El Brillo Way.

But no one complained? he was asked.

'I wish they had complained,' he said. 'Then I could have done something about it.' The crooked butler had got his dignity back.

The second young woman who gave evidence that Ghislaine had effectively groomed her for sex with Epstein was anonymised as 'Kate'. English, well-spoken, beautiful, blonde, Kate had high sculpted cheekbones and came across as the most elegant person in the courthouse. She explained that when she was hoovered up into Maxwelliana, her father was out of the picture, her mother troubled, ill, under a lot of stress, implying that she herself was a little broken. She was seventeen years old. As she was British and the age of sexual consent in the United Kingdom is sixteen, nothing criminal happened to Kate. But, against defence submissions, the judge allowed the prosecution to call her in evidence so long as the jury understood that they could not convict Ghislaine on what she told them alone.

Kate said she was on a trip to Paris with her then boyfriend, who was thirty-five and had been at Oxford with Ghislaine, when she bumped into the socialite. Later on, defence attorney Bobbi Sternheim described this man as an 'older prominent gentleman', but we never learnt the identity of the dirty old goat – sorry, the distinguished Oxonian goat.

Ghislaine had struck Kate as sophisticated, elegant. She gave her number on a piece of paper. A few weeks later Kate, who lived with her mother and stepfather in London's Belgravia, was invited round the corner to Ghislaine's mews flat for tea. 'I was quite excited to be friends with her.' She paused and then said with a catch in her throat: 'She seemed to be everything that I wanted to be.'

At Ghislaine's, Kate saw lots of photos of her with an older man with pepper hair. Ghislaine explained that this was Jeffrey Epstein and that he was a rich and generous man. Kate shared her troubles with Ghislaine. She had been offered a place at Oxford to read law but fancied ditching that in favour of getting into the music business, except that she was worried about telling her folks of her change of heart. Ghislaine said it would be really wonderful for Kate to meet Epstein. A few weeks later Ghislaine called, urgency in her voice, telling her to visit. This was the first time Kate met Epstein. He was on the phone, dressed in a hoodie. Call over, Ghislaine introduced them, saying that Kate was strangely strong for her size. Ghislaine suggested that Kate give his feet a squeeze to show him how strong she was.

Thus far, Kate's evidence had ticked every single box on the steps to grooming set out by the psychologist Lisa Rocchio: first contact by proxy female; victim established as troubled, unstable, from a broken home; massage introduced. Not that long after, Ghislaine called again, Kate said, explaining that Jeffrey's massage therapist had cancelled and could Kate please do her a favour and come over because she had such strong hands. Ghislaine was excited when Kate turned up, and led her upstairs to a small dimly lit room with a massage table. Epstein was inside the room, wearing a robe. He took it off and stood there, naked. Ghislaine gave Kate some massage oil and closed the door on the forty-something-year-old rich man and the seventeen-year-old girl. The cycle of abuse was established and continued. At one time Ghislaine chirped after a sex massage: 'Did you have fun? Oh you are such a good girl. I'm so happy.'

Ghislaine would exclaim, said Kate: 'boys and their willies!' The court heard that 'willies' was Ghislaine's euphemism for penis, but Kate said the word so softly that afterwards the court reporters argued whether it was 'weenies' – American slang – or the correct, English-English version, willies. She would talk about 'how demanding Jeffrey was. She would ask if I knew anybody who could come and give Jeffrey a blow job because it was a lot for her to do. She said, "You know what he likes. Cute, young, pretty, like you."'

Kate told prosecutors that on one visit she saw another girl downstairs with Ghislaine and Epstein, blonde, slim, around seventeen years. Ghislaine often spoke of sex and when she did, Kate said, 'it was almost like a schoolgirl, and I always felt like she was younger than me. It was odd. Everything was fun and everything was silly. Everything was just very exciting and everything seemed to be like a fun silly joke.'

So here we have a seventeen-year-old telling the court that she felt older than a woman roughly twice her age: that's Ghislaine's arrested development right there. On her eighteenth birthday, Kate said she received a Prada bag from Ghislaine, after she had had sex with Epstein.

Hooked on the high life, Kate soon found herself jetting around the world on Epstein's dime, travelling to Epstein's houses in New York and Palm Beach and to his island in the Caribbean. One day in Palm Beach she found a schoolgirl's outfit laid out on her bed: short pleated skirt, white socks, white panties and a shirt. Ghislaine explained: 'I thought it would be fun for you to take Jeffrey his tea in this outfit.'

Kate had put the schoolgirl outfit on, she explained to the jury, because 'I did not know how to say no to that', adding she did not know where she was or what might happen if she didn't. When she went to deliver the tea, she found Epstein working out with his personal trainer. Following a short pause, the trainer left and Epstein sexually abused Kate. Ghislaine, later, asked 'if I had had fun and told me that I was a good girl and that I was one of his favourites'.

Along the way, Kate became addicted to cocaine, sleeping pills and alcohol. With great pride in her voice, she said she had been clean since 1 May 2003. You would have to be a hard soul on the jury not to get it that Kate had had her demons and that, in shunning the booze and the drugs, she had confronted them. And, perhaps, that in coming to court and giving her evidence against Ghislaine Maxwell, she was confronting the biggest demon in her life of all.

Questioned by prosecutor Lara Pomerantz as to why she maintained the relationship with Epstein for more than a decade, she said that at first she believed Ghislaine was her 'friend' but that she had later become fearful of 'how connected they both were'.

Up popped Bobbi Sternheim for the defence, setting out that Kate's stepfather was a wealthy man with his own plane, that she had been a model in Milan, Paris and London and had worked for a British lingerie company: 'It folded almost as soon as it began,' Kate replied, downbeat. Under cross-examination, Kate admitted that she sent Epstein emails while he was in prison in 2008 for soliciting under-age girls for sex. She'd offered to send him pictures of herself, though she never actually did. Kate confirmed that she signed off the emails: 'Best love always, Kate.' She admitted that in 2011 she asked to stay with Epstein, even after he had come out of prison, at his home in New York, but he wasn't there at the time, so the visit did not happen. The last contact Kate had with Epstein was in 2012 when she became a mother, she said.

Sternheim said that although Kate was testifying under a pseudonym, she had spoken publicly in court after Epstein died in 2019 and had appeared on television with other alleged victims and that she had been awarded $2.25 million by the Epstein victims compensation fund. Gold-digger hung in the air, again.

That evening Ghislaine's brother, Kevin, who had been in the public gallery with his sister, Isabel, gave an impromptu press conference on the steps of the court, condemning the government's treatment of the accused: 'She's on trial for her life' but from 6.30 in the morning until 7.30 p.m. when returned to jail 'she receives a boiled egg, she is lucky if it's not mouldy, she receives a couple of pieces of bread, maybe a Kraft slice and a banana or an apple'. Kevin complained that bringing Ghislaine from the remand prison in Brooklyn to the court in lower Manhattan and back at the end of the day in shackles was an abuse: 'She has been bruised, she has even bled. And you really have to ask yourself, in 2021 what on earth is the government doing shackling a fifty-nine-year-old woman in this way, every day?'

On that, one could only agree with Kevin Maxwell.

The third woman who says she was groomed by Ghislaine and sexually abused by Epstein was Carolyn. The court, to give her some privacy, accepted her request to use only her real first name. Carolyn had a single-parent mother who was an alcoholic and a drug addict and she became an alcoholic and a drug addict herself; she left school when she was young, and did not, said her ex-boyfriend Shawn, have the reading ability to say Ms Maxwell's first name, Ghislaine. So Carolyn called her Maxwell.

Jane was a famous American actor, Kate a sometime-famous English singer and model, but Carolyn was someone who both looked and sounded like she was from the wrong side of the tracks. As she was. She told the court that at one time Ghislaine had asked her about her life. Carolyn responded: 'My mom was an alcoholic, and I had been molested, and just random personal things.'

Prosecutor Maurene Comey asked: what conversations did she remember having with Ghislaine Maxwell about her experience of sexual abuse?

'I remember telling her that I had been raped and molested by my grandfather, starting at the age of four,' said Carolyn.

What conversations did Carolyn have about travel with Maxwell?

'I couldn't travel because I couldn't get a passport because I was too young. And my mom, no matter how messed up she was, there was no way I would be able to leave the country.'

How did that topic come up?

'I was invited to go to an island . . . I told her that I was too young, and there is no way in hell my mom was going to let me leave the country.'

Did you tell her how old you were?

'Yes.'

What did you say?

'I told her I was fourteen.'

You could hear the scratch of the reporters' pens across paper and only that.

So, her evidence went, one decade after Carolyn's grandfather raped her when she was four years old, it was the turn of Epstein and Ghislaine Maxwell to break this child.

Carolyn said of the woman whose first name she couldn't articulate, Ghislaine, that she booked her for sex massages with her lover and once came into the massage room in the Epstein mansion in Palm Beach and molested her: 'I was fully nude and she [Ghislaine] came in and she felt my boobs and my hips and my buttocks and said that . . . I had a great body for Mr Epstein and his friends.'

Carolyn said that she had been introduced to Epstein and Ghislaine by her older friend, Virginia Roberts – now Virginia Roberts Giuffre. 'I was young and $300 was a lot of money to me,' Carolyn said of Virginia's offer. Sex was not mentioned at the get-go, she said. In the end, she gave Epstein about a hundred massages, all of them sexual, all of them ending with him masturbating. Ghislaine, she said, handed her $300 a few times after the sex and, during one visit, asked for her address. Epstein sent Carolyn a massage book 'for dummies', concert tickets to the rock band Incubus and lingerie from Victoria's Secret via FedEx.

The raw detail of Carolyn's testimony was grim.

Prosecutor Maurene Comey: 'Can you describe the vibrating thing that he tried to put on your vagina?'

Carolyn: 'It looked like what now I know – it looked like –'

Comey: 'Like a penis?'

Carolyn: 'Yes. Sorry.'

Comey: 'Did he actually touch that vibrator onto your vagina?'

Carolyn: 'Yes.'

Comey: 'How did every massage you ever gave Jeffrey Epstein end?'

Carolyn: 'With him masturbating until he ejaculated.'

Comey: 'Were there ever massages you provided Jeffrey Epstein where nothing sexual happened?'

Carolyn: 'No. Something sexual happened every single time.'

Carolyn managed to escape the dark world of Epstein and Ghislaine for a time. When she was sixteen, she and her boyfriend Shawn, then nineteen, stole her mother's car and drove to Georgia. Soon after, she became pregnant and had her baby in March 2004. Back in Florida, broke, and desperate to provide for the baby, she returned to Epstein's home to try and make some money: 'He asked me if I had younger friends and I said no.'

Prosecutor Comey asked why she stopped going to the home on El Brillo Way.

'I became too old.'

'How old were you?' Comey asked.

'Eighteen,' Carolyn replied.

The prosecution knew that the defence would bring up the dirt on their witnesses, so they did it first.

Had Carolyn ever been arrested for drug use? Yes, she said, for cocaine in 2011. What happened that led to her getting arrested?

'I handed the officer the drugs.'

'Why did you do that?'

'Because I'm an idiot.'

There was something heroic about Carolyn's bleak self-knowledge. The defence's hope that they could undermine her credibility sunk right there. She was more than willing to admit to her own grisly failures in life. Her honesty made her an impregnable witness. Especially amid the tedious legal to-and-fro, some members of the jury looked bored to tears. But not while Carolyn was on the stand.

She admitted that in 2013 she was arrested for possessing stolen property, her son's Xbox, which she had taken to the pawnshop because she was broke. The story behind the story was that her boyfriend Shawn had stolen the Xbox, but Carolyn was the one who did the time, fifty-two days in jail. Afterwards, she did a drug rehab course. Currently, she told the jury, she is on the following medications: methadone, Xanax, doxepin and Vyvanse. This was a second moment when the trial of a British socialite tunnelled a shaft of light down into the bleak bedrock of American life in the twenty-first century. No American dream for Carolyn; none at all.

Enter defence attorney Jeffrey Pagliuca. He read out Carolyn's surname by mistake. He'd also read out the true first name of the first female witness, 'Jane'.

Pagliuca is extraordinarily fluent, brutal even, when flaying the skin of a woman who left school at the age of fourteen. He brought up a 2007 interview Carolyn had given to the FBI, before the infamous sweetheart deal that saw Epstein serve a farcically short time in prison for being a serial paedophile.

The mechanics of this are worth noting: time and again Pagliuca would rattle out the document number, the page, the paragraph, a particular sentence and then stick it to Carolyn: 'If we can show the witness 005, page 1, third paragraph, first sentence, please . . .' As she stumbled to reconcile what the FBI noted down more than a decade ago with her evidence for this trial, the attorney was kind of suggesting – without actually articulating it – that when there was a discrepancy in her evidence she had either been lying then or was lying now.

Lost in the legal weeds, Carolyn started to retreat into her own misery, sometimes saying 'I don't recall', sometimes barking at him like a cornered animal, sometimes muttering a mute sob.

Watching how Ghislaine's defence lawyers earnt their big money, how they used their wits to trash sad and broken women, my pity for Ghislaine Maxwell shrivelled with every passing minute. Despite Pagliuca at his worst, Carolyn kept coming back at him and didn't back down on the central point: that she had been sexually abused by Jeffrey Epstein and Ghislaine Maxwell when she was fourteen years old. She came across as a broken, troubled but wholly authentic human being.

Pagliuca noted that Carolyn had been paid $3.25m from Epstein's estate after the paedophile's suicide. Pagliuca prodded Carolyn as to whether there was an 'incentive for you to stick to your story' after she got her money. Carolyn shot back: 'The only thing Ms Maxwell was involved in was fondling my breast and my buttocks, and for that my soul is broken and so is my heart. Money will not ever fix what that woman has done to me.'

Prosecutor Comey stood up and took Carolyn back to the time when she was paid $300 a pop for giving sex massages to Epstein. 'What did she spend the money on?' 'I spent it on drugs,' she replied, weeping out loud at her own foolishness, at how she had been played.

'Did anyone tell you what to say here?' Comey asked.

'No . . . What she did was wrong.'

Not long afterwards, the prosecution put up a J.P. Morgan banker, who said that Epstein banked with them. Epstein paid Ghislaine $18,300,000 in 1999; $5,000,000 in 2002; and $7,400,000 on 15 June 2007 for a green executive Sikorsky 57c6 helicopter for Air Ghislaine Inc. So Ghislaine had received $30m in three dollops from Epstein when he was very much alive. A victim, perhaps, but a very rich one. So, once more the idea of a gold-digger hung in the air, but this time the boot was on the other foot.

Carolyn could have been a fantasist, generating fake memories of sexual abuse. But a witness took the stand who bore her out, her one-time boyfriend Shawn. Like his ex, he didn't go for full anonymity but asked to be identified by his first name only. Asked to describe their courting, Shawn was matter-of-fact: 'drive around; smoke pot'. Readers will be aware that West Palm Beach, inland, away from the ocean, is where the trailer trash live; Palm Beach island was home to the likes of Jeffrey Epstein and Donald Trump, mansion trash. Shawn was asked to explain the difference: 'Money's no object over there.' He said that he and his crowd very rarely ventured into Palm Beach because 'I didn't have enough money to buy anything in the gas station.'

But he started going to Palm Beach a lot more often when he drove his fourteen-year-old girlfriend, Carolyn, so that she could give sex massages to Jeffrey Epstein. The problem was that Carolyn was routinely paid something like $300 in $100 bills and back in West Palm Beach 'they don't accept hundred-dollar bills', Shawn said. It was the kind of grim financial reality check that one felt the jury would recognise from their own experience; a third window into the harshness of life for America's great unrich.

I have no great vivid recollection of Shawn's physical presence but his voice sticks in the mind: it had a slight but discernible Deep South tang, as flat as flat can be, devoid of any expression or nuance. Most of the time when he agreed with an attorney, he would just say: 'Yes, Ma'am.' There's no way that Shawn would be faking his evidence. He just was not that kind of person.

Shawn was cheating on Carolyn at the time with two other girlfriends. He pimped out all three to Ghislaine and Epstein. Of Carolyn, he said: 'She was a child', one who, 'only had two jobs ever. She worked at Arby's [a US fast-food combine] and she worked for Jeffrey [Epstein].' He met Epstein once in the driveway of the El Brillo Way house when the multi-millionaire showed off his Shelby Cobra sports car to the boy from the wrong side of the causeway. People from the house would phone Carolyn, her mother and him to arrange massage appointments. He would routinely wait around an hour before Carolyn would emerge with $300. He remembered that at one point Carolyn got a present of lingerie delivered by FedEx, a gift from Epstein.

Later, a FedEx worker produced the waybill proving the link

between Carolyn, her address and Epstein's office in New York and the year in which she was fourteen. A small detail, you might think, but this was evidence of commerce between states, buttressing the prosecution's argument that this was federal crime.

Shawn later went to prison for a few years for unlawful possession of a gun. He told the court that he no longer had any contact with Carolyn. In the bleakness of his testimony, it was easy to overlook the big picture: that her loveless convict ex-boyfriend had corroborated her story.

Period.

When I arrived in New York for the trial, I started tweeting bits and pieces about the case and a new podcast I was making; Hunting Ghislaine: The Trial. An American journalist got in touch with me via my website, noting that I was in Manhattan. She wanted to meet me because of Belarus. I had been there undercover in 2012, written a short book, *Big Daddy*, about the dictator who rules the country, Alexander Lukashenko, and had recently been interviewed for a podcast called The Hated and the Dead. She wrote: 'I heard your episode on Lukashenko for The Hated and the Dead, and I would love to talk to you about your work related to the financial institutions that keep authoritarians like him wealthy . . . Will you have time for a coffee or a limoncello, on me, while you are in the city?'

On Twitter, The Hated and the Dead podcast has ninety-seven followers. For her to have listened to it, to have worked out that I believe the tragedy of Belarus is under-reported and that my favourite shot is limoncello was perceptive – very. We arranged to meet in an Italian restaurant she chose, had dinner, then went to a bar. The Italian was high-end, not the kind most freelance journalists would choose. She was an attractive woman but not in the least bit interested in Belarus. She did not ask me for any of my contacts in the old and new opposition. She did have a book with her, a series of essays on Nabokov, the author of *Lolita*. The moment I saw it I said, with my characteristic diplomacy: 'What are you reading that rubbish for?'

I went to the loo, switched on the recorder on my phone and

secretly taped our conversation. She seemed far more interested in Ghislaine Maxwell than Belarus and her stance was unusual: that Ghislaine had been wronged. After a time, I explained that she hadn't asked about Belarus, and that I didn't agree with her about Ghislaine. I gave her my share of the money for the drinks, made my excuses and left. It was odd – very.

chapter thirteen

The Church of BugsBunnyology

How do you defend Ghislaine Maxwell? The obvious strategy would be to paint a chasm between Jeffrey Epstein and his evil works and Ghislaine Maxwell, innocent and unaware of the true nature of the man. To scotch that, the prosecution put up a number of FBI officers, one of whom had been in charge of the raid on Jeffrey Epstein's mansion in Manhattan in the summer of 2019, seizing computer hard drives and boxes of CDs, a second who had gone through the digital treasure. The jury and the media were then treated to Epstein and Ghislaine's personal photo album, showing images that had not been aired in the public domain before. The chain of undated photographs starts when Ghislaine still looks markedly young, in her early thirties, placing them from the early 1990s, say 1992; the magic Epstein money tree offerings go up to 2007, locking Ghislaine firmly inside Epstein's world for fifteen years, cross-hatching the years when the four victims say they were sexually abused. For Ghislaine, there is no way out. The money and the photos paint a damning image of long-term social and financial intimacy that makes the suggestion that she knew nothing of the true nature of the man absurd.

But the photographs are not just damning. They're also profoundly sad. You're looking at, looking into, flicking through, the photo album of a dead man and a deeply troubled woman when they were still very much in love. Or, rather, she in love with him.

The prosecution submitted the photos with no dates or places, but there's an early one when Ghislaine looks very young, still in

her twenties or very early thirties, riding on the back of a motor-
bike driven by Epstein; neither are wearing crash helmets. In none
of the photographs does their essential dynamic change: she's got
the hots for him; he isn't bothered. The 'Easy Riders' photo looks
as though it was shot around the start of their love affair in 1991
or 1992: the precise years may be wrong but that era. His hands
are clasped on the handlebars, manly, in control; she's riding
pillion, her hands on his ribs. He is in a black jumper, she's wearing a pale green shirt. Epstein is growling at the camera, a wolf
beginning to take notice; she is laughing at the comedy of the
moment, but you can see that she is really in love with him. More
than any other moment during the trial, this photograph led me
to feel real sorrow for Ghislaine. There is an innocent joy about
Ghislaine's expression that is, now that we know what we know,
kind of heart-breaking. Her love for this man was real. It has
indeed ruined her life.

But that of too many others, too.

There are shots of them skiing somewhere, then one of them
enjoying drinks on a veranda that looks like it was taken at the
Palm Beach house. Another shows them lounging in a field, with a
dog, people, Epstein holding a pair of ear defenders in his hand,
suggesting that this might have been taken at the shooting weekend at Sandringham when they were guests of Prince Andrew in
2000. The next interesting one is of the couple sitting in a log cabin
somewhere, her hand resting on his knee. It turns out it's not any
old log cabin but Glenbeg and there is a picture of the Queen sitting
in that self-same spot, part of her Balmoral estate in Scotland.

Perhaps the tackiest is of Ghislaine, looking significantly older
than she does in the 'Easy Riders' photo, sitting on a fur pouffe
opposite Epstein on the Lolita Express massaging his naked right
foot, the buttons of her blouse undone, her cleavage leaving little
to the imagination, staring directly into the camera while her
master's eyes are semi-closed in exquisite rapture. There's another
shot in the same series that shows Jean-Luc Brunel on the next
seat along to Epstein, dating the picture roughly from the start of
the millennium or later. A second photo shows Ghislaine with her

arms locked around Epstein, in the background the dock of the bay. It's somewhere hot but hard to tell where, exactly.

A third captures Ghislaine kissing Epstein on the cheek, the background suggesting somewhere in the south of France. There's a car with a French number plate and four matelots wearing the white bonnets centred with a distinctive red bobbly bit of the Bagad de Lann-Bihoué, the French naval bagpipe band, originally from Brittany. Their daft hats make them look like Bakewell tarts. I put that photo up on Twitter and within minutes someone called Dave Standard had geo-located it to St Tropez. Then Philippe Berry, a French reporter, confirmed the location and suggested that the photo was most likely taken at the 'Bravade', an annual local festival, on 16 May 2002.

In the photo, Ghislaine is needily affectionate, he's guarded, tolerating her but colder. Same old; same old. We know Epstein and Ghislaine were lovers up to around 1997 and then, from the email traffic dug out by the researchers for BBC *Panorama*, that another woman steps into his life. From the evidence of this photo, if the 2002 dating is correct, the love affair is back on, as least as far as Ghislaine is concerned.

There's a shot of the two of them in a helicopter together when they're much older than the 'Easy Riders' photo; the roofing webbing material and the seat-belt she's wearing do not suggest an executive helicopter but something military, so it's not impossible that the photo was taken in Colombia in 2002 where Ghislaine was said by Vikram the Dog Torturer to have blown up a tank.

The last witness who says she was sexually molested by both Epstein and Ghislaine was Annie Farmer. Thus far, the court had heard from three women who had all confessed to addiction problems. Annie, forty-two, told the jury she had got a PhD and used the phrase 'pro bono', causing a lawyer to ask her to explain what the Latin meant: that your lawyer works for free, out of the goodness of his or her heart, if such an entity exists.

Annie was different; Annie was just the same. Her story was that she was sixteen, living with her mum and younger sister in

Arizona. The prosecution showed photographs of her at the time, a beautiful, blonde, thin, pale young woman. Her parents had got divorced and money was tight. Her older sister, Maria, was working as a receptionist in Epstein's mansion in Manhattan. In December 1995, Epstein paid for Annie to fly to New York to spend time with her sister. Ghislaine wasn't around, presumably in London where brothers Ian and Kevin spent an anxious Christmas waiting to learn that they had been found not guilty of defrauding the *Mirror* pensioners of £400 million.

Back in Arizona, word reached Annie that Epstein was interested in paying for her education through university. In America, such a golden opportunity should never be missed. To begin with everything went beautifully. She and sister Maria went to his home, he was friendly, down-to-earth, dressed casually, handing out champagne: 'I had never been to a private residence so large.' He treated them to tickets to *A Night at the Opera*, making sure his driver drove them to the theatre. A few days later he took them to see the science fiction movie *12 Monkeys* about a plague from the future: 'When the lights went down . . . he reached over and put his hand on the arm rest between our seats and started to reach for my hand and caressed my hand, interlocking his hand with mine and holding my hand.'

Annie recalled him crossing his legs, so that he 'was rubbing the bottom of my shoe and rubbing my foot and my leg . . . I was very surprised and anxious. I felt sick to my stomach. It was not something I was expecting. I noticed that when he interacted with my sister he'd stop doing that. When he was looking forward again he would return to touching me.'

At the time she kept a diary and the jury heard an entry about Epstein's creepy behaviour at the movies, 'the one thing that kind of weirded me out'. But Annie stayed mum about it because she did not want her sister to lose her job.

In the spring of 1996 Annie was invited to spend a weekend at Epstein's Zorro ranch in New Mexico with twenty or so other young men and women, all potential recipients of an Epstein travel scholarship scheme. Annie didn't get this directly from

Epstein but through her mother, Jan Swain, who later testified to that effect. The key facts that swung the trip for Annie and her mother were: (1) the presence of the score of other students; (2) her sister Maria was coming too; and (3) Epstein assured Annie's mother, that his 'wife' Ghislaine would be there too.

But when Annie got there, she found there were only three guests, Epstein, then aged forty-three, Ghislaine, then thirty-five, and herself, sixteen. The New Mexico desert is one of the creepiest places on earth. I know because, by strange coincidence, I have been there myself. About a hundred miles due west of Epstein's Zorro ranch is Trementina Base, where the Church of Scientology have sealed the wisdom of L. Ron Hubbard on discs of gold in an argon-sealed, H-bomb-proof vault. To make things easier for space aliens, they have put up two large traffic signs, only to be viewed from space, alerting bug-eyed monsters to the Church's secret base. If you're that interested, you can see the short film that ex-Scientologist Marc Headley and I made about the trip. It's on YouTube under 'Church of Fear' trailer.[1] I found the desert empty, creepy and scary. To be there, on your own, with only Epstein and Ghislaine for company, must have been quite terrifying.

The couple took her horse-riding and into town to go shopping. Annie felt a confusing mess of emotions: cool that the two adults paid her attention, went to the stores with her; creepy that they wanted to spend time alone with her. Ghislaine bought Annie a fancy pair of black cowboy boots she has to this day. Annie explained to the jury how Epstein and Ghislaine mucked about like teenagers, with Ghislaine trying to pull down Epstein's trousers as they queued up to buy tickets at the cinema. They went to see *Primal Fear*, a 1996 movie starring Richard Gere about child sex abuse and the Catholic Church. Epstein sat in the middle between Ghislaine and Annie: 'He right away began to hold my hand, caress it, rub on my foot and on my arm . . . It was more blatant' than the previous 'weirding out' in New York during *12 Monkeys*.

When the threesome got back to Zorro, Ghislaine encouraged Annie to give him a foot massage: 'I felt very uncomfortable . . . I

did not want to be touching his feet.' After that, Ghislaine asked
Annie if she herself had had a massage, and when she said no,
Maxwell insisted on giving her one. They went to Annie's room,
Ghislaine pulling out a fold-up massage table. She put a sheet on
top and told Annie to get on it.

'I was wearing nothing. She told me to get undressed and lay
under the sheet and I did,' Annie said. 'She started rubbing my
body, rubbing my back and she's making small talk and then at
some point she had me roll over so I was laying on my back. She
pulled the sheet down and exposed my breasts and started rubbing
on my chest and upper breasts'.

Prosecutor Lara Pomerantz asked what was Annie's reaction:
'When she pulled down the sheet I felt frozen because it didn't
make sense to me. I was surprised and I wanted so badly to get off
of the table and have that massage be done.'

Asked who was in the room, Annie said just Maxwell, but 'the
door to the room was open and I was fearful, especially at that
moment. I had this sense that Epstein could see me.'

Creepy and creepier.

The next morning as Annie lay in bed, Epstein bounced into
her room, got into her bed and proclaimed that he wanted to
cuddle her. Annie said that he wrapped his arms around her and
pressed his body against hers. She went to the bathroom, locked
the door and hid: 'I wanted to be in there long enough that this
whole situation would be over.'

Later, she tried to engage Ghislaine on the whole point of her
being there, to talk through education possibilities, in particular
to chat about an English literature essay she was working on. But
Epstein and Ghislaine couldn't give a damn: 'They had a very
different interest in me. She seemed very disinterested . . . She
didn't care.'

That summer, Epstein paid for Annie to go to Thailand and
Vietnam. The jury was shown a photo of her mucking about with
elephants somewhere in the jungle, classic gap-year stuff. She
could never have gone on such a trip without Epstein's generosity
but she hoped never to meet the couple again.

Defence attorney Laura Menninger sauntered into the attorney's glass box and battle commenced. Annie was a strong woman, an academic, not easily knocked off her perch. The argument the defence used against her was that her contact with Ghislaine was minimal, non-sexual and that she, too, had gold in her sights. Menninger's first line of attack was to create clear blue water between Ghislaine and Epstein. Ghislaine had not organised her ticket to New York; nor had she been present there. Menninger established that there had been no sexual activity in Epstein's New York home. No one had shown her vibrators, massagers or anything like that in Epstein's Manhattan palace. Nor had Ghislaine organised her visit to New Mexico; Ghislaine had not called Annie's mother to lie about the large group of fellow students going to Zorro too; neither had she run the hare that Annie's college education could be funded by the rich man. All of that was the work of Epstein or his office so Ghislaine was in the clear.

Then it was time for the court to focus on the cowboy boots.

> **Menninger:** 'You mentioned the boots. But on the trip you spent a significant amount of time horseback riding.'
>
> **Annie (heroically):** 'Is that a question?'
>
> **Menninger:** 'You told the FBI that in 2006, right?'
>
> **Annie:** 'Yes.'
>
> **Menninger:** 'Are these the boots?'
>
> **Annie:** 'Yes.'
>
> **Menninger:** 'You decided to wear the boots, even when you knew they were evidence. You wore them frequently?'
>
> **Annie:** 'I didn't wear them to work. I wore them when I was two-stepping.'

It's not the done thing to clap a witness in a courtroom, but if I could have done, I would have led a standing ovation for Annie Farmer. What the defence was trying to do, it seemed, was to make

Annie out to be less credible or even dishonest in that if she was really upset about what had happened in New Mexico she wouldn't have worn the boots. But Annie was having none of that. She had been abused, but it did not stop her wearing the boots. Yet again in the trial, class had reared its unpretty head. If you have a ton of money, you can afford to throw away boots with ugly memories. If you're poor, you can't. I put all the crap about boots as a win for the prosecution, as did all the other reporters I spoke to.

And then there was the diary. Menninger stuck the boot in – not the cowboy boots, obviously – noting that although Epstein's weird hand-holding and footsie game in New York made Annie's diary, the much more serious alleged abuse in New Mexico was not written up. In their darkly comic but always compelling podcast on the Epstein–Ghislaine saga, TrueAnon, hosts Liz Franczak and Brace Belden make the point that the first three victims all presented as middle-aged women. So did Annie Farmer, but as Liz and Brace say, the loopy teenage girl handwriting in her journal takes you right back to the world of a sixteen-year-old girl.[2] They both found it entirely reasonable for Annie to write up the weird stuff in New York but leave out the darker happenings in New Mexico. And so do I. It's not what you put in teenage diaries.

Menninger's third play was more brutal: that what had happened in New Mexico wasn't sexual; that Annie was making it up. The attorney pointed out that Ghislaine didn't touch Annie's nipples but rather her upper chest. Then Menninger moved on to Epstein coming into her bedroom and the forced cuddling session at the Zorro ranch.

> **Menninger:** 'You testified on direct [Annie's evidence to the prosecution] that he pressed his body into you, is that right?'
> **Annie:** 'That's right.'
> **Menninger:** 'You did not feel an erect penis in your back?'
> **Annie:** 'I did not – I do not – I couldn't say whether he had an erect penis.'

Menninger: 'You do not recall him pressing an erect penis into your back, correct?'

Annie: 'Yeah, I recall him pressing his body. I do not recall an erect penis.'

On and on it went, Menninger the 'Erect Penis' obsessive digging up a previous interview Annie had given the prosecution, seeking to undermine her evidence that anything of note had happened at Zorro. But Annie was adamant: she had not been raped in New Mexico but she had been sexually abused. After a break, when Menninger got into the glass box, Annie smiled at her. Of all the four victims, Annie was the strongest, the least perturbed by the defence's tricksiness.

Manhood had thus far put on a pretty dismal showing at the trial. There had been Epstein, dead, but a dark presence throughout; the pilot who saw nothing; the butler who had seen the dildos and the women who looked too young but had never dared to do anything about it; Shawn, Carolyn's pimp, who stole an Xbox and watched the mother of his child go to prison for it. But when Annie Farmer's high-school boyfriend, David Mulligan, took the stand, masculinity got a breather. The prosecution went through his CV, seeing that he had a degree in educational psychology. Do you still do that now? 'No, I'm a baker,' said David, giving the court a rare moment of light comedy as welcome as rain in the desert.

And then it got a lot more grim very quickly. Anne had gone to New Mexico in the spring of 1996 and she and David became more than friends that autumn. Annie told him that Epstein had 'touched her leg in the theatre and that she didn't want to say anything because Epstein was helping her sister Maria's artistic career'.

Did Annie tell him that Ghislaine Maxwell had touched her breasts during the massage? 'Yes,' said David.

What had happened at Zorro came up when he and Annie, young lovers, started to become intimate, David told the court. He didn't go into detail; he didn't have to. He corroborated Annie's story to the hilt.

Since Ghislaine Maxwell had vanished off the face of the earth in July 2019, I had been waiting to hear her side of the story. The opening of the defence on trial day eleven was Ghislaine's big moment, the day the world could first hear her witnesses speak truth to the heavy artillery of the prosecution case.

First on was Cimberly Espinosa. Cimberley – with a C, but pronounced as with a K – was a charming, sweet-voiced, nice Hispanic lady, still beautiful in middle age, with a sunny expression out of kilter with the mood of the courtroom. She had been Ghislaine's personal assistant back in the day, before leaving after 9/11 to go home to her native California. She had worked in Jeffrey Epstein's Madison Avenue office from 1996 to 2002 and had never seen anything untoward. But the victims – Jane, Kate, Carolyn and Annie – never said anything happened to them in Epstein's office on Madison Avenue. Carolyn never went to New York. Most of the sexual abuse happened at the Palm Beach house. In the cross-examination, the prosecution asked Espinosa:

'Have you ever been to Palm Beach?'
'No.'
'No further questions.'

The second witness was a travel agent who booked flights for Team Epstein from 1999 onwards. Jane, Kate and Farmer all flew on Epstein's dime in the mid-1990s. That is, the travel agent's evidence turned on events too late in the day to have any bearing on the trial. Carolyn never flew because she was, in her mother's view, too young at fourteen to get a passport. So the travel agent was irrelevant to the killer point a good defence would seek to make: that the victims and/or Epstein and Maxwell were in a different place when the abuse was supposed to have taken place.

The third witness was Professor Elizabeth Loftus, a psychologist and specialist in false memory. An expert witness in perhaps as many as three hundred trials, she asserted that fake facts could be implanted in people: 'False memories . . . can be very vivid, detailed. People can be confident about them, people can be emotional about them, even though they're false.' She told the jury, 'emotion is no guarantee that the memory is authentic'.

Prosecutor Lara Pomerantz noted that Loftus was being paid $600 an hour by the defence and that she'd written a book, *Witness for the Defense*.

'You haven't written a book called "Impartial Witness", right?' said Pomerantz, whose voice is sometimes so high-pitched she sounds like a very scary bat.

'No,' said Loftus, glumly.

Pomerantz moved on to Loftus's research.

> **Pomerantz (lethally):** 'One of your experiments
>   involves Bugs Bunny, right?'
> **Loftus:** 'A bunny.'
> **Pomerantz:** 'Bugs Bunny?'
> **Loftus:** 'Bugs Bunny, yes.'

The prosecutor reminded the professor of one of her research studies that had shown that 16 per cent of people said they'd seen Bugs Bunny at Disneyland, a false memory because the fictional rabbit is a Warner Bros character. Loftus defended the study, showing that 16 per cent of people claim that they shook his hand: 'others claim they touched his tail or touched his ear or heard him say, "What's up, Doc?"'

The reporters in the overflow rooms started to snigger, then giggle out loud. Hanging in the air was the thought that 84 per cent didn't see Bugs Bunny at the wrong theme park, that this was featherweight stuff, that getting the prof to go 'What's up, Doc' was a nice piece of legal footwork by prosecutor Pomerantz, that she had made the star defence witness out to be something from the Looney Tunes back catalogue.

Next, we were on to a second study, where Loftus and co. had tried to implant the false memory of people having had a rectal enema. No one falsely remembered having had a rectal enema when they hadn't had one, the point being that people remember trauma – horrible, nasty things – or not having trauma clearly.

False memory, the Church of BugsBunnyology, did not have a good day in court.

At the end of the defence's first day, once judge and jury had left the courtroom, Ghislaine was seen holding her hands up in despair at her fancy attorneys who have cost her, according to her own estimate, some $7m. We had listened to a nice lady who worked in an office, an irrelevant travel agent and a professor who had been made to look a fool.

Yes, the prosecution have got to prove their case and juries in US federal trials must be unanimous, that is twelve to nil, and it only takes one fruitcake on the jury to throw the trial, but at the end of her first big day, things looked bleak for Ghislaine, as bleak as bleak can be.

No wonder Ghislaine seemed distraught.

The defence's second day was no better than the first. It got off to a wretched start when one potential witness refused to respond to a subpoena, a second said they would take the fifth and so was not called, and a third proved kind of pointless. He was Kevin Moran, the pub landlord of the Nag's Head, the boozer immediately opposite Ghislaine's house in Belgravia, London. In the legal argy-bargy before the jury were summoned that morning, the defence team said that he would testify that Ghislaine only lived there from 1997 onwards, supposedly giving the lie to Kate's evidence that she had sex with Epstein there in 1994. Kate, who had been seventeen at the time, had said that Ghislaine wanted a massage and led her upstairs to a room where Epstein stood naked, closing the door behind her.

Ghislaine's team produced land records showing she took ownership of the house in 1997. Before accepting them as evidence, Judge Nathan asked if Maxwell might have lived there without owning the house, snapping: 'They don't rent places in London?'

They do.

The prosecution were on the case, flagging a deposition Ghislaine had given in 2019, in which she said she lived at the house from 1992 onwards. Her lawyers said she had made a mistake because she did not have records in front of her. The jury weren't in on this discussion but Ghislaine's minor loss of memory for a precise point in a time sequence struck me as exactly the same kind of mistake the four victims might have been accused of. That's not false memory for a horrible event, but the very human flaw of getting a precise sequence wrong. Team Ghislaine said she had not lived on Kinnerton Street but somewhere else, close by, in 1994. Even if that were true, so what? The actual post-code of the house in Belgravia was not the issue, but what had happened inside it. And if Ghislaine herself had got her true address wrong in 1992, that sank the whole argument. None of the reporters were surprised when the defence gave up on arguing for the pub landlord.

At the next break Josh Chaffin from the *Financial Times* turned to me and said, 'Nag's Head?' – suggesting that we go there for a pint. I grinned at him – Josh is gloriously funny, the only person I know who's written a zombie novel set inside the European Union headquarters in Brussels, and the idea of a drink inside the Nag's was kind of tempting. On reflection, writing this section of the book a few weeks later, it's true to say that I have got smashed out of my head in some of the worst drinking establishments, whole planet. But the Nag's Head in Belgravia is not my kind of boozer.

As far as the reporters in court were concerned, it looked to us that Team Ghislaine were struggling to find anyone who could lay a glove on the prosecution case.

The key witness that second defence day was Eva Dubin, a former Miss Sweden, ex-girlfriend of Epstein and long-time friend of Ghislaine. A handsome woman at sixty, she had dated Epstein from 1983 until 1991, for eight years. He had encouraged her to drop her modelling career and paid her way through medical school so that she could become a doctor. She had been on his private planes many times, never seen any sexual abuse, never seen anything untoward.

After she split up with Epstein, she went out with, then married Glenn Dubin, who has become a Wall Street Master of the Universe worth unknown billions of dollars. The Dubins have three children who called Epstein 'Uncle F'.

But the spell of Happy Families with Uncle F was broken by the defence team itself. Shown a photograph of her youngest daughter with Epstein, which the reporters could not see but was shared with the jury under seal, Eva appeared shocked.

Pagliuca asked: 'I'm assuming you know that Mr Epstein had this picture.'

Eva looked grim as she said: 'I have never seen this picture before.'

Shown a second photograph, this time featuring her eldest daughter, which had been on one of Epstein's bookshelves, she said: 'I have never seen this photo before.' I remember thinking that this was lousy planning by the defence to have managed to upset their own witness.

For the prosecution, Jane had given evidence that she had taken part in orgies with other young women and one of those was called Eva. When asked about the flight log for a May 1998 trip from Palm Beach to Teterboro, New Jersey, that included Jane, Epstein, Ghislaine and Eva, she couldn't remember the flight.

Pagliuca showed Eva a photo of Jane. Eva said, 'I don't recall ever meeting this person.'

'Have you ever been in a group sexual encounter with the person that we are calling Jane?'

'Absolutely not,' Eva replied.

When it was Prosecutor Alison Moe's turn to speak from the glass box, it was clear she was in no mood to take prisoners. She got Eva to confirm her name was Eva, then asked: 'Are you the only person named Eva in the whole wide world?'

Eva conceded it was a very common name in Scandinavia, in northern Europe, in the United States; that she had met many people called Eva. Pagliuca popped up to object to the relevance of the line of questioning. Judge Nathan overruled him as if she were squashing a bug.

'Do you know the first name of every person Jeffrey Epstein ever met?' asked Moe, her voice oozing sarcasm.

'Absolutely not,' said Eva.

But as the cross-examination got under way, the defence's

weakness became more starkly etched. Prosecutor Moe asked, silkily: 'Dr Dubin, are you having some issues with your memory?'

'Yes, I do,' said Eva. 'It's very hard for me to remember from far back. Sometimes I can't remember things from last month . . . my family notices it.'

What's the good of a defence witness if she tells the prosecution that her memory is shot to pieces?

Back in the day, Eva Dubin was loyal to Epstein to – no – beyond a fault. After he had been convicted of being a paedophile in 2008, Eva and Glenn Dubin invited Epstein to their home for Thanksgiving in 2009. Eva wrote to Epstein's probation officer: 'I am 100 per cent comfortable with Jeffrey Epstein around my children.'

Being a child under the law and comfortable around Epstein was not in everyone's gift. In 2019, a slew of court records relating to Virginia Roberts Giuffre suing Epstein were unsealed. One story from that source turned on what the Dubins' butler saw. The billionaire couple's one-time house manager, Rinaldo Rizzo, said that in 2005 he found a fifteen-year-old girl from Sweden sobbing her heart out in the Dubins' kitchen in their house in New York. Shaking and crying, she told Rizzo and his wife that she had just come back from a trip to Little St Jeffs. This is what the butler said: 'She proceeded to tell my wife and I . . . "I was on the island and there was Ghislaine, and there was Sarah," and she said, "They asked me for sex. I said no."'

The girl claimed that Sarah Kellen had taken her passport off her and Ghislaine had threatened her not to tell anyone what happened. Rizzo said that he stopped talking to the girl once Eva Dubin walked into the room.[3] Eva was not questioned about this but, as an old-school reporter, I think she should have been.

After a break, with the jury out, the issue of whether Ghislaine would give evidence herself came up. In an English accent so upper-cut it could chisel bone china, she told the judge: 'Your honour, the government has not proven its case beyond a reasonable doubt and so there is no need for me to testify.'

The moment I heard that, I thought, that's the jury's job.

After two not full days, the defence was done. In the lift on the way out, I was holding forth to some other reporters, saying that the reason there is no defence is because there is no defence; that is, Ghislaine Maxwell is guilty, full stop.

Then the lift door opened and her sister Isabel Maxwell got in and we all fell silent.

chapter fourteen

To the Bone Pit . . .

Guilty, five times over, Ghislaine Maxwell in manacles and shackles sat in the sweat box as it crawled over Brooklyn Bridge along with the rest of the rush-hour little people she used to fly over, saying a last goodbye to the imperial city's billion-dollar stalagmites. The one-time Princess Mwah-Mwah was now the Demon Queen, facing sixty-five years, the rest of her life in prison, not some Disneyland of right-wing fantasy but a bone pit of the bad, the mad and the broken locked up in faecal squalor until old age and then the only end of age.[1]

She has a secret key that could unlock her shackles. What if she sings, tells the feds what she knows, gives up the over-mighty men who, along with her one-time lover Jeffrey Epstein, abused women more child than adult back in her pomp? She could cut her jail time down to ten years and be out in seven, thanks to good behaviour.

But to do that, Ghislaine would have to admit that she had been Epstein's $30m pimp, that she treated a host of under-age women as nothings, trash, that she did great wrong, that she was sorry.

No sign of that. Given the dark chasm between how Ghislaine's life had been and the wretched place she was in now, I felt some pity for her, but her lack of remorse, her failure to address reality, her unwillingness to express a smidgen of regret to her victims hardened the heart.

Her first chance at coming clean was in 2002 when reporter Vicky Ward was checking out Annie Farmer's story that she had been sexually abused in New Mexico when Ghislaine gave her a massage with Epstein watching. To Ward, Ghislaine said: 'I can guarantee that I didn't give her a massage ... It is wrong! ... Disgusting.'

Having sat through Annie Farmer's evidence, I had no doubt that Ghislaine was lying then and, through her not-guilty plea, lying now.

Ghislaine's second chance to set evil to rights was in October 2005 when the Palm Beach police department raided Epstein's house on El Brillo Way. The socialite who got a countess to write a fifty-eight-page manual on such things as how full a box of tissues had to be before it was thrown away never noticed the fresh child factory production line of under-age girls coming and going, more than a hundred of them according to the brilliant reporting of Julie K. Brown. But Ghislaine would have heard about the police raid, surely? Would, perhaps, have wondered what had happened to all the house's computer hard drives, including, one might think, her own, when they were mysteriously removed before the raid, as if a bent copper in on the police investigation had forewarned Team Epstein? Nothing from Ghislaine then.

Not a word in 2007 when she got her final dollop of Epstein's $30m, a single $7m transfer for a helicopter to be owned by her own company. Silence in 2008 when her ex was convicted of procuring an under-age girl for prostitution, effectively that he was a paedophile. She was still taking his money in 2009, by her own account. In 2016 she swore on oath, in a civil suit brought by Virginia Roberts Giuffre, that there had been no under-age sex, nothing to see here, folks. She was still watching the paedophile's back.

Silence, too, in 2019 when Epstein was arrested a second time in July. Silence one month later when he killed himself. Just like her father, Ghislaine did not face the music. Instead, she ran to her hideout in New Hampshire where she wrapped her mobile phone in tinfoil, only to be caught and tried.

She could have told the jury to their faces that she was inno-cent, that the four women who said they had been abused were making it up, as were their three boyfriends, as was the butler,

Juan Alessi. They were all liars. The chain of photographs showing an intimacy with Epstein from the early 1990s: all lies too. The chain of money transfers proving that Epstein paid her $30m over eight years for being a fancy janitor: more lies.

The twin chains of photographs and money lock her to her paedophile for fifteen years. Had she dared to take the stand, then she would have had to explain to the prosecution exactly why Jane and Kate and Carolyn and Annie and Matt and Shawn and David and Alessi and the photographs and the money had false memories. Dollars in their tens of millions are not easily forgotten, as the banker witness from J. P. Morgan proved. The victims, too, had no reason to make things up, still less to go through the torture of cross-examination, of two of them having their full names read out by Pagliuca, unless they came to court to tell the truth. Nor had the ex-boyfriends reason to lie; nor had the butler. Had Ghislaine taken the stand, she would have been ripped to shreds and she knew it. Instead, she held her tongue, only telling the judge that the case against her had not been proved beyond reasonable doubt.

Her bark of arrogant command echoed her father, Robert Maxwell, the first monster in her life, a man who stole £400m from his pensioners, who took pride in pissing off the roof of his helicopter pad in the heart of London, who evacuated his bowels within earshot of reporters, who used to wipe his bottom with cloth towels and let the maids pick them up. Her pattern of denial over two decades suggests that his daughter will find it impossible to do a plea bargain with the feds and so her future the moment she was convicted looked impossibly bleak. And that could only be down to her, and the rest of the Maxwell family.

Though she was found guilty on five of the six charges, Kevin Maxwell said of her: 'she is not the Demon Queen'.

One can only ask the Maxwell family why did Epstein pay their sister $30m after they had stopped being lovers? They never address that question. Perhaps because they can't. The prosecution case was, simply put, that no sixteen-year-old girl would fly to the middle of nowhere in New Mexico to spend a weekend with

Epstein, but if her mother were told that Ghislaine Maxwell was going to be there, then they might. The same goes for the other three victims: Jane and Kate and Carolyn. Ghislaine got her $30m and in return she provided cover for the paedophile. I sat through the evidence and came to the conclusion that she was as guilty as sin. So did the other reporters. So did the jury.

That said, it made me deeply uneasy that while Maxwell was facing a long, slow, grey death inside, I was faced with two anxieties that she may have suffered an injustice.

The first is the question of perception, of viewpoint. Throughout this saga, not just the trial, I have always worried that we might be judging Ghislaine Maxwell unfairly, using the #MeToo glasses of 2022 to look at the world of the 1980s and 1990s. Ghislaine sketching the sketchers is, perhaps, a metaphor for that quandary: that if perception changes, so does reality. Sexual mores were quite different thirty years ago than they are today. That is true. But for a middle-aged woman to groom a fourteen-year-old girl to have sex with a middle-aged man was evil back then, is evil now.

The second anxiety is greater: that while Ghislaine faced life and death in jail, the alpha males in our dark fairy tale were walking free.

In a twenty-first-century version of Dante's *Inferno*, there are circles and circles of hell. On the outer circle are people who did not get too close but nevertheless had contact after Epstein's conviction in 2008. Step forward Amazon tsar Jeff Bezos, electric car wizard Elon Musk and Google honcho Sergey Brin. These three were at a billionaire's dinner in Long Beach, California, in 2011; so was Jeffrey Epstein.[2] That same year Microsoft creator Bill Gates was photographed at Epstein's home in Manhattan, and there is evidence of several other meetings too, leading to reporting that Melinda French Gates divorced him because of his friendship with Epstein.[3] Musk, Bezos, Gates and Brin have seven hundred billion dollars right there and none of them had the sense to work out that hanging out with a convicted paedophile does not look good.[4] They all deny wrongdoing.

There's the folk who did serious business with Epstein, people like Leon Black and Jes Staley, both of whom deny serious wrong-doing, both of whom had to step away from businesses they created because of their links to the paedophile. They deny wrongdoing.

And then in the inner circle of hell are the folk who flew on the Lolita Express or went to Little St Jeffs or palled around with Epstein and Ghislaine on many occasions. They all deny wrongdoing.

There is, of course, no suggestion that Presidents Bill Clinton and Donald Trump committed any wrongdoing. They both deny any wrongdoing.

Three men stand in their own little circle of hell. They, too, deny any wrongdoing. Jean-Luc Brunel denies wrongdoing but faces charges in France of having sex with minors. Harvard lawyer Alan Dershowitz vehemently denies wrongdoing. His primary accuser, Virginia Roberts Giuffre, stands by her story that she was required to have sex with him on multiple occasions. Her civil case against Dershowitz continues. Once again, Dershowitz denies any wrongdoing.

Virginia also accuses Prince Andrew, the Duke of York, saying she was forced to have sex with him three times in 2001. The prince strongly denies any wrongdoing.

The prince does not face criminal charges in London. This is because he denies Virginia's allegations and there is no compel-ling evidence of the sex act. There is, however, a difficult photo-graph for the prince taken in Ghislaine's house which shows him with his hand round Virginia's waist. She is wearing a cropped top. He says he has no memory of meeting Virginia and has suggested the photo may have been doctored. On criminal charges, legally, he is in a strong position: if Virginia was trafficked, he did not know of it or there is no evidence of that; she, at seventeen, was above the legal age of consent in Britain, sixteen; and the alleged sex acts took place two years before the Sexual Offence Act of 2003 which covers sex trafficking was passed. You can't try people for crimes before they are made law.

Virginia's civil suit against Prince Andrew in New York did not go well for the royal. At a pre-trial hearing in January 2022, his lawyers told Judge Kaplan that because the prince was a 'potential co-defendant' he was protected by a $500,000 deal between Epstein and Virginia in 2009. That is, the prince maintains his innocence while his lawyers were seeking to hide behind a deal made by a convicted paedophile. The prince's lawyers further argued that Virginia's case was vague. The judge knocked that back, telling them: 'that is a dog that is not going to hunt'.[5] A few days later Judge Kaplan rejected the attempts by the prince's lawyers to have the case struck out, setting out a schedule for a trial in the autumn of 2022. Buckingham Palace signalled its displeasure by announcing that Prince Andrew would no longer be able to use the title of 'His Royal Highness' in any official capacity and he would be stripped of all his military titles, a blow that the *Sunday Mirror* reported left him in tears.[6]

As this book went to press, the Queen died. Her seven decades of service to our country meant that her passing was genuinely mourned up and down the land. The very idea of a man on the stamps and the money seems absurd. The one great blot on her record was standing by her second son for far too long. That said, she signed off on the decision to strip Andrew of the HRH title. And a mother's love for a wayward son is a thing that afflicts rich and poor alike.

The prince's two primary defences to Virginia's claims, from his own mouth – first, that Virginia must be wrong that he had sex with her that night as he was not where she claims he was, but instead went to the Pizza Express with his daughters in Woking; second, that she said when they danced at Tramps nightclub he sweated disgustingly, and he can't sweat because he was shot at during the Falklands War – have led to derision. Headline writers made much of sweaty Andrew sweating it out, sweatily.

He denied any wrongdoing. In my personal view, his denials were as convincing as a gimp photographed in a gimp suit denying he's a gimp.

And then the prince settled. All his denials came to naught. If you're an innocent party, do you give millions to some chancer?

Has Virginia been telling the truth all along?

Ghislaine Maxwell was convicted on Wednesday 29 December 2021. One week later, her lawyers wrote to the judge calling for a mistrial because a juror, now known by his first names Scotty David, had told reporters that his experience of being sexually abused helped to sway the jury to convict. Some of them had expressed doubts because of concerns about false memory, that the victims could not remember details of the abuse. He had told his fellow jurors that he had vivid memories of abuse, but could not remember some aspects of it, just like the victims.

The problem is the answer Scotty David gave to one of the fifty questions potential jurors were asked at the pre-trial jury selection process was: had they been sexually abused? He ticked no and later realised that he should have ticked yes.

Ghislaine's defence lawyers argued that the juror was prejudiced against her and argued for a mistrial. In April, Judge Nathan threw that out, finding that the juror had made a mistake but had not lied. Ghislaine Maxwell was guilty, full stop.

In the meantime, Prince Andrew was stripped of most but not all of his royal titles and shuffled off into the dim twilight of his dim life. Jean-Luc Brunel hanged himself while awaiting trial in Paris.

In late June 2022 Ghislaine returned to court to hear some of the victims set out their agonies at her hands. Of the four of them, Annie Farmer's voice was the clearest when she told Judge Nathan: 'I ask you to bear in mind how Maxwell's unwillingness to acknowledge her crimes, her lack of remorse, and her repeated lies about her victims created the need for many of us to engage in a long fight for justice that has felt like a black hole.'

And then Ghislaine Maxwell addressed the court. Dressed in dowdy prison garb, her ankles shackled, her voice was prim, befitting her Marlborough public school education. Her manner was unsettled and unsettling, dabbing her hair, touching her neck and gazing at her twin sisters, Isabel and Christine and brother Kevin. Brothers Ian and Philip and sister Ann were no-shows.

Ghislaine said: 'Your Honour, it is hard for me to address the court after listening to the pain and anguish expressed today. The terrible impact on the lives of so many women is difficult to hear and even more difficult to absorb, both in its scale and extent. I acknowledge their suffering and empathise deeply with all of the victims in this case. I also acknowledge that I have been a victim of helping Jeffrey Epstein commit these crimes.'

Not a perp, but yet another victim. The crowning problem with this approach is that for at least ten years Ghislaine had denied the truth of what victims had been saying and that only months before her own lawyers had been trying to break them into little pieces. This was far too little, far too late. It was insulting. Judge Nathan looked on, impassive, her gown shimmering like the wing of a raven hoarse with the croak of doom.

Ghislaine continued: 'I realise I have been convicted of assisting Jeffrey Epstein to commit these crimes. My association with Epstein will permanently stain me. It is the biggest regret of my life that I ever met him.'

Once again, far too little, far too late. Had Ghislaine articulated this regret on the day he killed himself, then things might have turned out less bleakly for her. Instead, she had vanished.

Some of what she said was true enough: 'I believe Jeffrey Epstein fooled all of those in his orbit. His victims considered him a mentor, friend, lover. It is absolutely unfathomable today to think that was how he was viewed contemporaneously. His impact on all those close to him has been devastating. And today, those who even knew him briefly or never met him but were associated with someone who did, have lost relationships, jobs, and had their lives derailed. Jeffrey Epstein should have stood before you. In 2005. In 2009. And again in 2019. All the many times he was accused, charged, prosecuted.'

True.

'He should have spared victims the years of chasing justice.'

True, but not good enough. From 2005 onwards, Ghislaine could have helped Epstein's victims. Instead, she dallied and parried and, when deposed in 2016, told lies to cover up her own complicity.

'But today is ultimately not about Epstein. It is for me to be sentenced and for the victims to address me alone in court. To you I say: I am sorry for the pain you experienced.'

But not for the pain she made them experience. Then she slipped into self-pity.

'I hope my conviction along with my harsh incarceration brings you closure. I hope this brings the women who have suffered some measure of peace and faintly to help you put those experiences of so many years ago in a place that allows you to look forward and not back. I also acknowledge the pain this case has wrought to those I love, the many I held and still hold close, the relationships I have lost and will never be able to regain. It is my sincerest wish to all those in this courtroom and all those outside this courtroom that today brings a terrible chapter to an end. And to those of you who spoke here today and those who did not, may this day help you travel through darkness into the light.'

Judge Nathan was having none of Ghislaine's tea-towel aphorism banality. She called her actions 'heinous and predatory', telling the court Ghislaine 'worked with Epstein to select young victims who were vulnerable and played a pivotal role in facilitating sexual abuse'.

Her sentence? Twenty years. Noting that Ghislaine had received a $10 million bequest from Epstein after his death, the judge also fined her $750,000.

After the sentencing, Ghislaine's lawyer Bobbi Sternheim told the press that her client had been vilified, pilloried and would appeal the guilty verdict. Two weeks later Ghislaine sacked Sternheim, so the appeal will be led by someone else. In August 2022 news broke that Haddon, Morgan and Foreman, the Colorado based law firm where Laura Menninger and Jeffrey Pagliuca worked, were suing Ghislaine Maxwell, her brother Kevin and her estranged husband, Scott Borgerson, for $878,000 in unpaid fees.

Ghislaine may die in the bone pit. That seems harsh, cruel even, but no one who sat through the trial and watched her fancy lawyers pick great holes in the victims can forget that in persisting in her innocence – and therefore, their guilt as dishonest witnesses – Ghislaine was harsh and cruel to them, time and again. Reflecting on what Sarah Ramsden wrote, for those who knew the gracious

Ghislaine, twenty years may seem grotesquely unfair; for those who knew the conniving tyrant, twenty years may seem fair enough.

Ghislaine's father was a monster.

So was her lover.

Ghislaine was both the double victim of monsters and, to those without power and money and connections, a monster in her own right.

Thinking about Maxwell and Epstein and Ghislaine, a line from *The Great Gatsby* by F. Scott Fitzgerald comes to mind, how the rich 'smashed up things and creatures and then retreated back into their money'. Nothing good came of that. Or them.

The story of Ghislaine Maxwell is, then, a dark fairy tale for our time where no one at all ends up happily ever after.

Notes

Introduction

1 Archive film seen by the author.
2 Mike Molloy, *The Happy Hack: A Memoir of Fleet Street in its Heyday*, p. 278.
3 *The Sunday Times*, 14 March 2021, https://www.thetimes.co.uk/article/ian -maxwell-on-ghislaine-my-sister-is-not-a-monster-5kdnq33fx.
4 Sarah Ransome, *Silenced No More*, p. 150.
5 *The Sunday Times*, 14 March 2021, https://www.thetimes.co.uk/article/ian -maxwell-on-ghislaine-my-sister-is-not-a-monster-5kdnq33fx.

Chapter One

1 At the time of writing, January 2022.
2 Ian Maxwell in *The Sunday Times*, 14 March 2021, https://www.thetimes. co.uk/article/ian-maxwell-on-ghislaine-my-sister-is-not-a-monster -5kdnq33fx.
3 Betty Maxwell, *A Mind of My Own: My Life With Robert Maxwell*, p. 377.
4 *Daily Mirror*, 27 June 1963.
5 Betty Maxwell, p. 308.
6 John Preston, *Fall: The Mystery of Robert Maxwell*, p. 46.
7 *Daily Herald*, 28 June 1963.
8 *Daily Mirror*, 27 June 1963.
9 *Birmingham Daily Post*, 24 March 1965.
10 Betty Maxwell, p. 308.
11 *Daily Mail*, 10 September 2011, https://www.dailymail.co.uk/news/article -2035902/Whats-vegetable-doing-dining-room-Robert-Maxwells-reac- tion-meeting-new-granddaughter-revealed-sons-ex-wife-20th-anniversary -death-approaches.html.
12 Gyles Brandreth, *Breaking the Code*, p. 60.
13 Greenslade, *Maxwell's Fall: The Appalling Legacy of a Corrupt Man*, p. 12.

14 Greenslade, pp. 13–14.
15 Stott, *Dogs and Lamposts,* p. 231.
16 Nicholas Davies, *The Unknown Maxwell,* p. 186.
17 Davies, p. 82.
18 Betty Maxwell, p. xi.
19 Betty Maxwell, p. 535.
20 *Private Eye: The First Fifty Years,* p. 184.
21 Berry, *My Unique Relationship with Robert Maxwell: The Truth at Last,* p. 28.
22 Berry, p. 46.
23 Davies, pp. 14–16.
24 Davies, p. 14.
25 Davies, p. 183.
26 Davies, p. 83.
27 *BBC Newsnight* Donald Trump's business links to the mob, March 4 2016
28 Preston, p. 134.
29 Molloy, p. 258
30 Betty Maxwell, p. 41.
31 Betty Maxwell, p. 167.
32 Haines, *Maxwell,* p. 95.
33 Haines, p. 97.
34 *Desert Island Discs* with Robert Maxwell, https://www.bbc.co.uk/programmes/p009mllg.
35 Haines, p. 105.
36 Joe Haines, *Daily Mirror,* 24 February 1988.
37 Betty Maxwell, p. 349.
38 Sam Jaffa, *Maxwell Stories,* p. 57.
39 Stephen Clackson in conversation with the author. Plus Nicholas Davies, p. 168.
40 Edited conversation between Ingrams and the author, taped.
41 Taped conversation with the author.
42 Taped conversation with the author.
43 Jaffa, p. 131.
44 Betty Maxwell, p. 531.
45 Hunting Ghislaine podcast, Epilogue.
46 Betty Maxwell, pp. 347, 348.
47 Betty Maxwell, p. 355.
48 Betty Maxwell, p. 358.
49 Betty Maxwell, p. 444.
50 *The Sunday Times,* 9 September 2018, https://www.thetimes.co.uk/article/ian-and-kevin-maxwell-robert-maxwell-was-a-crook-but-to-us-he-was-dad-and-our-rock-lrgb6rg08.
51 Betty Maxwell, p. 445.
52 Betty Maxwell, p. 445.
53 Betty Maxwell, p. 445.

54 Betty Maxwell, p. 462.

55 Betty Maxwell, p. 450.

56 *The Times*, 4 June 2016, https://www.thetimes.co.uk/article/wendy-leigh
    -0lw7nl5n2.

57 Wendy Leigh, *Unravelled*, Kindle.

58 Tom Bower, *Maxwell: The Final Verdict*, p. 163.

59 Davies, p. 66.

60 Betty Maxwell, p. 453.

61 Davies, p. 81.

62 Peter Thompson and Anthony Delano, *Maxwell: A Portrait of Power*, p. 23.

63 Berry, p. 76.

64 Roy Greenslade, taped, for HG podcast.

65 *The Sunday Times*, 14 March 2021, https://www.thetimes.co.uk/article/ian
    -maxwell-on-ghislaine-my-sister-is-not-a-monster-5kdnq33fx.

66 Berry, p. 37.

67 Berry, p. 38; also *Daily Telegraph*, 13 August 2019, https://www.telegraph.
    co.uk/women/life/ghislaine-maxwell-did-go-socialite-shadowy-figure-sex
    -crime/. Also *The Tatler*, 3 July 2020, https://www.tatler.com/article/where
    -on-earth-is-ghislaine-maxwell.

68 Berry, p. 70.

69 Interview with the author, taped.

70 *The Sunday Times*, 14 March 2021, https://www.thetimes.co.uk/article/ian
    -maxwell-on-ghislaine-my-sister-is-not-a-monster-5kdnq33fx.

71 Brian Basham to the author, email.

Chapter Two

1 Gerald Ronson, *Leading from the Front*, p. 74.

2 Ronson, p. 72.

3 Nicholas Coleridge, *The Spectator*, August 2020.

4 Betty Maxwell, p. 333.

5 *Newsweek*, 20 December 2020, https://www.newsweek.com/ghislaine-
   maxwell-losing-weight-hair-prison-jeffrey-epstein-charges-lawyer-bobbi-
   sternheim-1553810.

6 Betty Maxwell, p. 335.

7 Preston, p. 67.

8 Betty Maxwell, p. 400.

9 Thompson and Delano, p. 179.

10 Betty Maxwell, p. 396.

11 Betty Maxwell, p. 398.

12 Betty Maxwell, p. 412.

13 Ben Macintyre, *The Times*, 4 July 2020, https://www.thetimes.co.uk/article
    /the-daddys-girl-with-a-monstrous-legacy-f2z2wsjbh.

14 Betty Maxwell, p. 412.

15 *Oxford Mail*, 3 August 2020, https://www.oxfordmail.co.uk/news/ 18624525.jeffrey-epstein-ghislaine-maxwell-oxford-united-director/.
16 Private conversation with the author.
17 Macintyre, *The Times*, 4 July 2020, https://www.thetimes.co.uk/article/the -daddys-girl-with-a-monstrous-legacy-f2z2wsjbh.
18 Tim Willis, *Tatler*, November 2019, https://www.tatler.com/article/friend-ship-ghislaine-maxwell.
19 Mark Edmonds, *Tatler*, 3 July 2020, https://www.tatler.com/article/where -on-earth-is-ghislaine-maxwell.
20 Vassi Chamberlain, *The Sunday Times*, 26 July 2020, https://www.thetimes. co.uk/article/inside-ghislaine-maxwells-dark-web-greed-sex-and-daddy-issues-32fnmhjzp.
21 Edmonds, *Tatler*, 3 July 2020, https://www.tatler.com/article/where-on-earth-is-ghislaine-maxwell.
22 Email to author.
23 Email to author.
24 Anne McElvoy, *Evening Standard*, 3 July 2020, https://www.standard.co.uk /news/world/ghislaine-maxwell-anne-mcelvoy-a4488011.html.
25 George Monbiot, Twitter, https://twitter.com/GeorgeMonbiot/status/ 1278919055362097152.
26 Rachel Johnston, *The Spectator*, https://www.spectator.co.uk/article/it-s-hard-not-to-pity-ghislaine-maxwell.
27 Taped, aired on Hunting Ghislaine podcast.
28 Tim Willis, *Tatler*, November 2019, https://www.tatler.com/article/friend-ship-ghislaine-maxwell.
29 *The Sunday Times*, 14 March 2021, https://www.thetimes.co.uk/article/ian -maxwell-on-ghislaine-my-sister-is-not-a-monster-5kdnq33fx.
30 *Vanity Fair*, March 1992, https://archive.vanityfair.com/article/1992/3/ the-sinking-of-captain-bob.
31 Berry, p. 56.
32 *Daily Mail*, 10 September 2011, https://www.dailymail.co.uk/news/article -2035902/Whats-vegetable-doing-dining-room-Robert-Maxwells-reac-tion-meeting-new-granddaughter-revealed-sons-ex-wife-20th-anniversary -death-approaches.htm.
33 *Daily Mail*, 10 September 2011.
34 *Daily Mail*, 10 September 2011.
35 Davies, p. 81.
36 Email to author.
37 Edmonds, *Tatler*, 3 July 2020, https://www.tatler.com/article/where-on-earth-is-ghislaine-maxwell.
38 Edmonds, *Tatler*, 3 July 2020, https://www.tatler.com/article/where-on-earth-is-ghislaine-maxwell.
39 Willis, *Tatler*, November, 2019, https://www.tatler.com/article/friendship -ghislaine-maxwell.
40 Conversation with author.

41 Chamberlain, *The Sunday Times*, 26 July 2020, https://www.thetimes.co.uk /article/inside-ghislaine-maxwells-dark-web-greed-sex-and-daddy-issues -32fnmhjzp.

42 Edmonds, *Tatler*, 3 July 2020, https://www.tatler.com/article/where-on-earth-is-ghislaine-maxwell.

43 Edmonds, *Tatler*, 3 July 2020, https://www.tatler.com/article/where-on-earth-is-ghislaine-maxwell.

44 *Daily Telegraph*, 4 July 2007, https://www.telegraph.co.uk/news/obituaries /1556420/Count-Gottfried-von-Bismarck.html.

45 W. C. Sellar and R. J. Yeatman, *1066 and All That*, p. 35.

46 Nick Richardson, *LRB*, 8 October 2015, https://www.lrb.co.uk/the-paper/ v37/n19/nick-richardson/short-cuts.

47 *The Times*, 5 October 2006, https://www.thetimes.co.uk/article/death-at-bismarck-flat-happened-after-gay-orgy-xkw9zbz8bwl.

48 *Independent*, 20 October 2007, https://www.independent.co.uk/news/uk/ crime/bismarck-died-after-injecting-cocaine-every-hour-for-a-day-394620.html.

49 McElvoy, *Evening Standard*, 3 July 2020, https://www.standard.co.uk/news /world/ghislaine-maxwell-anne-mcelvoy-a4488011.html.

50 *Observer*, 17 February 2002, https://www.theguardian.com/media/2002/ feb/17/newmedia.business.

51 *Vanity Fair*, July 2020, https://www.vanityfair.com/style/2020/07/inside-ghislaine-maxwells-life-on-the-lam.

52 Conversation with the author.

53 Email to author.

54 Hunting Ghislaine podcast.

55 Anthony Storr, *The Art of Psychotherapy*, p. 67.

Chapter Three

1 https://it.m.wikipedia.org/wiki/Cicogna-Mozzoni.

2 *Mail on Sunday*, 15 November 1992, https://www.reddit.com/r/Epstein/ comments/ch6g3r/the_mystery_of_ghislaine_maxwells_secret_love/.

3 Adam Roberts, *The Wonga Coup*, p. 211.

4 Conversation with author.

5 *Il Fatto Quotidiano*, 9 July 2012, https://www.ilfattoquotidiano.it/2012/07/ 09/la-morte-in-diretta-di-gianfranco-cicogna/288262/.

6 Vassi Chamberlain, *The Sunday Times*, 26 July 2020, https://www.thetimes. co.uk/article/inside-ghislaine-maxwells-dark-web-greed-sex-and-daddy-issues-32fnmhjzp.

7 Chamberlain, *The Sunday Times*, 26 July 2020, https://www.thetimes.co.uk /article/inside-ghislaine-maxwells-dark-web-greed-sex-and-daddy-issues -32fnmhjzp.

8 *Independent*, 25 October 1994, https://www.independent.co.uk/life-style/ the-beast-and-his-beauties-robert-maxwell-mesmerised-and-bullied

-women-but-betty-his-wife-for-nearly-50-years-remained-loyal-her-auto-biography-will-be-her-first-public-breach-of-that-loyalty-sandra-barwick-reports-1444890.html.

9 Molloy, p. 274.

10 Hunting Ghislaine podcast, Episode 1.

11 *Private Eye*, February 1983.

12 *Private Eye*, March 1983.

13 *Private Eye*, December 1986.

14 Bower, *The Outsider*, pp. 429–30.

15 MacQueen, *Private Eye: The First Fifty Years*, p. 191.

16 Hunting Ghislaine podcast, Episode 1.

17 Hunting Ghislaine podcast, Episode 1.

18 Sweeney, *The Life and Evil Times of Nicolae Ceausescu*, 1991, p. 13.

19 Russell Davies, *Foreign Body: The Secret Life of Robert Maxwell*, 1995, p. 66.

20 Hunting Ghislaine podcast.

21 Conversation with the author.

22 Conversation with the author.

23 Tom Bower, *Maxwell: The Final Verdict*, p. 9.

24 Hunting Ghislaine podcast.

25 Preston, p. 231.

26 Greenslade, p. 315.

27 Tom Bower, *Maxwell: The Final Verdict*, p. 166.

28 Christina Oxenberg, *Trash: Encounters with Ghislaine Maxwell*, p. 42.

29 Conversation with author.

30 *Vanity Fair*, March 1992, https://archive.vanityfair.com/article/1992/3/the-sinking-of-captain-bob.

31 Davies, p. 108.

Chapter Four

1 Kenny Lennox, taped conversation with author for Hunting Ghislaine podcast, for this whole section. Much of it broadcast.

2 Betty Maxwell, p. 5.

3 Hunting Ghislaine podcast, Episode 1.

4 *Irish Times*, 19 February 1997, https://www.irishtimes.com/news/daughter-denies-maxwell-suicide-1.44338.

5 *The Sunday Times*, 14 March 2021, https://www.thetimes.co.uk/article/ian-maxwell-on-ghislaine-my-sister-is-not-a-monster-5kdnq33fx.

6 Associated Press (AP), 9 January 1992, https://apnews.com/article/c85719fa04d85a950c7a22a83f14b8ed.

7 Dylan Howard, Melissa Cronin and James Robertson, *Epstein: Dead Men Tell No Tales*.

8 Consortium News, 18 June 2020, https://consortiumnews.com/2020/06/18/epstein-case-documentaries-wont-touch-tales-of-intel-ties/.

9 Craig Unger, 'The trouble with Ari', *The Village Voice*, July 1992.

10 Joint report of the Task Force to Investigate Certain Allegations Concerning the Holding of American Hostages by Iran in 1980 ('October Surprise Task Force'), p. 148.

11 Unger, 'The Trouble with Ari' *The Village Voice*, July 1992.

12 Hunting Ghislaine podcast, broadcast.

13 Davies, p. 2.

14 Hunting Ghislaine podcast, broadcast.

15 Hunting Ghislaine podcast tape, not broadcast.

16 Brandreth, p. 115.

17 *Mail on Sunday*, 23 January 2021, https://www.dailymail.co.uk/news/article-9179679/Was-Robert-Maxwell-murdered-JOHN-PRESTON-casts-new-light-mystery.html.

18 Stern, *Dr Iain West's Casebook*, p. 34.

19 *Office of National Statistics* https://www.ons.gov.uk/peoplepopulationand-community/birthsdeathsandmarriages/deaths/bulletins/suicidesintheu-nitedkingdom/2017registrations.

20 *Office of National Statistics* https://www.ons.gov.uk/peoplepopulationand-community/crimeandjustice/articles/homicideinenglandandwales/yearendingmarch2020.

21 Betty Maxwell, p. 533.

22 Betty Maxwell, p. 199.

23 John Sweeney, *The Church of Fear: Inside the Weird World of Scientology*, p. 2.

24 Betty Maxwell, p. xi.

25 Betty Maxwell, pp. 199, 355, 450.

26 *The Sunday Times*, 9 September 2018, https://www.thetimes.co.uk/article/ian-and-kevin-maxwell-robert-maxwell-was-a-crook-but-to-us-he-was-dad-and-our-rock-lrgb6rg08.

27 *The Sunday Times*, 14 March 2021, https://www.thetimes.co.uk/article/ian-maxwell-on-ghislaine-my-sister-is-not-a-monster-5kdnq33fx.

Chapter Five

1 *Vanity Fair*, July 2020, https://www.vanityfair.com/style/2020/07/inside-ghislaine-maxwells-life-on-the-lam.

2 *Vanity Fair*, March 1992, https://archive.vanityfair.com/article/1992/3/the-sinking-of-captain-bob.

3 Betty Maxwell, p. 516.

4 *Tatler*, 3 July 2020, https://www.tatler.com/article/where-on-earth-is-ghislaine-maxwell.

5 *Vanity Fair*, July 2020, https://www.vanityfair.com/style/2020/07/inside-ghislaine-maxwells-life-on-the-lam.

6 Vassi Chamberlain, *The Sunday Times*, 26 July 2020, https://www.thetimes.co.uk/article/inside-ghislaine-maxwells-dark-web-greed-sex-and-daddy-issues-32fnmhjzp.

7   *Sydney Morning Herald*, 31 January 2020, https://www.smh.com.au/
    national/the-rise-and-fall-of-socialite-ghislaine-maxwell-jeffrey-epstein-s-
    best-friend-20200103-p53omx.html.
8   *Vanity Fair*, March 1992, https://archive.vanityfair.com/article/1992/3/
    the-sinking-of-captain-bob.
9   Photographs posted by @KirbySommers on Twitter. Author has screenshots.
10 *NYT*, 12 July 2019, https://www.nytimes.com/2019/07/12/nyregion/
    jeffrey-epstein-dalton-teacher.html.
11 *Vanity Fair*, 6 August 2020, https://www.vanityfair.com/hollywood/2020/
    08/ghislaine-maxwell-jeffrey-epstein-birthday-gift.
12 *Daily Mail*, 5 August 2020, https://www.dailymail.co.uk/news/article-
    8596003/Ghislaine-Maxwell-friend-write-creepy-poem-Jeffrey-Epsteins-
    birthday.html.
13 *New York Times*, 15 July 2019, https://www.nytimes.com/2019/07/15/us/
    ghislaine-maxwell-epstein.html.
14 *Daily Mirror*, 15 December 2005, https://www.mirror.co.uk/3am/celebrity
    -news/beckham-exclusive-posh-off-569257.
15 James Patterson, John Connolly and Tim Malloy, *Filthy Rich: The Shocking
    True Story of Jeffrey Epstein*, p. 100
16 Edward Jay Epstein, *Daily Mail*, 19 July 2020, https://www.dailymail.co.uk
    /news/article-8537413/EDWARD-JAY-EPSTEIN-investigates-seemingly-
    unsolvable-mystery-Jeffrey-Epstein-fortune.html.
17 Mick Brown and Harriet Alexander, *Daily Telegraph*, 12 December 2019,
    https://www.telegraph.co.uk/news/2019/12/13/ghislaine-maxwell-went-
    daddys-girl-epsteins-right-hand-woman/.
18 Chamberlain, *The Sunday Times*, 26 July 2020, https://www.thetimes.co.uk
    /article/inside-ghislaine-maxwells-dark-web-greed-sex-and-daddy-issues
    -32fnmhjzp.
19 Hunting Ghislaine podcast, broadcast.
20 *SEC News Digest*, 18 February 1994, https://www.sec.gov/news/digest/
    1994/dig021894.pdf.
21 https://int.nyt.com/data/documenthelper/1494-epstein-wexner-power-
    of-attorney/04e6cef6bfb8b25c8684/optimized/full.pdf.
22 *Business Insider*, 8 August 2019, https://www.businessinsider.com/victorias
    -secret-head-les-wexner-letter-about-jeffrey-epstein-2019-8?r=US&IR=T.
23 *Mail on Sunday*, 15 November 1992, https://www.reddit.com/r/Epstein/
    comments/ch6g3r/the_mystery_of_ghislaine_maxwells_secret_love/.
24 https://www.youtube.com/watch?v=AUDr_c2PalI.
25 *New York Times*, 9 July 2019, https://www.nytimes.com/2019/07/09/us/
    politics/trump-epstein.html.
26 *Business Insider*, 7 July 2019, https://www.businessinsider.com/jeffrey-
    epstein-trump-link-liking-women-on-the-younger-side-2019
    -7?r=US&IR=T.
27 *Mail on Sunday*, 15 November 1992, https://www.reddit.com/r/Epstein/
    comments/ch6g3r/the_mystery_of_ghislaine_maxwells_secret_love/.

28 *Vanity Fair*, August 2019, https://www.vanityfair.com/news/2019/08/curious-sociopathy-of-jeffrey-epstein-ex-girlfriends.

29 *Vanity Fair*, August 2019, https://www.vanityfair.com/news/2019/08/curious-sociopathy-of-jeffrey-epstein-ex-girlfriends.

30 Christina Oxenberg, p. 75.

31 *The Sunday Times*, 14 March 2021, https://www.thetimes.co.uk/article/ian-maxwell-on-ghislaine-my-sister-is-not-a-monster-5kdnq33fx.

32 *The Times*, 10 August 1996.

33 Nazir Afzal, email to researcher Daisy Bata.

34 *The Sunday Times*, 14 March 2021, https://www.thetimes.co.uk/article/ian-maxwell-on-ghislaine-my-sister-is-not-a-monster-5kdnq33fx.

35 *Vanity Fair*, July 2020, https://www.vanityfair.com/style/2020/07/inside-ghislaine-maxwells-life-on-the-lam.

36 Sarah Ransome, p. 148.

37 *Vanity Fair*, March 2003, https://www.vanityfair.com/news/2003/03/jeffrey-epstein-200303.

38 *Vanity Fair*, March 2003, https://www.vanityfair.com/news/2003/03/jeffrey-epstein-200303.

39 *New York Times*, 31 July 2019, https://www.nytimes.com/2019/07/31/business/jeffrey-epstein-eugenics.html.

40 Stat News, 5 August 2019, https://www.statnews.com/2019/08/05/citing-nerd-tunnel-vision-biologist-george-church-apologizes-for-contacts-with-jeffrey-epstein/.

41 Bloomberg News, January 2003, https://www.bloomberg.com/news/videos/2019-08-14/epstein-i-was-always-good-at-mathematics-video.

42 *New York Times*, 31 July 2019, https://www.nytimes.com/2019/07/31/business/jeffrey-epstein-eugenics.html.

43 *New York Times*, 6 August 2019, https://www.nytimes.com/2019/08/26/us/epstein-farmer-sisters-maxwell.html.

44 *New York Times*, 26 August 2019, https://www.nytimes.com/2019/08/26/podcasts/the-daily/epstein-maxwell-farmer-sisters.html?showTranscript=1.

45 *Sun*, 7 July 2020, https://www.thesun.co.uk/news/12056474/ghislaine-maxwell-jeffrey-epstein-school-girls-maria-farmer/.

46 *Reuters*, 6 July 2020, https://news.yahoo.com/whats-case-far-against-ghislaine-173137653.html?guccounter=1&guce_referrer=aHR0cHM6Ly93d3cuZ29vZ2xlLmNvbS8&guce_referrer_sig=AQAAAGMnLeqKd-2uubfw5hwAgfmO4fzC2W0Fn5UAtfsbO3DQHCzPKAmnDvPSm0lAcOkw4ZOzTagA5fsjY4IUcOjFhT-qMqN04t316wWcvSXUG-1oVki-YEHroF8TAbvGwlJ90_dzp2QKmMfgi298FnO76_fKtR18NXRglIlF7T825Cpsy.

47 *New York Times*, 26 August 2019, https://www.nytimes.com/2019/08/26/podcasts/the-daily/epstein-maxwell-farmer-sisters.html?showTranscript=1.

48 *The Sunday Times*, 26 July 2020, https://www.thetimes.co.uk/article/inside-ghislaine-maxwells-dark-web-greed-sex-and-daddy-issues-32fnmhjzp.

49 *NPR*, 22 August 2019, https://www.npr.org/2019/08/22/753337520/why -the-media-didnt-pay-much-attention-to-jeffrey-epstein?t= 1621352634946.

50 *NPR*, 22 August 2019, https://www.npr.org/2019/08/22/753337520/why -the-media-didnt-pay-much-attention-to-jeffrey-epstein?t= 1621352634946.

51 *Vanity Fair*, March 2003, https://www.vanityfair.com/news/2003/03/ Jeffrey-epstein-200303.

52 *Vanity Fair*, March 2003, https://www.vanityfair.com/news/2003/03/ Jeffrey-epstein-200303.

53 Graydon Carter, *Page Six* website, July, 2021, https://pagesix.com/2021/07 /15/maria-farmer-slams-vicky-wards-jeffrey-epstein-podcast/.

54 *CBS*, 18 November 2019, https://www.cbsnews.com/news/jeffrey-epstein-accuser-maria-farmer-says-his-house-under-constant-tv-surveillance/.

Chapter Six

1 *Mother Jones*, 9 October 2020, https://www.motherjones.com/politics/ 2020/10/i-called-everyone-in-jeffrey-epsteins-little-black-book/.

2 *The Spectator*, 18 July 2020, https://www.spectator.co.uk/article/how-did-i -end-up-in-epstein-s-little-black-book-.

3 *The Spectator*, 15 August 2020, https://www.spectator.co.uk/article/nicho-las-coleridge-the-ghislaine-maxwell-i-knew.

4 R. L. Moseley, R. Hitchiner and J. A. Kirkby, 'Self-reported sex differences in high-functioning adults with autism: A meta-analysis', *Molecular Autism*, 18 May 2018.

5 Daniel Schöttle, Peer Briken, Oliver Tüscher and Daniel Turner, 'Sexuality in autism: hypersexual and paraphilic behaviour in women and men with high-functioning autism spectrum disorder', *Dialogues of Clinical Neuroscience*, December 2017.

6 *Miami Herald*, 28 November 2018, https://www.miamiherald.com/news/ local/article219494920.html.

7 *Guardian*, 12 December 2019, https://www.theguardian.com/us-news/ 2019/dec/12/she-was-so-dangerous-where-in-the-world-is-the-notorious-ghislaine-maxwell.

8 *New York Times*, 15 July 2019, https://www.nytimes.com/2019/07/15/us/ ghislaine-maxwell-epstein.html.

9 *Miami Herald*, 28 November 2018, https://www.miamiherald.com/news/ local/article219494920.html.

10 *New Yorker*, 29 July 2019, https://www.newyorker.com/magazine/2019/08 /05/alan-dershowitz-devils-advocate.

11 *Daily Telegraph*, 25 May 2020, https://www.telegraph.co.uk/news/2020/05 /25/prince-andrew-flew-paul-daniels-queens-helicopter-late-show/.

12 *The Sunday Times*, 24 August 2019, https://www.thetimes.co.uk/article/ prince-andrew-breaks-silence-over-epstein-friendship-0c3f3glcv.

13 *PRNewsWire* https://www.prnewswire.co.uk/news-releases/statement-on-behalf-of-ghislaine-maxwell-156665045.html.

14 *Epstein Flight Logs* https://assets.documentcloud.org/documents/1507315/epstein-flight-manifests.pdf.

15 *Daily Mail,* 13 March, 2011, https://www.dailymail.co.uk/news/article-1365733/How-Prince-Andrew-shared-room-Epsteins-Caribbean-hideaway-busty-blonde-claimed-brain-surgeon.html.

16 *Daily Mail,* 13 March 2011, https://www.dailymail.co.uk/news/article-1365733/How-Prince-Andrew-shared-room-Epsteins-Caribbean-hideaway-busty-blonde-claimed-brain-surgeon.html.

17 *Daily Mail,* 30 August 2019, https://www.dailymail.co.uk/news/article-7409279/PICTURED-Jeffrey-Epstein-Donald-Trump-Melania-Mar-Lago-2000.html.

18 *Daily Mail,* 19 August 2019, https://www.dailymail.co.uk/news/article-7373055/Flight-logs-prove-Duke-Yorks-Epstein-girl-key-locations.html.

19 https://www.youtube.com/watch?v=8ydVbn0gMk4.

20 BBC, 2 December 2019, https://www.bbc.co.uk/news/uk-50607705.

21 BBC, *Panorama,* 3 December 2019, https://www.bbc.co.uk/news/uk-50633640.

22 Sam McAlister, *Scoops: Behind the Scenes of the BBC's Most Shocking Interviews.*

23 BBC, 18 November 2019, https://www.bbc.co.uk/news/uk-50451953.

24 Hunting Ghislaine podcast, broadcast.

25 *Sunday Times,* 8 July 2020, https://www.thetimes.co.uk/article/prince-andrews-sexual-appetite-was-always-his-blind-spot-nlwxtfwlv.

26 Bradley Edwards, *Relentless Pursuit,* p. 269.

27 *Daily Mail,* https://www.dailymail.co.uk/news/article-8925269/Prince-Andrew-remembered-seeing-Spitting-Image-doll-centre-grope-claim-claims-Steve-Wright.html.

28 *New York Post,* 21 April 2000, https://nypost.com/2000/04/21/andrews-lovey-dovey-lunch-date-with-ghislaine/.

Chapter Seven

1 Flight logs, 2002 https://assets.documentcloud.org/documents/1507315/epstein-flight-manifests.pdf.

2 *Daily Mail,* https://www.dailymail.co.uk/news/article-7231935/Epstein-female-executives-call-24-7-paid-200-000-let-fly-private-jet.html.

3 Taped conversation with author.

4 Alana Goodman and Daniel Halper, *A Convenient Death,* p. 121.

5 *Daily Mirror,* 22 October 2020, https://www.mirror.co.uk/news/us-news/ghislaine-maxwell-12-key-things-22891262.

6 *Daily Mail,* 16 August 2019, https://www.dailymail.co.uk/news/article-7360597/Jeffrey-Epstein-paid-Ghislaine-Maxwell-pilots-license-ferry-girls.html.

7 Flight logs https://assets.documentcloud.org/documents/1507315/epstein-flight-manifests.pdf, p. 18.

8 *Daily Mail*, 18 October 2016, https://www.dailymail.co.uk/news/article-3849498/Hotel-heir-Vikram-Chatwal-arrested-setting-dogs-fire.html.

9 *New York Observer*, November 2002, https://observer.com/2002/11/vikram-chatwal-turban-cowboy/.

10 https://twitter.com/AndresPastrana_/status/1161656189236719617.

11 *Daily Mail*, 19 August 2020, https://www.dailymail.co.uk/news/article-8639501/Bill-Clinton-smiles-receiving-neck-massage-Jeffrey-Epstein-victim.html.

12 *New York Times*, 9 July 2019, https://www.nytimes.com/2019/07/09/nyregion/bill-clinton-jeffrey-epstein.html.

13 NPR, 2 September 2019, https://www.npr.org/2019/09/02/756823299/chauntae-davies-describes-coming-forward-as-epstein-accuser?t=1621965119792.

14 BBC, 2 October 2002, http://news.bbc.co.uk/1/hi/uk_politics/2294147.stm.

15 *Daily Telegraph*, 3 July 2020, https://www.telegraph.co.uk/news/2020/07/03/exclusivehow-ghislaine-maxwell-kevin-spacey-relaxed-buckingham/.

Chapter Eight

1 *Miami Herald*, 28 November 2018, https://www.miamiherald.com/news/local/article214210674.html.

2 Hunting Ghislaine podcast.

3 Hunting Ghislaine podcast.

4 *Miami Herald*, 28 November 2018, https://www.miamiherald.com/news/local/article214210674.html.

5 *Miami Herald*, 28 November 2018, https://www.miamiherald.com/news/local/article214210674.html.

6 *Daily Mail*, 24 September 2019, https://www.dailymail.co.uk/news/article-7499171/Ex-cop-MI6-fears-leaked-secrets-Prince-Andrews-friendship-Jeffrey-Epstein-breaks-silence.html.

7 *Miami Herald*, 28 November 2018, https://www.miamiherald.com/news/local/article214210674.html.

8 *Daily Mail*, 9 March 2011, https://www.dailymail.co.uk/news/article-1364171/Females-Jeffrey-Epstein-The-damning-telephone-log.html.

9 Brad Edwards, p. 108.

10 *Miami Herald*, 28 November 2018, https://www.miamiherald.com/news/local/article214210674.html.

11 *Miami Herald*, 28 November 2018, https://www.miamiherald.com/news/local/article214210674.html.

12 Getty Images, 15 March 2005, New York City.

13 *Chicago Tribune*, 2 March 2005, https://www.chicagotribune.com/news/ct-xpm-2005-03-02-0503020018-story.html.

14 *Daily Mail*, 17 July 2020, https://www.dailymail.co.uk/news/article-8510925/Parents-Ghislaine-Maxwells-lieutenant-fear-charged-Epsteins-sex-ring.html.

Chapter Nine

1 Michael Gross, *Model: The Ugly Business of Beautiful Women*.
2 Alan Dershowitz, *Guilt By Accusation: The Challenge of Proving Innocence in the Age of #MeToo*, p. 7.
3 *Dateline NBC*, 20 September 2019.
4 Hunting Ghislaine podcast, broadcast 2020.
5 *New Yorker*, 29 July 2019, https://www.newyorker.com/magazine/2019/08/05/alan-dershowitz-devils-advocate.
6 *Mail on Sunday*, 29 April 2007, https://www.dailymail.co.uk/news/article-451372/Prince-Andrews-billionaire-friend-accused-preying-girl-14.html.
7 *New Yorker*, 29 July 2019, https://www.newyorker.com/magazine/2019/08/05/alan-dershowitz-devils-advocate.
8 *Daily Mail*, https://www.dailymail.co.uk/news/article-7412517/Peter-Mandelson-Jeffrey-Epstein-Ex-Labour-minister-shopping-depraved-financier-2005.html.
9 BBC, 16 November 2019, https://www.bbc.co.uk/news/uk-49411215.
10 Sarah Ransome, p. 128.
11 Sarah Ransome, p. 148.
12 Sarah Ransome, p. 153.
13 Sarah Ransome, p. 177.
14 *The Sun*, 8 January, 2022 https://www.thesun.co.uk/news/17262658/peter-mandelson-jeffrey-epstein-after-paedophile-underage-sex-probe/
15 *New York Times*, https://www.nytimes.com/2019/07/13/nyregion/jeffrey-epstein-new-york-elite.html.
16 Hunting Ghislaine podcast, broadcast.
17 *Metro*, 5 June 2020, https://metro.co.uk/2020/06/05/jeffrey-epstein-assistants-sarah-kellen-nadia-marcinkova-ghislaine-maxwell-12802148/.
18 *CBS*, 26 May 2020, https://www.cbsnews.com/news/jeffrey-epstein-netflix-filthy-rich-sarah-ransome-ghislaine-maxwell/.
19 Hunting Ghislaine podcast, broadcast.
20 *The Daily Beast*, 9 July 2019, https://www.thedailybeast.com/jeffrey-epsteins-sick-story-played-out-for-years-in-plain-sight.

Chapter Ten

1 Julie K. Brown, *Perversion of Justice*, paperback edition, p. 168.
2 Edward Jay Epstein, *Daily Mail*, 19 July 2020, https://www.dailymail.co.uk

/news/article-8537413/EDWARD-JAY-EPSTEIN-investigates-seemingly-unsolvable-mystery-Jeffrey-Epstein-fortune.html.

3 Tim Willis, *Tatler*, 3 July 2020, https://www.tatler.com/article/friendship-ghislaine-maxwell.

4 *Daily Mail*, https://www.dailymail.co.uk/news/article-10199007/Ex-Barclays-boss-denies-using-snow-white-codewords-emails-Jeffrey-Epstein.html.

5 *New York Times*, https://www.nytimes.com/2021/01/25/business/leon-black-apollo-jeffrey-epstein.html.

6 https://www.youtube.com/watch?v=cJkc3Z1w5qU.

7 Hunting Ghislaine podcast.

8 BBC, *Newsnight*, 17 November 2019, https://www.bbc.co.uk/news/uk-50449339.

9 *The Sunday Times*, 8 July 2020, https://www.thetimes.co.uk/article/prince-andrews-sexual-appetite-was-always-his-blind-spot-nlwxtfwlv.

10 Hunting Ghislaine podcast.

11 *Sunday Telegraph*, 7 August 2010, https://www.telegraph.co.uk/news/uknews/theroyalfamily/7932529/Revealed-how-the-Duchess-of-York-was-led-to-the-brink-of-ruin.html.

12 *Guardian*, https://www.theguardian.com/uk/2010/aug/08/sarah-ferguson-bankrupt-debts-millions.

13 Hunting Ghislaine podcast.

14 *Daily Mail*, 7 March 2011, https://www.dailymail.co.uk/news/article-1363838/Prince-Andrews-ex-Sarah-Ferguson-Paedophile-Jeffrey-Epsteins-15k-error-judgement.html.

15 Hunting Ghislaine podcast.

16 *Sunday Times*, 8 July 2020, https://www.thetimes.co.uk/article/prince-andrews-sexual-appetite-was-always-his-blind-spot-nlwxtfwlv.

17 *New Republic*, 22 August 2019, https://newrepublic.com/article/154826/jeffrey-epsteins-intellectual-enabler.

18 BBC, 3 December 2019, https://www.bbc.co.uk/news/uk-50633640.

19 Edwards, p. 108.

20 NPR, 22 October 2020, https://www.npr.org/2020/10/22/926590153/jeffrey-epstein-update-read-the-deposition-that-ghislaine-maxwell-fought-to-hide?t=1622393138163.

21 See NPR above and also https://www.justice.gov/usao-sdny/press-release/file/1291491/download.

22 Hunting Ghislaine podcast.

23 Edwards, p. 108.

24 NPR, 22 October 2020, https://www.npr.org/2020/10/22/926590153/jeffrey-epstein-update-read-the-deposition-that-ghislaine-maxwell-fought-to-hide?t=1622393138163.

25 *Daily Mail*, 31 July 2020, https://www.dailymail.co.uk/news/article-8579099/Jeffrey-Epstein-told-Ghislaine-Maxwell-wrong-unsealed-court-docs-reveal.html.

26 https://www.youtube.com/watch?v=3pUzcRORDIg.

27 *New York Times*, 14 August 2019, https://www.nytimes.com/2019/08/14/style/ghislaine-maxwell-terramar-boats-jeffrey-epstein.html.

28 *The Sunday Times*, 14 March 2021, https://www.thetimes.co.uk/article/ian-maxwell-on-ghislaine-my-sister-is-not-a-monster-5kdnq33fx.

29 Conversation with author.

Chapter Eleven

1 *New York Times*, 7 July 2019, https://www.nytimes.com/2019/07/09/business/media/miami-herald-epstein.html.

2 *Fox News*, 30 October 2019, https://www.foxnews.com/us/forensic-pathologist-jeffrey-epstein-homicide-suicide.

3 *Axios*, 4 August 2020, https://www.axios.com/trump-ghislaine-maxwell-jeffrey-epstein-1b313a9d-13c0-45f6-8975-26de2e1559aa.html.

4 *New York Times*, 17 August 2019, https://www.nytimes.com/2019/08/17/nyregion/epstein-suicide-death.html.

5 Hunting Ghislaine podcast.

6 MedPage, 1 November 2019, https://www.medpagetoday.com/blogs/working-stiff/83087.

7 BBC, *Newsnight*, 17 November 2019, https://www.bbc.co.uk/news/uk-50449339.

8 *Daily Mail*, 18 August 2019, https://www.dailymail.co.uk/news/article-7367943/The-tantalising-mystery-Ghislaine-Maxwells-burger-bar-makeover.html.

9 *Mail on Sunday*, https://www.dailymail.co.uk/news/article-10198943/Ghislaine-Maxwell-team-hired-DOUBLES-brother-Kevin-stroll-Paris.html.

10 *Daily Mail*, 6 July 2020, https://www.dailymail.co.uk/news/article-8494411/Ghislaine-Maxwell-secret-stash-Jeffrey-Epsteins-sex-tapes.html.

11 *Guardian*, 10 April 2021, https://www.theguardian.com/us-news/2021/apr/10/ghislaine-maxwell-prosecutors-defend-new-indictment-july-trial-.

12 *Daily Mail*, 4 January 2021, https://www.dailymail.co.uk/news/article-9112613/FBI-located-Ghislaine-Maxwell-obtaining-warrant-track-cell-phone-data.html.

Chapter Twelve

1 Ian Maxwell to BBC Radio Four's *Today* programme, 10 March 2021; https://www.bbc.co.uk/news/av/world-56347316.

2 *Daily Mail*, 2 January 2022, https://www.dailymail.co.uk/news/article-10361777/Ghislaine-Maxwell-learned-husband-moved-yoga-instructor-call-bars-says-friend.html.

3 Seth Stevenson in *Slate*, 30 November 2021: https://slate.com/news-and-politics/2021/11/ghislaine-maxwell-trial-day-two-jane-bill-clinton-donald-trump-prince-andrew-pilot.html.

4 All quotes from court proceedings taken from court transcripts.

5 *Tatler*, July 2020; https://www.tatler.com/article/countess-of-iveagh-flights-on-jeffrey-epsteins-lolita-express-questioning.

6 Joshua Chaffin, 14 December 2021, *Financial Times*, https://www.ft.com/content/0b9d93da-1687-4eb1-bd53-0a84a1b40dff?accessToken=zwAAA
X3QJeB4kc8LnZPaFodOsdO9UwqEobQN_w.MEUCIASJw5PvFscF_
14c1ZEVHCi5t0pQ7KhzquC86--UkUCvAiEA2GX1ovqcwoHpl5QPjt1f-
IFVyOpfq_38XoV5ZX39W98&sharetype=gift?token=2b5f1e65-e577-
47e9-b0bb-1c7a0151f478.

Chapter Thirteen

1 *Church of Fear* trailer, 2013, https://www.youtube.com/watch?v=YtLuQ01rpwk.

2 TrueAnon, https://open.spotify.com/show/0LYHwc0D2JbZGvd4dyKsiz.

3 *The Daily Beast*, https://www.thedailybeast.com/epsteins-ex-girlfriend-and-miss-sweden-eva-andersson-dubin-denies-having-orgies-with-teen-girls.

Chapter Fourteen

1 I love Philip Larkin.

2 *Buzzfeed*, 9 September 2019, https://www.buzzfeednews.com/article/peteraldhous/jeffrey-epstein-bezos-musk-billionaires-dinner.

3 *The Daily Beast*, 7 May 2021, https://www.thedailybeast.com/melinda-gates-warned-bill-gates-about-jeffrey-epstein.

4 *Bloomberg Billionaires Index*, January 2022, https://www.bloomberg.com/billionaires/.

5 BBC, 4 January 2022, https://www.bbc.co.uk/news/uk-59865102.

6 *Sunday Mirror*, 15 January, https://www.mirror.co.uk/news/uk-news/prince-andrew-in-tears-queen-25957350

7 *Daily Mail*, 13 January 2022, https://www.dailymail.co.uk/news/article-10396753/Ghislaine-Maxwell-juror-recall-questions-assault-asks-judge-answers.html.

Acknowledgements

This book naturally flowed from my podcast series, Hunting Ghislaine but also from my time as a freelance in the early 1980s on the Street of Shame when the brave and good on the *Daily Mirror*, *Private Eye* and beyond told me the truth about the monster Robert Maxwell. Thanks to all those ghosts from Fleet Street who, when my luck was down, helped me get my mojo as a story-teller back. Tom Bower, Stephen Clackson, Roy Greenslade, Ian Hyslop, Richard Ingrams, Kenny Lennox, my old doorstep target Kelvin MacKenzie, Andy MacSmith, Andrew Morton, David Seymour, Noreen Taylor and Francis Wheen were generous with their time and reminded me that when Fleet Street was undermined by social media, we lost something precious and remarkable.

Understanding the strange brittle word of Ghislaine Maxwell is not easy. The following took time out to share their reflections with me, in person or otherwise: Nazir Afsal, Wendy Behary, Josh Chaffin, Nicholas Coleridge, Patrick Forbes, Jenni Frazer, Geordie Greig, Professor Ashley Grossman, Cordelia Grossman, Nicky Haslam, Jaysim Hanspal, Stephen Hoffenberg, Peter Jay, Simon Mann, Peter Mandelson and Anna Pasternak.

I am especially grateful to Nicola Glucksmann for her brave and empathetic reflections on Ghislaine. I don't agree with all of her conclusions but I admire her courage in setting out the case that not just Ghislaine knew about Epstein's child factory. Others did too.

Scores of people have written about Maxwells, Robert and Ghislaine. Thanks to everyone, living and dead, who have I quoted here, but in particular the late Richard Stott, the late Michael Molloy and the late Betty Maxwell. Her memoir of life with Robert Maxwell is the best defence of Ghislaine's ghastly conduct ever written. Emily Maitlis' astonishing interview with Prince Andrew is quoted at length. Thanks to her, Sam McAlister the producer who got the scoop, all my old colleagues at BBC Newsnight and BBC Panorama for their help. Laura Burns in particular helped me steer away from one disaster. My old paper, *The Observer*, ran my reports from the trial in New York which I draw on here. Thanks to everyone at *The Observer*.

An online talk I gave to a group of City University's investigative journalism students led to the following brilliant people helping me research this book: Daisy Bata, Bertie Harrison-Broninski and Emily O'Sullivan.

The victims of Jeffrey Epstein and Ghislaine Maxwell are extraordinary, ordinary people who suffered for far too long without their voices being heeded. Annie Farmer, 'Jane', 'Kate' and Carolyn gave evidence in court, Sarah Ransome gave a witness statement about the pain she endured and wrote a powerful book about it and Virginia Roberts Giuffre fought the longest for the truth to come out. My conversation with Michelle Licata stands out in part because she never knew the name of the man who abused her. Thanks to all the victims for their courage.

Hunting Ghislaine, the podcast, was commissioned by Chris Baughen at Global and produced by Chalk and Blade, where the executive was Laura Sheeter and the producer and my on-air friend Ruth Barnes. Laura and Ruth are a brilliant double-act, always on it and their fine judgments saved my bacon repeatedly.

Thanks very much to my publishers Rupert Lancaster and Ciara Mongey and my agent Humfrey Hunter.

As ever, my family have had my back: love to Sam, Lou, Shilah and Molly for their long-suffering and always amusing support. Families mould people. Ghislaine's broke her – and that is a tragedy for her and them too.